Endorsements

"I'm so glad that the rest of the world gets to read "Morning Manna" now. I have been built up, torn down, challenged, and amused through the years by the thoughtful musings from a true teacher. This compilation of Dr. Dan's Monday Morning Manna will give you a daily boost in your walk with the Lord."

Dave Butts, Chairman,
America's National Prayer Committee

"Dr. Crawford has been a friend whose advice I admire. His Morning Manna has encouraged me often when I needed something to cheer me and has convicted me when I needed to change. He delights in sharing fun facts and true words. I am thrilled that Dan's thoughts now fill a book that we can read every day!"

Sharon L. Gresham, Founder and Director of
Ashes to Crowns Ministries

"As you read this book, you will discover my friend and colleague Dan Crawford as a teacher-professor, a biblical-preacher, a story-telling writer, a "devoted to prayer" disciple. Every morning will be a brief but deep-in-the-soul adventure. And one of those days, you'll discover you too have a new friend and a colleague on your journey into Christ."

Phil Miglioratti, Community Coordinator,
Pray Network, Discipleship Network, and *LOVE2020.com*

"This book contains a generous supply of the wit, wisdom and inspiration I always receive from Dan Crawford's writing/teaching. I've appreciated Dr. Crawford's ministry for many years now, and know that this book is bound to bless!"

Eddie Smith, President,
U.S. Prayer Center

"*Morning Manna* delivers a good dose of wisdom served up with warmth and humor. Dr. Crawford draws from his years of walking with Jesus to share insights for daily life, leadership and ministry. Sure to delight and challenge!

Dr. Craig O'Brien, Pastor, Chaplain, Church Planter, Vancouver, Canada

"I have been reading Dr. Dan's Monday Morning Manna from the beginning, and have looked forward to receiving it each week. I have found it to be encouraging, humorous, inspiring, and thought provoking, and know you will enjoy using this book of morning manna."

Lynn Sasser, Pastor and Missionary, Mexico City

"Dr. Dan has shown daily discipline in writing concise spiritual explanations and illustrations of life in our real world. Those "Manna" musings have blessed, amused, challenged, convicted my wife and I to look at ourselves in God's mirror, and we need that. We are so happy they are now printed in this daily devotional."

Bob McEachern, Retired Missionary

"As a long-time reader of Dr. Crawford's online Monday Morning Manna, I'm thrilled to see this collection of inspiration, wit, and wisdom in book form. I can tell you to expect nuggets of spiritual truth in a concise, easy-to-understand format. You will enjoy and grow from this book."

Dr. Vicki Gilliam, Retired Educator

"Dr. Dan's Morning Manna is might near as habit forming as coffee-drinking, but it's a great way to start a day just as coffee! He writes in the manner of Erma Bombeck; somewhere along the way, his meanderings bring smiles. I'm a blessed person for the reading, just as I believe he's blessed for the writing. He's a good 'un!"

Dr. Don Newbury, Chancellor, *Howard Payne University*

"Dr. Dan has a gift for making a relatable point that lingers through the day. I am so glad that he has compiled *Morning Manna* into book form so I can review old favorites and be inspired again."

Elaine Helms, Author, *Prayer Without Limits*

"Dan Crawford's Morning Manna is a pithy and realistic collection of daily thoughts which have arisen out of his expansive life of service and study as a Christian leader. He tackles the difficult and practical issues with which we all have to deal with and for which we all need direction. His Texas humor is refreshing and is the 'spoonful of sugar that makes the medicine go down.' Read...reflect...enjoy."

Dr. Al Meredith, Senior Pastor, Retired

"Refreshing, creative, funny, thought-provoking, renewing...what a great way to begin each day in the presence of the Lord! Dan Crawford combines devotional thoughts with a lifetime of personal experience and ministry - the result is a smile, centering one's life in the love of God, and walking through the day with confidence and obedience. A great resource for daily reading and meditation!"

Bonnie E. Hearon, Strategy Coordinator, Global Gates

Morning Manna: Hidden and Unhidden

Dan R. Crawford

© Copyright 2016, Dan R. Crawford

All rights reserved. No part of this collection may be reproduced or transmitted in any form or by any means, electronic or mechanical, including photocopying and recording, or by any information storage and retrieval system, except in the case of brief quotations for use in articles and reviews, without written permission from the author.

Unless otherwise noted, all scripture is from *The Holy Bible: The New King James Version,* copyright 1979, 1980, 1982, 1988 by Thomas Nelson, Inc. Publishers. All rights reserved.

With grateful appreciation to Cindy Aday for proof-reading the manuscript.

Writings from the author's online website, *Dr. Dan's Monday Morning Manna* are used by permission.

**7710-T Cherry Park Dr, Ste 224
Houston, TX 77095
713-766-4271**

Paperback: 978-1-0880-0801-0

Table of Contents

Introduction 29

January 1 Another New Year 33

January 2 Giving It All We've Got! 33

January 3 Facebook Praying: Goals and Resolutions 34

January 4 Birthday Paranoia Cured 35

January 5 Plays and Plans that Work... 36

January 6 Infused 36

January 7 Merry Christmas, Again 37

January 8 All Things 37

January 9 Restored, Then Led 38

January 10 Standing on the Rock 39

January 11 Prescriptions 39

January 12 Connectivity 40

January 13 Mountain Tops and Flat Lands 41

January 14 Words 41

January 15 Interruptions 42

January 16 Wet feet 42

January 17 An Elijah Complex.. 43

January 18 Not Enough Jesus 44

January 19 Recognizing the Real 45

January 20 Be Ye Kind.. 45

January 21 Diversity... 46

January 22 Happiness 47

January 23 Remember Your Creator 47

January 24 Desperate for God 48

January 25 From These Hills 49

January 26 Removal... 49

January 27 What's the Point?... 50

January 28 No Hope and Hope 51

January 29 While I'm Thinking about It 51

January 30 Holiness 52

January 31 Honest Additions 52

February 1 God's Provision in the Wilderness 53

February 2 Past, Present, and Future 54

February 3 The Prayer of Jehoshaphat.. 55

February 4 Acceptance and Arrival 55

February 5 Joy Comes When? 56

February 6 Benchwarmers 57

February 7 Speaking in Songs... 57

February 8 Thinking and Praying 58

February 9 Super Silence 59

February 10 Super Perspective 59

February 11 Cancellation and Completion 60

February 12 Going Home Again 61

February 13 Footprints and Vision 62

February 14 Things of the Heart 63

February 15 When Mentors Fail 63

February 16 Bread and Water 64

February 17 Family Day 65

February 18 A New Season 65

February 19 Prayer for Friends 66

February 20 Mathematical Praying 67

February 21 Pleasing God 67

February 22 When Does a Day Begin? 68

February 23 Revelations and Applications 69

February 24 To Speak or Not to Speak 70

February 25 Unanswered Prayer 70

February 26 Urgencies and Emergencies 71

February 27 A Word Fitly Spoken . . . by Someone! 72

February 28 Staying in Touch 73

March 1 The Uniqueness of Indwelling	73
March 2 A Home in Glory Land	74
March 3 Mega-ego	75
March 4 God Knows	75
March 5 Wait to Worry	76
March 6 Satisfied or Content?	76
March 7 Prayer's Profit	77
March 8 My Favorite Teacher	78
March 9 Favorite Bible Verses	78
March 10 Blessed in Weariness	79
March 11 Endure Hardship	79
March 12 Rumors and Angels	80
March 13 Got Your Back	81
March 14 Survey Says . . . God Help Us!	81
March 15 March Meanings - A Sunday Fit for a King	82
March 16 3/16	83
March 17 Choosing Correctly	84
March 18 Twitter de, twitter dumb!	84
March 19 Disciplined Silence	85
March 20 Keep on!	86
March 21 Reclaim and Return	87

March 22 Sunday Tears 87

March 23 Because He Lives 88

March 24 Passing by 89

March 25 Worshipping a Listening God 89

March 26 God's Heart-beat 90

March 27 Servanthood and the Lack Thereof 91

March 28 Answered Prayer or Coincidence? 91

March 29 Cat Nap or Prayer Partner 92

March 30 The Priority of a Good Start 92

March 31 Faith that Releases Power 93

April 1 April Fools 93

April 2 The Road Goes on Forever 94

April 3 A Worthy Model 95

April 4 Opening Day and Worship Day 95

April 5 Adoration 96

April 6 Lifestyle 97

April 7 Lifestyle, Continued 97

April 8 Too Busy to Pray? 98

April 9 Leading with Eyes Wide Open 99

April 10 Leading With Eyes Wide Open, Continued 100

April 11 A Time to Laugh 100

April 12 Vapor View 101

April 13 Silence: Unbroken and Broken 102

April 14 Ego-buster or God's Selection Process? 102

April 15 Post-Easter Heartburn 103

April 16 With and Without Form 104

April 17 Home: Place or People? 105

April 18 A Lesson from my Cell Phone 105

April 19 Precious Memories 106

April 20 Play it where it Lies 106

April 21 The Fireworks were on Key 107

April 22 Earth Day Every Day 108

April 23 "When Your Prayers are Unanswered" 109

April 24 Now Abides Faith and Hope 109

April 25 Real, Relevant or Both? 110

April 26 Shipwrecked Faith 111

April 27 Called to Worship 111

April 28 Watching and Waiting 112

April 29 Ministry by Paranoia 113

April 30 Today and Tomorrow 113

May 1 Let the Children Come 114

May 2 Good, Better, Best 114

May 3 Reunion Anxiety 115

May 4 Progressive Dinner 116

May 5 Travail 116

May 6 Keep on Keeping On 117

May 7 Re-proving Truth.. 118

May 8 Two Heavenly Mansions; Two Earthly Saints 119

May 9 Praying in Sleepless Weakness 119

May 10 Reunion Attended 120

May 11 Coincidence 121

May 12 Mother Love 121

May 13 What Would Mother Say? 122

May 14 Jesus and Humor 123

May 15 When Knowledge Trumps Action 123

May 16 God's Requirements 124

May 17 The Cost of Love 124

May 18 Kindergarten Dreams 125

May 19 Back of the Line 126

May 20 Why so Many Intercessors? 126

May 21 The End is not Yet, but Could Be 127

May 22 Standing in Need of (Saturday Night) Prayer 128

May 23 Just in Case 129

May 24 Just Live the Golden Rule, or Not 130

May 25 When God Does Not Answer Immediately........................... 131

May 26 His Way in the Storms 132

May 27 Putters and Plumb Lines 132

May 28 Memorial Day Meaning 133

May 29 Another Soldier has Gone Home 134

May 30 The Windows of Heaven 135

May 31 Remembrance 135

June 1 Sorry, but You Can't Come In 136

June 2 A New Song 137

June 3 Agreement and Disagreement 137

June 4 Passing a New Way... 138

June 5 The Wind Beneath my Wings 139

June 6 Working on Becoming Young 140

June 7 Deceiving Looks 141

June 8 However You Pronounce It 141

June 9 Praying for the Pastor... 142

June 10 Faith in Action – Intensity or Consistency? 143

June 11 Second Chance to Follow 144

June 12 Necessary Edification 145

June 13 What it takes to be Happy... 145

June 14 Remember and Recommit 146

June 15 Fading Desires 147

June 16 A Symphony of Prayer 148

June 17 Truth or Fiction? 148

June 18 Keep Your Eye on the Ball 149

June 19 Polishing the Parts 150

June 20 God's Will and Boldness 150

June 21 The E's of Teaching 151

June 22 Honk or Pray? 152

June 23 Helping with Holiness 153

June 24 An Unmarked Grave 153

June 25 Night-time Aroma 154

June 26 God's Slow Response to our Prayer for Revival 155

June 27 You Never Know 156

June 28 Pilgrims on the Earth 156

June 29 Excellence is also in the Striving 157

June 30 The Mystery of the Gospel from two Perspectives 158

July 1 National Pride and Intercessory Prayer 158

July 2 Celebrating from a Distance 159

July 3 Birthday Losses 160

July 4 Happy Birthday America 160

July 5 Celebrating a Specific Freedom 161

July 6 Which Way to Go 162

July 7 Moving On 163

July 8 One Caffeinated Blue Jay 163

July 9 Tireless Praying 164

July 10 Feeble Knees and Facing Life 165

July 11 Praying Outside of God's Will 166

July 12 Re-connecting with Facebook Friends 166

July 13 Glory Up and Blessings Down 167

July 14 Memorizing with Meaning 168

July 15 Breathless or God-breathed? 168

July 16 Aging: Praying or Pouting? 169

July 17 When God Whispers 170

July 18 What We Leave Behind 171

July 19 Warnings 172

July 20 Left Behind 172

July 21 Will and Willingness 173

July 22 Ordinary and Encouraged 174

July 23 How Much is Enough? 174

July 24 Belonging 175

July 25 Living the Jesus Way 176

July 26 Tracks Left Behind 176

July 27 A Displeasing Voice.. 177

July 28 Playing the Part 178

July 29 A Home Where We've Never Lived 178

July 30 No Autocorrect with God 179

July 31 Mountain Top Encounters or Flatland Ministry? 180

August 1 Failure is Not Final 181

August 2 Morning Prayer or Night Prayer? 181

August 3 Self Made or Multi-made? 182

August 4 Sometimes there is Crying in Baseball 183

August 5 Faith and the Prosperity Gospel... 183

August 6 Giving Our Best.. 184

August 7 Too Much Vision... 185

August 8 A Wedding Prayer, Many Years Later................................... 186

August 9 Settled Before Sleep 186

August 10 Grieve in Grace 187

August 11 Precious Memories and Positive Eulogies.......................... 188

August 12 Some Ships Sail, Others Don't 188

August 13 An Unbeatable Formula 189

August 14 Double Discipleship 190

August 15 Reading about Prayer or Praying?...................................... 191

August 16 Age-related Smiles 191

August 17 Faith's Landing Place 192

August 18 Harvest-Field Praying 192

August 19 Getting Out or Getting Content 193

August 20 Upholding or Upheld? 194

August 21 Praying for Those for Whom We'd Rather Not Pray 195

August 22 When Baby and Body Belong to God 196

August 23 A Barnabas Word 196

August 24 This, That, and the Other 197

August 25 Sending Prayers Where? 198

August 26 Balancing Service and Rest 198

August 27 Thank God for God 199

August 28 Legion 200

August 29 A Ninety-One year Old Cadillac 200

August 30 Holy Boldness or Not? 201

August 31 Sentimental (Prayer) Journey 202

September 1 Gray Headed Declarations 203

September 2 My Retirement Office 203

September 3 Retirement, Promotion, Adjustment, or Transition? 204

September 4 Happy Labor Day 205

September 5 Rewind and Replay 206

September 6 God's Will . . . My Will 207

September 7 Understood 208

September 8 From Tablet to Tongue 208

September 9 You Jus' Like Us 209

September 10 Alone, but not Lonely 210

September 11 9/11 Plus 210

September 12 Looking Beyond in Joyful Praise 211

September 13 God on Speed Dial 212

September 14 Decisions During the Journey 213

September 15 Laughter Lines 213

September 16 Joy Entered In 214

September 17 A Tribute to my Professor 215

September 18 Decision Making: Faith or Sight? 216

September 19 Morality, or Spirituality, or Both? 216

September 20 Lo and Behold! 217

September 21 The Levity of Brevity 218

September 22 Number One or Other 219

September 23 Declaring Kindness and Faithfulness with and without Music 219

September 24 Making Satan Mad 220

September 25 A Helpful Refuge in Hard Times 221

September 26 Further Along 222

September 27 But, What About My Left Hand? 222

September 28 The Lost Art of Loyalty 223

September 29 Back of the Line 224

September 30 God's GPS 225

October 1 When Should a Pastor be Appreciated? 226

October 2 A Gift for Pastor Appreciation Month 227

October 3 Pastor Appreciation Night 228

October 4 Minister Appreciation 228

October 5 Called or Not? 229

October 6 Give the World a Smile 230

October 7 Comments and Compliments 231

October 8 Fuel for the Journey 231

October 9 ACTS or MIGHTY ACTS? 232

October 10 Agreeing to Disagree Without Being Disagreeable 233

October 11 Known by Our Office 233

October 12 That Could Have Been 234

October 13 Sleepless, but not Prayerless 235

October 14 Canadian Thanksgiving 236

October 15 Following God's Call with Passion 237

October 16 Anxious Reunions 238

October 17 Golden Friendships 239

October 18 Sabbath Rest.. 239

October 19 The Long and Short of Separation 240

October 20 Fight or Focus? 241

October 21 God's Got This! 241

October 22 When Noise Needs a Silence Break..................................... 242

October 23 A Personal Benediction 243

October 24 Loving in the Day; Singing in the Night.............................. 244

October 25 You Can't Judge a Book, or a Person, by the Cover 244

October 26 Walking by Faith 245

October 27 Influence That Continues 246

October 28 Patience When Needed.. 247

October 29 Serenity or Courage? 247

October 30 A Little-Celebrated Special Day 248

October 31 Facing Fear with Faith 249

November 1 Day of the Dead and the Living... 249

November 2 Praying Through 250

November 3 Praying for Pastors and Football Coaches 251

November 4 Explosivity... 252

November 5 Is Praying "Thank You" Really Enough?............................ 253

November 6 Eating and Sinning 254

November 7 Making Melody in Your Heart 254

November 8 Pressing On in a Slow Burn 255

November 9 The Sweet Aroma of Friendship 256

November 10 Productive Sleep 257

November 11 Responsibility and Reason 257

November 12 Coping with Conflict 258

November 13 What I Teach in my Class on Prayer 259

November 14 Jim Didn't Quit! 260

November 15 Loyalty, Where Have You Gone? 261

November 16 When Life Gives You a Parenthesis 261

November 17 Proper and Improper Celebration 262

November 18 Redeeming the Time 263

November 19 When the Spirit Departs 264

November 20 From This River 264

November 21 Death, Where is Your Calendar? 265

November 22 Trust in God and Push Along 265

November 23 Thanking a Teacher 266

November 24 Expressions of Gratitude 267

November 25 Thanksgiving – A Shared Blessing 268

November 26 Making an "F" on Thanksgiving 269

November 27 One Out of Ten 269

November 28 A Gratitude Attitude 270

November 29 Given and Required 271

November 30 Post-Thanksgiving Praying 271

December 1 The Uncommon Use of Common Sense 272

December 2 Background Checks and Second Chances 273

December 3 Mountains and Canyons 274

December 4 Why I Like Senior Adults 274

December 5 Honored with Honors 275

December 6 Determining Attendance at a Funeral 276

December 7 Quietly Pointing to the Victor 277

December 8 Bright, Shiny Faces 277

December 9 Not Everything is a God Thing 278

December 10 Faltering Near the Finish Line 279

December 11 Introductions 280

December 12 Remembering Home Again 281

December 13 The Full Presence of God 282

December 14 A Christmas Prayer 283

December 15 Do You Sing What I Sing? 283

December 16 My Christmas List 284

December 17 What's in a Baby's Name? 285

December 18 What to do With Glory 285

December 19 The Cost of Christmas 286

December 20 Another Way 287

December 21 A Pin Dropped 288

December 22 God with Us.. 288

December 23 Who's Watching O'er the Sheep?................................. 289

December 24 An Embarrassing Christmas Moment 290

December 25 The Changing and the Unchanging 291

December 26 Christmas Forever Changed 292

December 27 A Second Meaning of the Manger 293

December 28 Remember the Reason 293

December 29 Caught on Christmas.. 294

December 30 The Spirit of Christmas Past 295

December 31 Last Year . . . Next Year 295

Morning Manna – Scripture Appendix 297

**Dedicated to my wife, Joanne,
with whom I have been privileged to
share "Manna" for more than 50 years.**

Introduction

The real challenge of living the Christian life is that it is so daily. Yesterday is a part of reflection, victories celebrated, mistakes made, lessons learned. We build on it, but we can't live in it. Tomorrow is a part of hope, victories anticipated, goals attained. We can anxiously await it but we can't live there. Today is where we live. Today we need commitment. Today we need inspiration. Today we need challenge. Today we are called by God to intimacy, to service, to minister. Today we need God's provision. In the past, God's daily provision was given in the form of "manna" provided each morning, as nourishment for the day, with enough only for that day.

In the Old Testament days, as the Israelites wandered in the wilderness, God provided daily nourishment for them, called "Manna." It was provided each morning, just enough for that day, except on the sixth day when two days' supply was provided, so as not to violate a Sabbath law (Exodus 16:23-24). "Manna" is a Hebrew word described in the Bible as "a small round substance, as fine as frost on the ground" (Exodus 16:14) and further, "it was like white coriander seed, and the taste of it was like wafers made with honey" (Exodus 16:31). Its provision was described as, "when the dew fell on the camp in the night, the manna fell on it" (Numbers 11:9). The Scripture says, "They gathered it every morning, every man according to his need. And when the sun became hot, it melted" (Exodus 16:21). Numbers 11:8 adds, "People went about and gathered it, ground it on millstones or beat it in the mortar, cooked it in pans, and made cakes of it." Exodus 16:15 tells us that "when the children of Israel saw it, they said to one another, 'What is it?' For they did not know what it was". The word "manna" is believed to have been derived from the question "man hu" meaning "what is it." Moses informed them, "This is the bread which the Lord has given you to eat" (Exodus 16:15). This provision of manna continued for forty years until the Israelites reached the promise land (Exodus 16:35) after which a small amount was kept in a golden pot in the Tabernacle (Exodus 16:32-34).

In the biblical days following, the Psalmist wrote that God, "rained down manna on them to eat, and gave them of the bread of heaven. Men ate angels' food" (Psalm 78:24-25). The disciples reminded Jesus, "Our fathers ate the manna in the desert" (John 6:31). The writer of Hebrews wrote of "the ark of the covenant overlaid on all sides with gold, in which were the golden pot that had the manna" (Hebrews 9:4). Through the years of Christian history, manna has been a symbol of God's divine provision of spiritual nourishment.

However, Revelation 2:17 presents a new idea related to manna, "To him who overcomes I will give some of the hidden manna to eat." What is "hidden manna" and how does it relate to the manna given by God in Old Testament days? The theories vary.

The idea of the manna being "hidden":

- may be an allusion to the manna which the Hebrews ate in the wilderness, not knowing what it was when they first observed it;

- or because it was preserved in a golden pot, and kept in the holy place, where it was a secret that only the high priest could see and know;

- or perhaps, because it was at first hidden under the dew for according to the account the Jews gave of it, a dew first fell on the ground, then the manna on top, and then another dew fell upon the manna; so that there was a dew under it, and a dew over it, hidden.

One theory proposes that those who are overcoming will be nourished through this earthly existence with "hidden manna," that is, they will be sustained along through the world's wilderness by the immediate presence and provisions of God.

Then there is the idea, that because the term "hidden manna" is mentioned in Revelation along with the word, "overcomes" it relates to a heaven and eternal reward. The idea is that the souls of those who "overcame" and gained the ultimate victory would be permitted to partake of that spiritual food which is saved for God's people, to which the angels have access, and they will be nourished forever.

There was, in fact, a tradition among the Jews that the ark of the covenant, the tables of stone, Aaron's rod, the holy anointing oil, and the pot of manna, were hidden by King Josiah when Jerusalem was taken by the Chaldeans; and that these would be restored in the days of the Messiah.

Then there are those who say the two ideas seem to be combined. Jesus Christ is the bread from heaven, the nourishment of the life of believers, the true manna, of which those who eat shall never die (John 6:31-43, John 6:48-51). He is now withdrawn from our sight, thus "hidden." Furthermore, the believer's life is hid with Him in God (Colossians 3:3). In this world the souls of believers are nourished with "hidden manna"; in heaven it will be their constant food for all eternity.

Other than the obvious purpose of sustaining the Hebrew people in their wanderings, God had another purpose for manna. God's pre-creation plan was that the Hebrew people would be a servant nation, a people though whom God could bless the nations. The modern application of this purpose is that once we are sustained, we are to serve, to minister, to bless.

So, this is a book of unhidden manna – truths revealed and shared – for daily sustenance and inspiration, motivating us to serve. Yet, even in each days writing, there is more than what is revealed. There is hidden manna. Thus the revealed manna – bits of spiritual insight designed to jump start a day of ministry and service – is followed with the hidden manna -- a prayer for the reader to complete. All designed to make us better servants of God, blessing the nations.

I challenge you to begin a year of more intense ministry as you partake of the daily manna – hidden and unhidden - provided in this book.

January 1 Another New Year

Today we turn a page on our calendars. A new year begins. Someone said an optimist stays up until midnight to greet the New Year. A pessimist stays up to be sure the old year departs. There are other differences between optimists and pessimists. Churches have both in their membership. I ask both groups: Is there a word from God for a new year? As a matter of fact there is and it comes from an ancient source. As Moses stood on Mt. Nebo and gave his farewell address, Joshua became the leader of God's people. It was Joshua, not Moses, who would take them into the Promised Land. The Old Testament book of Joshua begins with a message from God to Joshua and continues with Joshua's message to a people in transition. Joshua's words are fitting for a new year with all its excitement and uncertainties, its reasons for optimism and for pessimism. "Joshua said to the people, 'Sanctify yourselves, for tomorrow the Lord will do wonders among you'." (Joshua 3:5) As the calendar turns, what do you need to do to "sanctify" yourself so the Lord can do wonders in and through you in this new year?

Today's prayer to continue: Lord, I desire to be used for Your purposes this year, so I sanctify myself in the following ways . . .

January 2 Giving It All We've Got!

I have a number of favorite quotes displayed around my office. A particular one relates well to birthdays, and since I had one last week, I re-read the quote. No one really knows who originally said or wrote it. The most oft quoted version is from Hunter S. Thompson in his book "Hell's Angels" written in 1966. Other versions of the quote have been attributed to a Maxine cartoon, to novelist and screenwriter, Mike Frost, and to multiple bloggers with various adjustments to the original. The quote in my office says, "Life is not a journey to the grave with the intention of arriving safely in a pretty and well-preserved body, but rather to skid in broadside, thoroughly used up, totally worn out and loudly proclaiming–Wow! What a ride!" Maybe the origin of the quote, or at least the idea for the quote goes back to the Apostle Paul, who, toward the end of his life wrote, "I have fought the good fight, I have finished the race, I have kept the faith" (2 Timothy 4:7) or better yet, the paraphrase from "The Message," I've run hard right to the finish, believed all the way. All that's left now is the shouting—God's applause!" When the end is nearer than the beginning, one thinks of these things. As the new year begins, let's give it all we've got, full speed ahead! OK?

Today's prayer to continue: Lord, not only do I desire to live today well, but also to finish well. To that end I want to give it all I've got. Today that means . . .

January 3 Facebook Praying: Goals and Resolutions

Long ago I stopped making serious New Year's resolutions. Then a few years ago, my teenage granddaughter challenged me to "get with it and get on Facebook." I saw little value in some toy created by a Harvard sophomore, but I agreed to do so as a New Year's resolution. I had also set an earlier goal to spend more time praying for friends. The Bible says, "The Lord restored the fortunes of Job when he prayed for his friends" (Job 42:10 NAS). I certainly had no fortunes needing restoration, nor, fortunately, did I have any "friends" like Job had. I lost some things I wished to have restored and I wanted to do more praying for friends. Little did I know that Facebook would provide that opportunity. Once on Facebook, I added "friends" to my list, almost daily - some long-lost friends. Years later, I'm happy to report a host of Facebook friends for whom I pray on their birthdays, complete with a notice to them of my intercession. I've also grouped my friends into subgroupings that enable me to pray for them in a systematic manner. So thanks to my Facebook New Year's resolution, I have fulfilled my goal of spending more time praying for my friends. Why should satan be the only one using technology?

Today's prayer to continue: Today would be a good day, Lord, for me to add friends to my prayer life. Friends like . . .

January 4 Birthday Paranoia Cured

I celebrated another birthday last week. I never liked birthdays. When I was young, my birthday was always the occasion for someone else to have fun. On the first birthday I remember, my aunt stood me in front of the TV where some dumb looking clown called out my name, including middle name, in the birthday list. Everyone in the family laughed – except me. Middle name on TV! How embarrassing! One year my birthday party was a trip to the stables and horseback riding. Everyone had fun but me. I had never ridden a horse, have not ridden one since, and unless there are horses in heaven, I will never ride one again. Another year my birthday party was at Playland Park, the forerunner of AstroWorld in southwest Houston. We ate hot dogs and rode the Ferris wheel. I lost my hot dog somewhere on the sharp down-hill turn. As to ever riding another Ferris wheel, see my comment above on horses. Out of Birthday paranoia, I always insist that my birthday be low key with no parties. In fact, my favorite way to spend my birthday is with family, in a quiet restaurant that offers a free birthday meal. That was my story – until Facebook. I now receive hundreds of birthday greetings. Some bring laughter, others bring memory tears. So, I repent. Even birthdays are days that "the Lord has made . . . We will rejoice and be glad in it." (Psalm 118:24). OK, now I feel better.

Today's prayer to continue: I need to "rejoice" every day, not just on my birthday. So today, Lord, I rejoice as follows . . .

January 5 Plays and Plans that Work

"Sixty percent of the time, that play always works." I wondered if I heard that correctly. A football coach described a play that failed and put his team behind in the score. This time of year how many football games can one watch without going crazy? I'm not sure, but 34 bowl games, plus professional end-of-season and playoff games, plus a high school all-star game or two and I was close to overdosing on television football. But that's what he said. Come to think of it, I've had days like that, days when I just knew that I had prepared well and planned the day correctly. But at the end of the day, I thought "most of the time, those plans should have worked." We have plans for the year to come. They should work. They look good on paper. May your plans and mine work for the glory of God in this new year – at least 60% of the time. "May He grant you according to your heart's desire, and fulfill all your purpose" (Psalm 20:4).

Today's prayer to continue: Lord, I submit my plans to You. More than the fulfillment of these plans, I want to do Your will. However, "my heart's desire" today is . . .

January 6 Infused

Some dentists instruct patients to bite down on a tea bag if their gums are bleeding following extraction of a tooth. Other than that, a tea bag is of very little use alone. However, let the tea bag be infused with boiling water and the result is hot tea. This image is reflected in Paul's words in Philippians 4:13, "I can do all things through Christ who strengthens (infuses) me." We may not be able to do much with our circumstances, but when we allow our circumstances to be infused with God's strength, we are strengthened. Do you need to do anything today and not sure how to do it? Allow the Lord to infuse you with His strength. Now that's a truth on which you can bite down.

Today's prayer to continue: To be infused with Your strength today, Lord, that means for me to be . . .

January 7 Merry Christmas, Again

Merry Christmas! Am I late? I am if I celebrate Christmas according to the Gregorian calendar (which I do). While all Christians believe that Mary, "brought forth her first-born Son" (Luke 2:7), there is disagreement as to when that happened. Orthodox Christians in Central and Eastern Europe and other parts of the world celebrate Christmas on January 7, according to the Julian calendar. Christmas on January 7 is also known as Old Christmas Day. Eleven days were dropped to make up for the calendar discrepancy that accumulated with the Julian calendar when England and Scotland switched from the Julian to the Gregorian calendar in 1752. Many people, especially in rural areas, did not accept the loss of these 11 days and preferred to use the Julian calendar. Nevertheless, January 7 is a time of reflection, inner thoughts and healing in many eastern European countries. Many Orthodox Christians fast before January 7, which is a day for feasting and enjoying their friends' and family members' company. So Merry Christmas to my friends who live and serve in places where today is Christmas Day. And for everyone else, if you didn't get enough Christmas on December 25, you can celebrate again.

Today's prayer to continue: Today, Lord, I celebrate Your birth again. My gift to you on this day is . . .

January 8 All Things

In five verses, the Apostle Paul uses the phrase "all things" six times (Colossians 1:16-20). You don't need to have a theological education to know that when one writer uses a phrase that often in that short of a span, he is trying to communicate something about that phrase. In summary, Paul says God put "all things" together in the beginning, God holds "all things" together now and God will ultimately bring "all things" together. Do you have anything in your life that does not fit in the category of "all things"? If so, you can exclude it from the following application - surrender all things to the Lordship of Jesus Christ, who put all things together, holds all things together and will bring all things together and, He will "present you holy, blameless and above approach in His sight (Colossians 1:22)."

Today's prayer to continue: Lord, acknowledging You put "all things" together, I surrender some things to You today, like . . .

January 9 Restored, Then Led

While I've always believed that the Bible was fully inspired by God, lately I've been inspired by even the divine arrangement of ideas in the Bible. For instance, the Psalmist – in the Psalm without equal – proclaims God "restores his soul" then goes on to affirm that God leads him "in paths of righteousness" (Psalm 23:3). When I was young, there was a still-popular phrase, from a generation or two before me. Seems folks had a mental image of "getting the cart before the horse" and often warned against such an arrangement. In fact, as I made my plans for the future, my grandfather often cautioned me to avoid getting my cart before my horse. While I did not then, nor do I now, own a cart, nor a horse, I do have a similar problem with more modern terminology. Too often I get the order of scripture backwards. I want to be led in righteous paths, but I don't want to wait for my soul to be restored. So as you plan your day, be sure you have your cart in its proper alignment or your horse will have great difficulty in finding "righteous" paths.

Today's prayer to continue: Today Lord, I need to get my priorities in order and rightly aligned with Your priorities, such as . . .

January 10 Standing on the Rock

"I'm standing on the Rock" replied the quarterback following the championship football game last week. His answer was in response to a reporter who, for lack of any appropriate question to ask a young man who had just missed the biggest game of his life with an early game injury, asked what it was like to watch this last game in his school's uniform, from the sidelines. Makes me wonder how much education one has to have to be a sports sideline reporter. But I digress. The full quote was, "I always give God the glory. I never question why things happen the way they do. God is in control of my life, and I know that if nothing else, I'm standing on the Rock." Not everyone gets to play in the big game. Most don't make the headlines. The majority live in relative obscurity. To have a celebrity, a two-time Heisman Trophy candidate, a potential pro football player, testify to his faith in the midst of adversity, is a challenge to all of us, whatever team colors we wear and no matter how many fingers we hold up at the end of the game. I hope next time I get knocked down, I can say, "In the time of trouble . . . set me high upon a rock" (Psalm 27:5).

Today's prayer to continue: Right now Lord, I stand upon the Rock, before this day is over, I just might slip. When I slip, restore me, especially when my slipping involves . . .

January 11 Prescriptions

Doctors have given me prescriptions for things that ail me and prescriptions that supplement my lifestyle. I have needed both. So did John. Exiled on Patmos, he was hurting as well as in need of a supplemental spiritual boost. When he began to write the Revelation, he got both and in so doing offered us a prescription for praise. The very mention of the name of Jesus (Revelation 1:5) caused John to offer praise for three attributes of the Lord. John was reminded that Jesus loved him – past, present and future. Because of that love, Jesus had liberated, loosed, freed, and washed John from his sin. Having been loved and liberated, John then discovered that Jesus adopted him into His family and that lineage made him a priest able to communicate directly with God. Having praised the Lord, John had the curtain opened and God showed him what heaven would be like. That should have cured his ailments and supplemented his lifestyle! The Psalmist says God inhabits the praise of his people (Psalm 22:3). God sure inhabited the praise of John! So, take a praise prescription today and enjoy God's presence inhabiting your life.

Today's prayer to continue: Lord, acknowledging that praise has to do with Your attributes, I praise you today for being . . .

January 12 Connectivity

To the charge that I am computer illiterate, I plead guilty. However, as long as I have friends who understand computers and can keep me in line, I am okay. One thing that concerns me about computer people is their language. Not because it's obscene, but because it's unknown by most of the rest of us. Recently, a computer technician stopped by my office and asked, "How's your connectivity?" I thought of several cute responses but decided to not use any of them. Later I looked up "connectivity" in the dictionary and found: "The state of being connected." With that profound definition, I concluded that I am rich. No, not in possessions. Jesus said, "One's life does not consist in the abundance of the things he possesses (Luke 8:15)." I am rich in connectivity – to an awesome God, to a wonderful family, to a great church and to a host of faithful friends. How's your connectivity today?

Today's prayer to continue: Thank You Lord for allowing me to be connected to You. I am also thankful today for other connections like . . .

January 13 Mountain Tops and Flat Lands

It is so easy to prize the peaceful times of private, direct communion with God. The disciples of Jesus had such an experience on the Mount of Transfiguration (Luke 9:27-36). So satisfied with the feeling was Peter that he suggested building three tabernacles and staying on the mountain top – while the routine of life went on below. Peter either had not fully learned or temporarily forgot that life is not lived on spiritual mountain tops, but on the day-by-day flat lands below. On the other hand, daily routine is lived poorly by those who have spent little time with God on the mountain top. So, here's the strategy for living on the flat lands – divert daily, withdraw weekly to the mountain top and meet with God. When that becomes routine, the flat lands begin to look more heavenly.

Today's prayer to continue: I love being on the "mountain top" with You, Lord. Today, I ask that I be equally appreciative of Your presence on the flat lands of my life. Flat lands like . . .

January 14 Words

You don't really know what is in someone's mind until it comes out in words, (unless, of course, they are a pantomime artist). Jesus was a reality in the mind of God, but we didn't really know it for sure until the Father sent the Son as "the Word made flesh." As Jesus, the eternal Word, lived and taught, the message of the Father was communicated to mankind in a way that did not misrepresent God's plan. Recently, I sat on the Emergency Door row of an airplane. While waiting for take-off, I decided to read the emergency card in the seat pocket. "Do not sit on this row if: (You are physically unable to open the door, etc.) The last "If" on the list was, "If you cannot read English." Hmmmm! Barring a language barrier, words are helpful in clarifying thoughts. The Bible speaks of "a word fitly spoken" (Proverbs 25:11). As Jesus, the eternal

Word, lived and taught, He clarified the meaning of God. Watch your words today. They may clarify what's in your mind.

Today's prayer to continue: Today, I desire that my words clearly represent You, O Lord, especially related to . . .

January 15 Interruptions

The other morning I got up with a list of things that had to be done that day. When I lay down on the same bed that same night, none of the things I had planned to do had been done. Have you ever had a day when you never got to your "To Do" list because of interruptions? Some weeks, I have about three of those days. I hear the term "The Ministry of Interruptions" and it bothers me because I try to be so organized. How could an interruption be meaningful, much less ministry? But it was for Jesus. He had an entire of day of interruptions - a man named Legion with emotional issues, a government official named Jairus with a family concern, a woman with a physical problem that doctors couldn't solve, and a young girl that appeared to have died. I don't know what He had planned for that day, but if you'll read Mark 5, you will discover what Jesus did with the interruptions that came into His schedule. May you and I do as well with the interruptions that come our way today.

Today's prayer to continue: Help me today, Lord, to use my interruptions to serve others and glorify You, especially related to . . .

January 16 Wet feet

I've never walked on water, although I have gotten my feet wet a few times. As far as I can tell, Peter just had one chance to walk on water (Matthew 14:22-33). He made the most of it. There comes a time when you have to act, step out on faith, get your feet wet. Peter did. At one time Peter had wayward feet, but Andrew brought him to Jesus.

Then he had washed feet when Jesus knelt before him and washed his feet. He had wandering feet when he denied the Lord. He also had willing feet. "How beautiful are the feet of them that preach the gospel of peace" (Romans 10:15). Here, Peter had wet feet because he was attempting to walk on the water (He actually made one step on water, which is one more than I've made). When the opportunity comes your way to exhibit water-walking faith you too have to act. Such an opportunity may well only knock once. Sometimes I get stuff in the mail that says, "For a limited time only." That could be written over a lot of possibilities in life. Look for opportunities today - opportunities that may come your way only once - and if you can't walk on water, at least get your feet wet.

Today's prayer to continue: I'm looking for that once in a lifetime opportunity today Lord. When it comes, may I be found faithful and . . .

January 17 An Elijah Complex

Ever had an Elijah complex? Elijah was a 9th century prophet in Israel during the reign of King Ahab. At the darkest hour, God sent him to confront Ahab. There had been no rain for three years in Israel. Elijah had encountered the prophets of Baal on Mt. Carmel and killed all 850 of them before praying for rain. Ahab rushed to tell Jezebel with Elijah running alongside. Jezebel's message to Elijah was, "You're going to die!" Elijah sat under a broom tree and "prayed that he might die. (1 Kings 19:4)" Elijah made three symptomatic statements and added an additional statement in verse 10, all describing an Elijah complex:

- "It is enough."
- "Take my life"
- "I am no better than my fathers"
- "I alone am left."

Before the chapter ends there appears a cure for an Elijah complex. God told Elijah to get back to doing what he had been called to do. I have discovered when I am doing what God called me to do – no more and no less – I don't have to worry about the Elijah complex. How about you?

Today's prayer to continue: I want to follow Your leadership today, Lord, and not make excuses like . . .

January 18 Not Enough Jesus

I read with great interest the activities surrounding the dedication of the Billy Graham Museum in North Carolina. Proving that no family is perfect, the Graham family has had their disagreements aired in the media. Finally the Museum was dedicated and open to the public. The most interesting event to me was reported on Billy Graham's first visit to the Museum. Upon entering he reportedly said, "Too much Billy; not enough Jesus." The comment caused me to wonder where else that same quote might be used:

- Too much personality; not enough Jesus.
- Too much program; not enough Jesus.
- Too much building; not enough Jesus.
- Too much talking; not enough Jesus.
- Too much curriculum; not enough Jesus.

On the Mount of Transfiguration three disciples saw many extras. Moses and Elijah appeared after being dead a long time. There was a bright cloud and a voice coming out of the cloud. The extras caused them to fall on their faces. When they looked up again, Moses and Elijah were gone. The cloud was unseen and the voice unheard. Matthew 17:8 records that the disciples, "saw no one but Jesus only." With all the extras that surround me, I may not be able to see "Jesus only" today but at least I'm going to try to experience more of Jesus and not so much of the other. How about you?

Today's prayer to continue: Lord, today I really prefer to see only You, which is enough, not extras like . . .

January 19 Recognizing the Real

I returned from a convention meeting in San Antonio, Texas. More amazing to me than the inspiring sermons, the uplifting music, the debatable reports, and the non-binding resolutions, was hearing an experience from a colleague of mine. Staying in a hotel just a few block from the historic Alamo, this long-time John Wayne fan drove 127 miles to Brackettville, Texas to see the movie set of the film, "The Alamo." Never mind Davie Crockett, Sam Houston, William Travis, James Bowie, and a host of others, Brackettville is the location of the Alamo where the legendary John Wayne was. Amazing! One day, the disciple, Philip, said to Jesus. "Lord, show us the Father." Patiently (or maybe the Biblical record hides the Lord's frustration) Jesus replied, "Have I been with you so long, and yet you have not known me, Philip (John 14:8-9)?" Also amazing! Poor Philip! Like my colleague, he missed the real while looking for the spectacular. I pray that doesn't happen to you or me today.

Today's prayer to continue: Lord, block my eyes from seeking the spectacular today and help me to long for the real, such as . . .

January 20 Be Ye Kind

I have a younger brother of whom I am very proud. He is heavily involved in the Southern Gospel Music industry. If you log on to the Internet, you might hear him as Breakfast Bob. When Bob was young he came home from church one Sunday having memorized Ephesians 4:32, "Be ye kind one to another" from the King James Version of the Bible. There were a couple of other versions back then, but only liberals used them (or so we were told). Our parents were very proud of Bob for his scripture memory. I was not. Every time I started to hit him or do him some other bodily harm, he quoted that verse to me. What he was doing, although we were both too young to know it, was stabilizing our relationship before it needed repair. Most of us are not so fortunate. Our relationships need repair. I encourage you to repair some strained relationships today, or maybe stabilize a few before they need repair. "Be ye kind to one another" today.

Today's prayer to continue: Today Lord, I need Your help in being kind to . . .

January 21 Diversity

I compiled a book that includes multiple authors from various denominational backgrounds. Chapters from authors arrived daily. It caused me to wonder (and ask) why God chose eight or nine men (depending on who wrote Hebrews) to write the New Testament instead of just picking one and inspiring all of it through him. The second answer I was given (after the first answer of "We don't ask that kind of question.") was because God loves diversity. God knows, as I read the various writing styles and ideas of my contributors, I am trying my very best to love diversity or at least appreciate it. I need to. We all need to. Paul wrote, "we have many members in one body" (Romans 12:4). I keep reminding myself that there are no majority parts in the body/Body. We are each uniquely created by God and placed in the Body to accomplish a divine purpose. No two of us are exactly alike. This might be a good day to celebrate the diversity in the Father's forever family.

Today's prayer to continue: Help me today, Lord to celebrate the diversity of your Body, especially . . .

January 22 Happiness

Everywhere I've been I have discovered people to have at least one thing in common. Whether I've been in the over-crowded cities of the third world or the high-tech cities of North America; great urban centers or open-country, rural areas; among the very rich or the very poor; among the highly educated of academia or among those with little formal education; whatever the age group; whatever the economic level, I have found one thing in common with everyone I have met. Everyone has a desire to be happy. Not everyone defines happiness the same way, but all desire it. A formula for genuine happiness is stated in these words from Proverbs 3:5-6: "Trust in the Lord with all your heart, and lean not on your own understanding; in all you ways acknowledge Him, and he shall direct your path." It is my prayer that today will open up for you a deeper level of happiness than you have ever known before.

Today's prayer to continue: For me to be happy today, Lord, I need to . . .

January 23 Remember Your Creator

The writer of Ecclesiastes said, "Remember now your Creator in the days of your youth, before the difficult days come (Ecclesiastes 12:1)." We recently celebrated a grandchild's birthday. Someone said, "Grand kids are God's reward for not killing your teenagers." I'm not sure about that, but I am sure that our lives have been rewarded a hundred times over by our loving grandchildren. Actively involved at their Christian school and faithful to their church's activities, they consistently remember their Creator in the days of their youth. Most of you know that "difficult days" do come and one way to cope with them is by remembering the Creator's guidance in the past. This might be a good day to thankfully remember your Creator for His past leadership in your life and for assurance of ongoing divine direction.

Today's prayer to continue: Thank you Lord, for all that You have done for me in my past and for all You are doing today, especially . . .

January 24 Desperate for God

Don't you hate it when a song gets stuck in your head and won't go away? There is a Michael W. Smith song that keeps running through my mind. "This is the air I breathe . . . This is my daily bread . . . I'm desperate for You." When was the last time you were really desperate for God (Psalm 84:2)? I asked myself that question and the answer was a bit frightening. Abraham was desperate for God on Mt. Moriah. Moses was desperate for God up against the Red Sea. David was desperate for God when caught in multiple disobediences. Jonah was desperate for God while "vacationing" inside a huge fish. Daniel was desperate for God while visiting a lion's den. Paul was desperate for God . . . well almost every day of his Christian life. John was desperate for God on the Isle of Patmos. What about me? I desire God. I need God. Occasionally, I even long for God, but desperate for God? Sorry to say, it's been awhile. Too long. Part of the issue of prayerlessness (or prayer deficit) is that we are not desperate enough for God. We are self-satisfied and content with our lives as they are. I think we often wait for a crisis to be desperate. Why can't desperation for God be as common as breathing and eating? I think that question is why the song is stuck in my head. How about you and I trying to be as desperate for God today as we are in crisis times?

Today's prayer to continue: Lord, what would it take today for me to be desperate for You? Perhaps . . .

January 25 From These Hills

I've just returned from a week of refreshment high in the mountains. Every time I visit the mountains I look up and reflect on Psalm 121:1-2 – one of the first passages of scripture I memorized. The Psalmist must have been in a similar setting when he exclaimed, "I will lift up my eyes to the hills." As if someone might misunderstand and think he was worshipping the hills instead of the God who created the hills, he continued with a question, "From whence comes my help?" Then came the answer, "My help comes from the Lord, who made heaven and the earth." Last week was a good reminder that my Lord is God of the hills. Now that I am out of the mountains, I'm going to try real hard to remember that my Lord - since He made the "heaven and the earth" - is God of the valley as well. I invite you to join me in that remembrance.

Today's prayer to continue: Lord, today, as I live in the valley, I need to be reminded of . . .

January 26 Removal

Like a lot of people my age who grew up playing outside in the sun, I occasionally have to make a visit to the dermatologist and have him spray a bit of liquid nitrogen on my skin to remove the skin cancer spots. No one told me when I was young that this would be a problem. Of course, there are a lot of other things no one told me when I was young that I am discovering these days. The Apostle Paul told the young believers in Ephesus there were certain things that needed to be "put away from you" (Ephesians 4:31). Other translations say "get rid of" these things or "be banished from" these things. The most accurate translation is the Holman Christian Standard Bible that says, these things "must be removed." The word literally means "remove." Now the things Paul was referring to could not be removed by liquid nitrogen, nor can some of the unhealthy things in my life. Living in the presence of the Son causes these unwanted features to surface. In fact, the closer to the Son I live, the more things seem to surface. If I'll work with Him, God will "remove" these unnecessary things from my life. Now that I've had sun spots removed, this might be a good time to let the Son remove some other things. Join me?

Today's prayer to continue: Today, Lord, I ask You to remove the following things from my life . . .

January 27 What's the Point?

I'm not sure where the mistake was made - probably by me, perhaps by some well-meaning secretary, then again it could all be blamed on the computer. It doesn't really matter. The sermon outline that appeared in the bulletin on a recent Sunday had both of my main points listed as "II." There was no point "I" only two point "IIs." It was only frustrating because it was humorous. How can you preach a two-point sermon without point "I"? How can you proceed without a starting point? It reminded me of the cook book for newlyweds in which the first chapter is entitled, "Face the Stove." You've got to start at the starting point. Right? How silly for a football referee to announce on first down, "Second and ten!" Or for someone to mis-state the well-worn phrase, "Second things first!" Much worse for one to misquote Jesus in Matthew 20:16, "The last will be second, and the second last." Or to mistakenly identify our Lord in Revelation 1:11 as, "the Alpha and the Omega, the second and the last." So, what's the point? I went ahead with my sermon and preached both points and no one commented on the mistake. Maybe no one reads the bulletin. Maybe no one cares about the points. Now that's a scary point. What's your first point this today?

Today's prayer to continue: The first thing I need to do today, Lord, is . . .

January 28 No Hope and Hope

One of the indicators that the years are passing by is that you attend more funerals than you do weddings. I've attended my share of weddings, performed a few of them, and now the funeral count is catching up. I attended another funeral last week. If funerals must be attended (I only know of one way to avoid it and I'm not ready for my own funeral yet) I'd rather attend funerals of Christians than funerals of non-believers. I've been to both. While both involve grief, Christians do not grieve as, "others who have no hope" (1 Thessalonians 4:13). Certainly no less intense, Christian grief is different. It is mixed with hope. Both the music and the message of Christian funerals are hope-ful. Come to think of it what is the music of the non-Christian funeral? So in the midst of last week's funeral, of a faithful, long-time, servant of God, I received a new dose of hope. This then is not about death and funerals. It is about life – abundant and eternal – and the hope that is within us – hope for reunion and hope for reward. I'm sure of it! Aren't you?

Today's prayer to continue: Thank You Lord for the assurance of eternity with You. I celebrate that assurance today by . . .

January 29 While I'm Thinking about It

All along I thought I was having "senior moments." This past week a friend told me that he didn't have "senior moments," but rather suffered from "intellectual interruptions." Since I've had this problem long before I became a senior, I think I like the new term better. Whether your memory lapses are "senior moments" or "intellectual interruptions" or "losing the train of thought" or "drawing a blank" as my grandfather used to call it, the key is to re-focus. The mind is a wonderful gift from God, but it's a lot like that machine at the cleaners that takes my shirts around and around the building – when a shirt is missed, I must wait for it to come back around. Thoughts are similar, but the older one gets the slower that machine runs. The Bible tells us to use our minds to focus on "whatever things are true, whatever things are noble, whatever things are just, whatever things are pure, whatever things are lovely, whatever things are of good report . . ." So, while I'm thinking about it, I want to "think on these things" (Philippians 4:8). Would you join me today – as you remember to do so?

Today's prayer to continue: Today Lord, I need Your help as I think on . . .

January 30 Holiness

I've been thinking and reading about holiness lately. Holiness is not knowledge. Balaam had knowledge; nor great position-Judas Iscariot had position; nor doing many things-Herod did many things; nor zeal for certain religious matters-Jehu had zeal; nor outward respectability-the young ruler was respected; nor taking pleasure in hearing preachers-the Jews in Ezekiel's day enjoyed that; nor keeping company with godly people-Demas did that. Blood-parents cannot give it to their children by inheritance. Ministers cannot give it to their members by baptism. Holiness is the result of vital union with Jesus Christ. It is the fruit of being an abiding and living branch off the True Vine. He is the Physician to whom you must go if you would keep well. He is the Manna which you must eat, and the Well from which you must drink. He is the Rock on which you must rest. His arm is the arm on which you must lean. Paul encouraged his readers to, "be holy" (Ephesians 1:4). So, have a holy day.

Today's prayer to continue: OK Lord, I really want to be holy. To do so I today, I need to . . .

January 31 Honest Additions

Waiting in an airport terminal this past week for my connecting flight, I heard a familiar announcement with a new ending. The airline employee, with routine discipline, announced, "Ladies and Gentlemen, we are ready to begin boarding our flight. Please have your boarding passes out and ready for the gate attendant." Then with obvious negative experiences in her past, she added, "We are not taking a DNA test this morning, so please do not put your boarding pass in your mouth or under your arm." Now, with everyone's full attention, she added one final comment, "Besides, that's really gross!" Her professional training gave way to honest additions. Perhaps this was similar to what Paul was feeling when he wrote of his crowd that they were, "always learning and never able to come to the knowledge of the truth" (2 Timothy 3:7). Today thoughts are far too short for me to tell you how many times I've made a routine, traditional statement, and been tempted to add an honest addition. Well, maybe I'll share just one. I'll put my honest additions in parenthesis (where they belong). "It is time in our service for the offering (would someone cue the ushers they're already supposed to be down front), and I know you'll give generously as unto the Lord (besides part of this pays my salary so don't hold back!)." Maybe we ought to go ahead with the boldness of the gate attendant and share the "truth" of our honest additions (and then again maybe not).

Today's prayer to continue: Honestly Lord, I would like to serve You today, especially as I . . .

February 1 God's Provision in the Wilderness

Is there ever a time when God cannot provide? Have you ever doubted God's ability to provide? I have. I can now confess that I was not sure God could provide enough income for me in retirement. How foolish! In Psalm 78:20-33 others wondered if God could provide. This time there was doubt that God could provide a table in the wilderness. In spite of God's provisions in the past, the people still wondered. God had provided a miraculous exodus from Egypt as well as reminders of His presence along the way – water from rock, manna, etc. Their sin was not in wanting food in the wilderness, but in doubting God could provide food. It was not a sin against another person, but against the God, who had delivered them. They doubted that God, who had delivered them, could now provide them the basic necessities of life. Human nature is such that if God performs a miracle there, we doubt He will do it here and if He does one here, we doubt He'll do it again. Let's establish a fact: God provides, even in the wildernesses of our lives. He will provide for me today – and for you as well. Rejoice!

Today's prayer to continue: Lord, more than anything else, I need Your provision today related to . . .

February 2 Past, Present, and Future

Ideas from other cultures fascinate me. For instance, the Hebrews spoke of the future as though it was behind them, rather than in front, believing that you could see what was in front of you, but not what was behind you. Thus the unseen future was described as behind one, while the known past was described as in front of one. Maybe that's what inspired the intriguing quote by 19th century Dutch philosopher and theologian, Soren Kierkegaard, who said, "Life can only be understood backwards; but it must be lived forwards." I'm no philosopher and not much of a theologian, but I have learned this much along the way – the future, wherever it is perceived to be, is in God's hands. The Psalmist proclaimed that our God, "will be our guide even to death" (Psalm 48:14) and I'm fairly sure death is in the future, not the past. So, with your hand in God's hand, join me in having a good day – yesterday.

Today's prayer to continue: Lord, the past belongs to You as does the present. Help me to trust You with my future, especially related to . . .

February 3 The Prayer of Jehoshaphat

I just returned from a meeting with a great group of cross-denominational folks. I'm one of only a few from my denomination on the committee of approximately 100 and possibly the only one from the academic world. I love being with them. No one cares who I am or what I am. I'm just Dan. In one of the many prayer times, someone prayed the prayer of Jehoshaphat (could this be a new book title?) – "Lord, we don't know what to do, but our eyes are on You" (2 Chronicles 20:12). How many times have I felt this way, not knowing exactly what to do, yet trusting with all my being on God's directions? What an encouragement on days when confusion or uncertainty reigns. Jehoshaphat was troubled because a "great multitude" of the enemy was coming against him. Did God answer the prayer? Sure did! God sent Jahaziel to say, "Do not be afraid or dismayed because of this great multitude, for the battle is not yours, but God's" (2 Chronicles 20:15). Do you face a multitude of concerns today? How about joining me in praying the prayer of Jehoshaphat?

Today's prayer to continue: Lord, like Jehoshaphat, we don't always know what to do. Help us today to keep our eyes on You related to . . .

February 4 Acceptance and Arrival

"What if they don't accept me" the student asked. He had been invited to interview for a position and his anxious condition caused him to seek my advice. His concern was a universal one. Everyone seeks acceptance of some kind, even those who boast they don't care what anyone else thinks about them. Counselors tell us that acceptance is a necessary element in the development of our personality. People look to various sources to find this acceptance. Some seek it from other people. Some seek it from God. The apostle Paul tells us how to gain acceptance from God. It comes through Jesus Christ, "the Beloved." ". . . He (God) has made us accepted in the Beloved" (Ephesians 1:6). Once we feel accepted by God, it is easier to feel good about who we are. "So," I said to the student, "if you are accepted by God and you accept yourself as God made you, then leave the interview in God's hands." The real challenge is not acceptance. Jesus died to make that available for us. The real challenge is that acceptance is not equal to arrival. Through Jesus, God accepts us where we are, allows us to accept ourselves, and then walks with us along the way. Acceptance is the beginning of a wonderful journey; arrival is the end of the journey. The closer I get to the end, the more I appreciate the beginning. How about you?

Today's prayer to continue: Thank You Lord for accepting me as I am and for making me to become what You want me to be. I see that today in . . .

February 5 Joy Comes When?

On many an occasion, someone has quoted to me, "Joy comes in the morning" (Psalm 30:5). Why do you think the morning is so special? Why doesn't joy come in the middle of the afternoon or at midnight? Is there something about the night that generates joy, so that first thing in the morning we are joyful? Maybe we ought to look at the context of the statement. The Psalmist precedes this statement with the words, "weeping may endure for a night" (Psalm 30:5). Ah ha! Joy follows weeping. No! That can't be true. Sometimes night weeping is followed by morning weeping. Sometimes joy doesn't come in the morning. Sometimes joy comes at noon. Enough speculation! Joy does not usually come as a result of the trouble-free, casual times of life, but rather joy is distilled from a unique mixture of challenge, stress, risk, and hope. Helen Keller, who knew both joy and weeping, said, "We could never learn to be brave and patient if there were only joy in the world." So be patient, even in the midst of tears. Joy is on the way – and, like weeping, it may come when you least expect it.

Today's prayer to continue: I'd like to experience joy today, Lord, but first I think I need to . . .

February 6 Benchwarmers

I watched the Super Bowl last night. What a game! In the midst of all the on-field excitement and the funny commercials I couldn't help but notice that the camera kept showing the backup quarterback on the sidelines. He was excited and kept shouting encouragement to his teammates, even though there was little chance of him getting into the game. With the exception of born super-stars, most wannabe athletes have spent time "warming the bench." Somewhere I read that there are four stages of benchwarmers: (1) I can do better (2) Coach doesn't know what he is doing (3) I hope someone gets injured (4) I hope we lose. While the Christian life is often compared to a game, it is more. The last thing we need is benchwarmers. We need to clear the bench and get everyone in the game. After all, "we are members of one another" (Romans 12:5). I don't need you on the bench offering encouragement to me. I need you in the game, moving together toward the same objective. I stand amazed at how far we Christians have diverted from this simple truth.

Today's prayer to continue: Get me off the bench Lord. I want to be in the game with You and with . . .

February 7 Speaking in Songs

How many down times have been uplifted with a song? In my life the answer would be "many" times. It may be a song from my childhood or youth days in which case, it is classified as an old song. It may be a contemporary song that only recently has become a part of my memory bank of songs. The strange thing for me is that I am not a musician. I have a family full of them and many of my best friends are musicians, but not me. In my teenage years, my mother bought me a trombone but the teacher quit after only a few "lessons" with me. While I can carry a tune, I just can't release it very well. So here's my dilemma – I love music and find that it is most often music that makes my day, but I'm not musically inclined. That's why I got so excited reading Ephesians 5:19. I had read the verse before, several times, but never caught the right word – "speaking to one another in psalms and hymns and spiritual songs, singing and making melody in your heart to the Lord." In looking through a number of commentaries, apparently none of the commentary writers caught that word either, since most of the commentary related to defining and distinguishing between "psalms and hymns and spiritual songs." But I don't need a commentary to set me free. Since I speak far better than I sing, I now can "speak" a song and not worry about anyone quitting on me. Would you join me in "speaking" a song to someone today?

Today's prayer to continue: Lord, the song I want to "speak" to You and to someone else today is . . .

February 8 Thinking and Praying

Do you think much before you pray? How about thinking as you pray? I've observed several categories of pray-ers. Some just begin full speed ahead and spontaneously pray all over the place. Others seem so organized that even the Holy Spirit would have difficulty intervening. Still others simply string together learned phrases without much thought – "lead, guide and direct;" "bless the gift and the giver." Then again there are those who cannot pray a complete sentence without using the word "just" at least once – "just bless;" "just watch over us;" "just help us." I call it the Prayer of the Just. It is a biblical fact that God hears some prayers and chooses not to hear others (Isaiah 59:2; -John 9:31). It strikes me that perhaps the prayers that God chooses not to hear are the ones that are not divinely inspired to be offered. Valid, out-spoken prayers may be the result of quiet, in-spoken inspiration from God.

How else would God know what we need before we ask and be in the process of responding to us even as we intercede? So, maybe we should listen more and talk less. Sounds like what I was told as a child. Perhaps as a child of God, I need to be told again. How about you?

Today's prayer to continue: Lord, I need to learn how better to talk with You, Help me today specifically to learn . . .

February 9 Super Silence

It started two weeks in advance and escalated all the way to Super Bowl Sunday. It began again early on Sunday and continued right up to game time, resuming during half-time. It seemed that every former player, coach and wannabe was sharing Super Bowl opinions, theories, observations – on talk show panels, in interviews, and via social networks. A few were insightful, some were interesting, most were hot air. I was reminded of one of my favorite quotes, this one from Plato, "A wise man speaks when something needs to be said. A fool speaks when he needs to say something." Is there a religious lesson to be learned from this? Absolutely! One of the first verses I memorized (and I have long since forgotten why I did so) was James 1:19, "So then, my beloved brethren, let everyman be swift to hear, slow to speak, slow to wrath." One of my recent Scripture favorites is Zephaniah 1:7, "Be silent in the presence of the Lord God." There is a time for words. When that time comes, choose wisely. There is also a time for silence. Silence drives most fast-lane Americans crazy, but when the time comes, shhhh!

Today's prayer to continue: Not so much in silence, Lord, as in reverence, I ask you to show me today . . .

February 10 Super Perspective

I enjoyed the Super Bowl but I'm glad it's over and congratulations to the champions. A recent survey showed 66% of men would miss the birth of their first born child in order to watch the Super Bowl. A lot of faithful Christians missed a worship service for the same purpose. Or maybe their church cancelled services so they could all watch the Super Bowl. Don't get me wrong. I am a hopeless, helpless, sports fanatic. But enough is enough. I'm not really going anywhere super spiritual with this. So let me broaden the playing field (to stick with an analogy for one more sentence). It's not really about priority. It's more about perspective. Many years ago, I had a seminary professor who was totally against sports on Sunday. "Activity of the devil that hinders the worship of God on God's day" he said and I wrote in my notes. When one student asked him what he did on Sunday afternoons to enhance his worship, he admitted to listening to symphony music. So there you are. To each his own. Whether your Lord's Day extra-activity is sports or symphony, just remember it is "the day the Lord has made" (Psalm 118:24) and keep that thought in proper perspective. Now let's see where is the Super Bowl next year? Near my house? Someone remind me this time next year – perspective, perspective, perspective.

Today's prayer to continue: Help me remember Lord that every day is a day You made. In need to worship You more in the area of . . .

February 11 Cancellation and Completion

I cancelled a flight this week. A major airline has been recalling hundreds of its planes for inspections and thereby stranding thousands of passengers in airports far from home. I couldn't take a chance, needing to be back at home at exactly the time printed on my return flight itinerary. How did my calendar get so full anyway? Why is it that I needed to get back at a specific time so I could leave again at another specific time? Somehow I thought retirement would be less busy, less demanding. Don't misunderstand. I'm not ready to sit in a rocking chair all day, every day. But I did envision a slightly less-demanding schedule. My cancellation didn't leave anyone else disadvantaged. Conference phone calls often serve as an adequate replacement. Maybe I need to make more conference calls and fewer flight arrangements. Even with these issues, this much I can affirm: "He who has begun a good work . . . will complete it" (Philippians 1:6) and I'm totally committed to "completion." While retirement brings changes, the "work" continues. For one thing, I now pray more before saying "yes" to invitations. That can't be a bad thing, can it?

Today's prayer to continue: Thank You Lord for what you began in me. As You complete it in me, help me to . . .

February 12 Going Home Again

Thomas Wolfe wrote a classic book entitled, "You Can't Go Home Again." The idea is that things change. If you are away and return, it is never the same. The Hebrew children spent forty futile years trying to go home again. Their experience, recorded in Numbers, is summarized with the cry, "Let us select a leader and return to Egypt" (Numbers 14:4). So is it true that we can't go home again? Yes, if home is a place. I spent a recent weekend with 65 people to whom and with whom I ministered many years ago. We told many of the same stories, even if embellished a bit, laughed at the same jokes, grieved over the same recollections of sadness. True, it wasn't the same, but for a little while, it was close enough. It was close enough because ultimately home for Christians revolves, not around place, but around people. That being true, one of the awesome things about the family of God is that you can go home again. Anytime you're around God's people, you're around family and any time you're with family, you're home. For a few hours at least, it was good to be home again.

Today's prayer to continue: Realizing that "home" is people as well as place, I thank You Lord today for those who make-up my "home," especially . . .

February 13 Footprints and Vision

I've recently been out of the country, in an urban area where owning and operating a motor vehicle is cost prohibitive for many. Going only where public transportation can take them, their geographical world is small. They speak often of their "small footprint" a reference to the limited area of space they normally cover day by day. Church leaders in the area speak of small footprint, large vision. It occurred to me that there are really four categories of people:

• Small footprint, small vision – they go nowhere, see nothing, envision nothing, care little about the rest of the world.

• Small footprint, large vision – while confined to a small geographic area they envision the world and attempt to make some impact on it.

• Large footprint, small vision – These folks travel widely and are knowledgeable of the world, but don't really care about it.

• Large footprint, large vision – They travel widely, care deeply, attempt great things on a world-scale.

I realize these are huge generalities, but at least somewhat valid. The ideal for the Christian would be to have a large vision, regardless of the size of the footprint. Whether local, rural, metropolitan, or global, we need to remember that Jesus said, "The field is the world" (Matthew 13:38). How large is your footprint? How about your vision? Whichever category fits you, I challenge you to "lift up your eyes" and look beyond your footprint this week.

Today's prayer to continue: Increase my vision, Lord. Help me to see . . .

February 14 Things of the Heart

Today is Valentine's Day – a day to think about things of the heart. We speak of loving someone "with all our heart." Hallmark will make several million dollars selling cards with hearts on them. Many floral arrangement with include hearts along with the flowers. Some of us broke teeth on candy hearts given to us by friends, with cute sayings on them such as "Luv U." Long ago Valentine's Day was named after an early Christian martyr, Saint Valentine, and was established by Pope Gelasius I in 500 AD. But even before all of that, hearts were a popular subject. One day God was talking with Ezekiel about hearts and said, "Son of man, these men have set up their idols in their hearts . . . should I let Myself be inquired of at all by them" (Ezekiel 14:3)? In other words, if the heart is not filled with the right ingredients, God is not obliged to listen to our prayers. While Valentine's Day is a good time to express the love of your heart for others, it is also a good time to check on any idols that reside in your heart. Their presence may be why your prayer life is hindered.

Today's prayer to continue: Lord, please remove any thing in my heart that does not glorify you and serve others, specifically remove . . .

February 15 When Mentors Fail

The danger of spiritual role modeling is that the mentored often become like the mentor and stop there, rather than moving beyond to be like Jesus. Paul understood that concept and even though he instructed, "Brethren, I urge you to become like me" (Galatians 4:12) he also pointed them ultimately to Jesus. Spiritual mentoring can so easily and so quickly become dangerous. One is led to faith by a respected believer. Then that respected believer begins to mentor the new convert. The danger on the part of the mentor is an unhealthy ego trip that leads to foolish and unwise advice. The danger on the part of the mentored is a sometimes distorted focus on egotistical advice and ultimately a blind following of an ill-advised direction. How often and how recently have we seen this? And oh the pain of separation between mentor and mentored when realization leads to reality. Be careful who you allow to mentor you today. Be equally careful how you mentor another. Be sure the final model is not an imperfect human being, but rather the infallible Lord.

Today's prayer to continue: Lord, I want to be like You. Thank you for the mentors in my life that have helped move me in Your direction, especially . . .

February 16 Bread and Water

There are some things we simply cannot live without. They are so simple they amaze the intellects among us. In John 4:10, Jesus offers Himself as "living water" and two chapters later, in John 6:35, He describes Himself as, "the bread of life." Bread and water are the very basic, most essential, everyday necessities of life, without which we cannot live but a few hours. Some think of faith as a luxury, a Sunday delicacy, an acquired taste, take it or leave it. But to Jesus, faith was not defined by some super-imposed accessory. It was simply illustrated with bread and water. In a land where water was often unfit to drink and where wine was the substitute of choice, I find it interesting that on the night Jesus was betrayed, in an upper room with His disciples and one final teaching opportunity, He chose to illustrate His truth with bread and wine. We, who long so for the challenging, complicated things of life, may need to again hear Jesus say, "bread" and "water."

Today's prayer to continue: Lord, keep it simple. Today I just need bread and water, meaning, I need . . .

February 17 Family Day

My first clue was a note in the elevator that the hotel restaurant would be closing at 11am for Family Day. My second clue was the day-old newspaper in the restaurant (no paper printed on Family Day). When I asked Donna, my favorite Vancouver waitress, what was going on she replied, "It's Family Day! It's a national holiday in Canada. A day to be with the family and take part in activities for the family – you know, like Sunday used to be." Out of the mouths of babes and waitresses! Even though my Father was also my Pastor, I remember being with family on Sunday, at church, at home, at after-church gatherings, etc. Somehow the worship of God and the celebration of family were blended together. No, we didn't worship family and celebrate God. We had it in proper order. Strangely enough, the rather new holiday was opposed by the British Columbia Chamber of Commerce. Sounds like a very American business/profit mind-set. Same folks (Canadian and American) might have argued against closing stores on Sunday (anyone remember Sunday Blue Laws?). Anyway, the whole idea sounds biblical to me. "This is the written account of Adam's family line. When God created mankind, he made them in the likeness of God" (Genesis 5:1). Not only were family members created in God's image ("He made them") together, they were to become more like God.

Today's prayer to continue: Thank You, Lord for family. I am especially thankful today for . . .

February 18 A New Season

"Pitchers and Catchers report!" Baseball FANatics live for these words. It signals a new beginning when every team has a mathematical chance of being a champion. The past is forgiven, hope springs eternal. Even though baseball had not yet been invented, New Testament Christians understood the feeling. "Old things have passed away; behold all things have become new" (2

Corinthians 5:17). There is a new beginning when one becomes a believer in Jesus Christ. The past is forgiven. The future is one of great hope. But it doesn't end there, because sin doesn't end there. We continue to sin, mess up, and have bad seasons. God continues to forgive and offer fresh hope. As Major League Baseball's spring training begins again, it might be a good time to ask God to once again forget the last season of our life and fill us with new hope.

Today's prayer to continue: Today I ask forgiveness for the past and give thanks for the hope of the present and future. I will strive to follow You Lord in the following areas of my life . . .

February 19 Prayer for Friends

What do you do when you are having a difficult day? Whenever I think I'm having an especially tough time, I read Job. I find some measure of comfort in the fact that whatever my circumstances, Job had it worse. If you stay with Job to the end, you'll find an amazing fact. One of the things I love about the Bible is that you find some of the most profound truth in some of the most obscure places. Just seven verses from the end of the book, these words appear: "The Lord restored Job's losses when he prayed for his friends. (Job 42:10)" Since Job's "losses" included almost everything, this was no small replacement. And were these the same friends who assured Job that his "losses" were a result of sin in his life? How do you pray for friends like that? While I'm not sure exactly how significant Job's losses were and thus how amazing the replacement was I do take from this verse the importance of praying for "friends" – good friends and not-so-good friends. In fact, there is a hint of a promise here that praying for "friends" may improve our own situation. I believe I can think of a few "friends" I need to pray for today. How about you?

Today's prayer to continue: Lord, today, I pray for the following "friends" . . .

February 20 Mathematical Praying

I was never very good at mathematics and I have embarrassing academic transcripts to prove it. Last week I discovered mathematical praying. I'm not sure it will improve my mathematical skills, but it sure enhanced my prayer life. I was in the final stages of preparing to speak to a group of students who were in a three-day orientation time before leading revival meetings during the summer. I was asking God for anointing as I polished my notes one final time before actually speaking. As I thought about their overall orientation and my small part of it, I asked God to allow my presentation to ADD to their training and not SUBTRACT from it. Then I found myself asking God to guide me in "rightly DIVIDING the word of truth" (2 Timothy 2:15) in such a way as to MULTIPLY their summer ministry. I challenge you to practice mathematical praying today. Now if I could just master the Pythagorean Theorem!

Today's prayer to continue: Lord, I need You to add and subtract, multiply and divide, in my life today. Specifically, I'm asking You to . . .

February 21 Pleasing God

In what ways do you try to please God? Perhaps you try to please God through worship, or maybe Bible study, or even acts of ministry. Some seek to please God through prayer, or giving, or simply being obedient. Beware lest you select incorrect methods. Nadab and Abihu displeased God by offering a "profane fire before the Lord" and were destroyed. Then God spoke to Moses and said, "By those who come near me I must be regarded as holy; and before all the people I must be glorified" (Leviticus 10:3). Be sure that in your attempts to please God today, you regard Him as holy. Above all else make certain God is glorified.

Today's prayer to continue: Lord, I acknowledge You as holy, and ask that what I do today will glorify You, specifically as I . . .

February 22 When Does a Day Begin?

When does your day begin? I often wondered why the end of each of the six days of creation in Genesis closed with "the evening and the morning were the first day" (second day, third day, etc. Genesis 1: 5, 8, 13, 19, 23, 31). "Evening" normally denotes the end of the day, while "morning" is usually a reference to the beginning of the day. So, why did God begin with the evening? I knew it was a difficult question. I went to all of the Genesis commentaries on my shelf and all the online commentaries I could "Google" and could not find one explanation, although the question was raised in a few sources. Surely, it was not a reference to dark and light since the heavenly bodies were not created until the fourth day, thus separating the day from the night. Perhaps it referred to the fact that the Jews reckoned time "from evening to evening" (Leviticus 23:32) or that the works of God are works of light, not darkness (1 John 1:5). I really had not the time nor interest in reading much of the commentary as to whether these were twenty-four hour days or periods of time. What I wanted to know was why God began with the "evening." I reasoned as follows: the evening merges into night, and the night terminates with morning. By the time morning is reached, the day has ended ("the first day") and everything needs to be ready for the next day. Ah ha! There it was! When do you get ready for a new day, first thing in the morning? If so, you are already behind God's schedule. You say, "Jesus prayed early in the morning." No, Jesus prayed "a long while before daylight" (Mark 1:35). Maybe God's day begins with a late night/pre-dawn preparation for the next day. It is said that every morning in Africa, a gazelle wakes up knowing it must outrun the fastest lion to survive. Every morning a lion wakes up knowing it must outrun the slowest gazelle or starve to death. So, it doesn't matter if you are a gazelle or a lion. When the morning comes, you'd better be running.

Today's prayer to continue: Lord, it's probably too late to adequately prepare for this day, but please bless my efforts and help me to get a better start on tomorrow as I plan for . . .

February 23 Revelations and Applications

Have you ever noticed in the life of Jesus that mountain revelations were often followed by valley applications? No sooner had Jesus ended his spectacular sermon on the mount than, coming down, He was confronted by a leper (Matthew 8:1). Truth taught on the mountain, had to be applied. Later, the almost unbelievable experience of transfiguration, complete with the re-appearance of Moses and Elijah, was met on the down-side of another mountain, this time with a man crying for Jesus to help his son who was an epileptic (Matthew 17:15). The unique glory which had shown in the face of Jesus on the mountain now had to be applied to the daily hurt of the valley. Yet again, Jesus stood on an appointed mountain and delivered what we have labeled, "the great commission" (Matthew 28:19-20). But wait! Just as I was about to make an application, the Gospel of Matthew ended. What did Jesus do to apply His commission? Oh, He left the application to His disciples, you say? You mean we are the ones who are responsible for applying His mountain words - going, making disciples, baptizing, teaching, etc.? Bummer, just when I was enjoying the solitude of mountain revelations. Truth revealed on the mountain, can never camp out there for long. Calls from the valley hurry us downward.

Today's prayer to continue: Thank You, Lord for mountain-top revelations. Now, today, I ask for Your assistance with valley applications as I serve on the down-side of the mountain, especially, as I . . .

February 24 To Speak or Not to Speak

Have you ever balked at something God impressed upon you to say? Sure you have and so have I. Well, we're not the first to do so. Jeremiah's response to God's instructions was that he was too young to speak. You and I might respond that we are too old, too untrained, too unqualified, too inexperienced, too poor, too fearful, too intimidated, or a dozen other excuses. After God had chastised Jeremiah for his feeble excuse, there came a comforting promise, "Whatever I command you, you shall speak. Do not be afraid . . . for I am with you" (Jeremiah 1:8). Next time you feel led to speak, to one or to one thousand, first be sure both the prompting and the content have come from God, then speak boldly with full assurance that God is your commander, prompter, interpreter, defender, and strength.

Today's prayer to continue: Today, Lord, I may need to speak a word on Your behalf. Help me to know for sure, then guide me as I . . .

February 25 Unanswered Prayer

How many times have you used or heard someone use the phrase, "unanswered prayer." Where did that phrase originate? Not with Jesus. In His teaching on prayer, our Lord never once referred to unanswered prayer. Sometimes the answer is "no" as it was for Jesus when in Gethsemane, He asked the Father to let the Calvary cup pass from His lips. Sometimes God may ask us to wait for a better-timed answer, since His ways and times are not identical to ours. Sometimes, God doesn't answer our prayers in the way we asked them. But if we pray "in His name and for His sake," God will answer according to His will, not ours. So, God always answers prayer – even though sometimes different from our chosen response and often delayed according to our calendar. Otherwise, how do you explain, "Ask, and it will be given to you" (Matthew 7:7; Luke 11:9). We'd prefer the Scripture to say, "Ask and it will be given to you exactly as you prefer and precisely on your schedule." But then we would be conforming God to our image rather than being conformed to His image. So, pray on . . . and wait. God always answers the prayers of His children, even when we do not recognize the answers.

Today's prayer to continue: Lord, You know that prayer I've been praying for a long time and waiting for an answer? Help me to understand the answer that You are already giving, then help me to . . .

February 26 Urgencies and Emergencies

We live in a day of urgencies and emergencies. We have addresses but we may not be there. We have e-mail addresses but we may not answer. We have phone numbers but we also have answering machines to take our messages. Planned agendas often get bumped in favor of some sudden need either of our own or of someone needing us. In times like these, we find it incredibly difficult to "be still, and know" (Psalm 46:10) or as one translation words it, "cease striving and know." I have found three things to be non-negotiable in these current circumstances. My time in God's Word, the Bible, is invaluable. It really is my guide for faith and practice – "a lamp to my feet and a light to my path" (Psalm 119:105). Likewise I must have times – planned and unplanned – to communicate with God. Prayer is the priority of the Christian life. How can a student study without a teacher, an athlete perform without a coach, a musician play without a conductor, a worker toil without a supervisor? How can I serve without continual communication with my Lord? One thing more is needed. I must have the mentoring, advising, supporting, counseling, directing, of trusted friends. When the voices calling to me are many and diverse, not to mention mixed with the world's voices, I need help in hearing and discerning. Of the three this is the one most easily overlooked. The key word is "trusted." In these days of distrust and mistrust, "trusted friends" are hard to find and maintain. If you have them, rejoice. If not, seek them soon. May your urgencies and emergencies be few today.

Today's prayer to continue: Thank You Lord for Your Word, for allowing me to communicate with You, and for trusted friends who walk with me through this journey, especially for . . .

February 27 A Word Fitly Spoken . . . by Someone!

Recently, a friend shared a quote with me – "Prayer is the slender nerve that moves the muscle of omnipotence." I was impressed with the quote and being a professor who is in the habit of looking for footnotes, I asked who made the statement. He didn't know. In curiosity, I began a search. I "Googled it!" In various places I found the quote attributed to the following persons: Edwin Hartsell, Martin Farquhar Tupper, Charles Haddon Spurgeon, Jonathan Edwards, and Archbishop Seraphim. Variations of the quote were attributed to a half-dozen other persons. The entire process reminded me of a couple of things: (1) If something comes from God, it doesn't really matter who gets the credit; and (2) In a generation or two, most of what I say will either be lost or repeated by someone else. So if God has given you something to say, say it the way He said it to you, and let the credit go where it may. In Proverbs 25:11, Solomon (or perhaps someone before him) said, "A word fitly spoken is like apples of gold in settings of silver" whoever says it! (the last three words are mine – I think.)

Today's prayer to continue: Lord, direct me today in the words I say. May they be helpful, beneficial, uplifting, and most of all . . .

February 28 Staying in Touch

"I'll be in touch!" Ever hear that and then not hear from the person for days? I hear it all the time. At last count, I could be reached via three phone numbers, six E-mail addresses, three web sites, two post office mailing addresses, Facebook, LinkedIn, and Twitter. So, what's the problem? It's probably time management, hopefully not lack of interest. As frustrating as that is for me, it makes me wonder how frustrating it is for God when we do not communicate for days and days. God says, "Call to Me, and I will answer you" (Jeremiah 33:3). So, what's the problem? It's not God's problem, it's ours. God wants to communicate with us, invites us to communicate, and encourages us to communicate. What happens when we fail to communicate? Information is missed, connection is broken, relationship is stressed, friendship is . . . Well you get the idea.

Today's prayer to continue: I'm listening, Lord. Speak to me whenever You need to, and as often as You need to, and help me to . . .

March 1 The Uniqueness of Indwelling

I often lead prayer teams in a major North American city. Among other places visited, we tour an Islamic Mosque, A Hindu Center, A Sikh Temple, and a Buddhist Temple. We listen patiently and respectfully as their leaders tell us of their beliefs. Then we move to the parking lot, get in our van, and pray. We pray to the only Founder of a religion that claims its Founder lives in those who believe. In fact, this is one of the unique features of the Christian faith – "Do you not know yourselves, that Jesus Christ is in you" (2 Corinthians 13:5)? In a similar way that sap indwells the branch, producing fruit and blood indwells the body, manifesting itself in life, so our Lord indwells those who believe, reproducing Godly attributes in them. He has not always indwelled us. We had to invite Him in. We did not have to make a sacred pilgrimage, sacrifice another life, or vow to carry a weapon on our body at all times. Convicted of sin and with a repentant spirit, we simply had to invite the Lord into our lives and He began to indwell us. Rejoice with me today for our indwelling Lord.

Today's prayer to continue: Thank You Lord for indwelling my life. That fact alone, makes today . . .

March 2 A Home in Glory Land

I recently attended two funerals in the same week. In both and in most I've attended in my life, and in many obituaries I've read, I've heard and seen the phrase, "gone home to be with the Lord." Why do we use home as a reference for heaven? God's Old Testament people and many of God's New Testament people lived in tents. Few people are at home in a tent. Tent dwellers are continually on the move. People who live in homes are at home, or at least as close as one can get in this life. Really the only earthly home we have is our body. At least that's what Paul believed, but even then he wrote, "While we are at home in the body we are absent from the Lord" (2 Corinthians 5:6). The old spiritual said it best, "This world is not my home; I'm just a passin' through." We've heard that you can't go home again, but that all depends on where home is. If your earthly home is temporary – like your body is temporary – and your heavenly home is eternal, you can go home again. Indeed death is a home going . . . to be with the Lord . . . in the home He has prepared for us. I guess there was more theology than I knew in the songs I was taught as a child. "I've got a home in glory land . . ." How about you?

Today's prayer to continue: As much as I love my earthly home, Lord, I'm anticipating the one You have prepared for me in heaven, and so, today I . . .

March 3 Mega-ego

While mega-churches get most of the spotlight in our day, this is also a day of mega-egos, not necessarily connected to mega churches. After a stirring testimony of conversion, a young man was asked who was responsible for his decision. "I don't remember" he replied, "I only heard from God." Those of us who share the good news need to be reminded occasionally that we are not the good news, but the messenger of such. Paul said his decision to share came, "not from men nor through man, but through Jesus Christ and God the Father" (Galatians 1:1). The call to share is a high and holy calling, but it is the voice of God that needs to be heard when we share.

Today's prayer to continue: Lord, I need to share Your truth today, but help me to remember that I am only a messenger, as I share with . . .

March 4 God Knows

The old spiritual says, "Nobody knows the trouble I've seen . . ." While that may be true on a human level, it is not true when it comes to one's relationship with God. The Psalmist proclaimed, "O Lord, you have searched me and known me" (Psalm 139:1). It is impossible to hide our weaknesses, our failures, our pain, our mistakes, our inadequacies from God. The all-knowing God is aware of our ups and our downs, our victories and our defeats, our positives and our negatives. Absolutely nothing takes God by surprise. God plans our path (Psalm 139:3) and accompanies us along the way. I don't know about you but that affords me great comfort. With God, I do not have to prove myself, impress, cover-up, or justify my actions. I can relax in God's omniscience and I plan on doing just that today. Join me?

Today's prayer to continue: Thank You Lord for knowing all about me. I need to pass that wonderful news on to someone else today, perhaps to . . .

March 5 Wait to Worry

Like many of you I lose money occasionally in the stock market. To be quite honest, I lost a lot of retirement money a few years ago. In fact, I lost so much, I may need to un-retire at some future date. In the midst of my depression, God gave me a passage of scripture from the Sermon on the Mount. Actually, I was preaching through this sermon of our Lord and I was working on this text. "Therefore do not worry about tomorrow, for tomorrow will worry about its own things. Sufficient for the day is its own trouble" (Matthew 6:34) I remembered the advice of a friend in a similar concern in past years. He simply said to me, "Wait to worry!" That's the short version of what Jesus said. After all, worry does not lessen tomorrow's troubles; it only lessens today's energy. Still, I did a poor job of waiting. The only waiting I really did was waiting to get to sleep each night. Many friends sent me scripture verses and other words of encouragement. But then a long-time, dear friend sent me Philippians 4:19, "My God shall supply all your need according to His riches in glory." That night I slept. What an awesome promise and one I needed refreshed on my mind. Whether you lost money recently or face some other concern, you're welcome to claim this passage with me and join me in waiting to worry.

Today's prayer to continue: I seem to worry about a lot of things, Lord, and I can't stop. So today, would You help me wait to worry about . . .

March 6 Satisfied or Content?

The Apostle Paul said he had learned that in whatever circumstance he found himself to be "content" (Philippians 4:11). He didn't say "satisfied." There is a difference. Had Paul been willing to accept all his surroundings, positive as well as negative, he might have used the word "satisfied", meaning, "happy, gratified, pleased." Makes me wonder how he would have reacted to today's circumstances – or for that matter, the circumstances of any day -- satisfied or content? Are you satisfied with your circumstances? All of them? Since we are made for heaven, we will likely never be completely satisfied with earthly circumstances, but like Paul, we can and must learn to be "content" - the Greek word meaning, "independent of external circumstances."

Today's prayer to continue: I really want to be satisfied, Lord, but I'll be content to be content today, especially related to . . .

March 7 Prayer's Profit

Everyone who knows the Bible knows that Job had a truck load of problems. He also asked a few good questions. "Who is the almighty, that we should serve Him and what profit do we have if we pray to Him? (Job 21:15)" I think you know who the almighty is and why we should serve Him. But do you know what profit you have in prayer? One immediately thinks of the responses we get from prayer, but I think that is a self-centered answer. The real profit in prayer is not in the asking and receiving, but in the communion with God. It is in the kneeling, the pausing, the waiting, the praising, the listening, the speaking. It is in the time spent in the prayer closet or on the prayer bench. For it is in these moments that we find new resolve, fresh vision, renewed strength, deepened insight. It is in these times that we profit most from prayer. And that profit helps us cope with the Job-like problems that come our way.

Today's prayer to continue: Lord, my problems are minimal compared to those of Job, but I'd like to profit by communicating with You today about one specific problem . . .

March 8 My Favorite Teacher

We loved to hear sixth grade teacher Myrle Acton read to us from "Miss Minerva and William Green Hill," as she did each day following lunch. But it was the moments following the reading that I enjoyed most. In those moments, she talked personally to us, just love-words from our gentle teacher. She often said to us, "I believe there is greatness in this room." I knew what she apparently did not know; that she was the one exhibiting greatness. She knew what I did not know; that God had great things in store for me. I was positive she was talking about someone else in the room, but I knew that she believed in a group of twelve year olds and that was special to me. I've long since lost contact with the others in that class, so I'm not sure what degrees of greatness may have developed in them over the years. This much I know, whatever greatness I have achieved, I owe a great deal of it to the belief and affirmation of Myrle Acton. More than thirty years later I acknowledged her in my first book. Her son-in-law read the book and found me, connecting me with her by phone so she could thank me for including her in the book. When I reminded her of her "greatness" quote, I was amazed at her response. She said that I must be the one to whom she was referring, since no one else from that class had ever contacted her. That's when I should have said, "Your greatness has grown" (Daniel 4:22) for she taught me one last lesson: greatness and gratitude go together.

Today's prayer to continue: Lord, I don't need to be great, but I do need to be more grateful. Even though I haven't thought about this much lately, I am grateful for . . .

March 9 Favorite Bible Verses

The Christian Post conducted an Internet survey of 37 million Bible references and revealed that 87 of the top 100 favorites are in the New Testament with John 3:16 coming in on top, twice as popular as the second choice of John 1:1. The highest ranking Old Testament verse was Genesis 1:1 finishing in 7th place on the list. My favorite Old Testament verse came in at 28th – "Trust in the Lord with all your heart, and lean not on your own understanding; in all your ways acknowledge Him, and he will direct your paths (Proverbs 3:5-6). My favorite New Testament verse ranked 14th in the top 100 – "We know that all things work together for good to those who love God, to those who are called according to His purpose" (Romans 8:28). The top ranking book in the Bible was Ephesians. The survey counted how many times a specific verse was referenced on the web. Very interesting.

Today's prayer to continue: Lord, I thank You for Your Word, the Bible, but today, I want to thank you for my favorite verse . . .

March 10 Blessed in Weariness

Ever grow weary in well-doing? Paul referenced that idea in Galatians 6:9 and again in 2 Thessalonians 3:3. Most have experienced it. In our instant everything society, we mistakenly think we can plow, plant, nurture, and reap all at the same time. When that doesn't happen, we grow weary. Part of the problem is that once the seed is planted and disappears, we don't see it again for a while. In the absence of seed, we grow weary waiting. But, if we know for certain that the plowing, planting, and nurturing will bring forth fruit, we can be blessed even in the weariness of waiting. The Psalmist said, "Those who sow in tears shall reap in joy. He who continually goes forth weeping, bearing seed for sowing, shall doubtless come again with rejoicing, bringing his sheaves with him" (Ps. 126:5-6). So keep plowing, planting, and nurturing. Harvest joy is not far away.

Today's prayer to continue: Some days Lord, I do get tired waiting, but today, I want to experience joy with You, as I . . .

March 11 Endure Hardship

It's so easy to be passionate about spiritual influences, but it takes a heart totally in love with Jesus to put feet in His footprints. It's fun to be thrilled by spiritual successes, but difficult to walk in lock-step in the midst of hardship. Paul told Timothy to "endure hardship as a good soldier of Jesus Christ" (2 Timothy 2:3). If a soldier is not willing to give up life, he or she has no business enlisting as a soldier. We are here to be totally loyal to Jesus, even unto death. Every emotion, every impulse, every thought, every energy must be in sync with God's will and purpose. Hardships– adversities of life that are difficult to endure – are necessary parts of our existence. We can't avoid them. Uncle Remus said, "You can't run away from trouble. There ain't no place that far." An African Proverb says, "Smooth seas do not make skillful sailors." So don't run from today's hardships. Endure them.

Today's prayer to continue: Today, I am keenly aware of hardships. I need Your help Lord as I endure . . .

March 12 Rumors and Angels

"So live that when the rumors begin, no one will believe them." I said that to every class of students I had in my teaching career. In recent days I have seen the truth of that affirmed again. Few of us will avoid being the subject of rumors. We must remember that ultimately it is less important what people say about us than what people believe about us. However people do talk and words do damage and some people will believe anything. In the secular world, one is innocent until proven guilty. Often times in the religious world, one is guilty until proven innocent – unless you have friends who simply refuse to believe the rumors. So what do you do when you are the subject of rumors, half-truths, falsehoods, slander? When Jesus was being falsely accused, He told Peter to put away his sword because the Father would provide "twelve legions of angels" (Matthew 26:53) for protection. You might ask the Father if he could spare maybe half a legion of angels just for you.

Today's prayer to continue: Lord, whether it's angels or Your divine presence, I do need help when people talk about me, especially when they say . . .

March 13 Got Your Back

"I've got your back" is a popular way of assuring someone that you are watching out for them. According to "The Urban Dictionary" the phrase comes from making sure you are safe by watching what's behind you when you're busy looking ahead. Isaiah knew who had his back. "Your ears shall hear a word behind you saying 'This is the way, walk in it'" (Isaiah 30:21). The emphasis is on the preposition. When you hear God's words directing you to God's way, you walk in that way, not around it, not past it, not over it, not under it, not avoiding it, not ignoring it. As you walk in God's way, you walk guarded, equipped, challenged, and protected – even from your back. So walk boldly today!

Today's prayer to continue: Thanks, Lord, for covering my back – and every other part of me. Today I would appreciate it if You would protect me from . . .

March 14 Survey Says . . . God Help Us!

A recent survey asked more than 800 pastors to name the critical ministries of their churches by listing the top five. Only five percent of participating pastors listed prayer/prayer ministry/prayer groups in the top five. Do they not know that exclusive of the Psalms, which is a prayer-book of its own, the Bible records 650 definite prayers, 450 of which have recorded answers? Do they not know that the most widely used verb in the ministry of Jesus was the verb "to pray?" Do they not know that almost every great spiritual leader in Christianity has listed prayer as utmost important in their life? Do they not know that the countries in the world where Christianity is growing fastest are countries where prayer is paramount in the churches? The answer is that they do not know. Or at least, if they know, they forgot when they took the survey. No wonder the majority of churches in America are either plateaued or declining. No wonder ministerial burn-out is at an all-time high. No wonder theological schools are forced to teach conflict management courses while ignoring courses on prayer. Jesus said, "Therefore, pray . . ." (Matthew 9:38). God help us!

Today's prayer to continue: Lord, I'm not sure what the top five critical ministries are in my life, but I want prayer to be one of them, so help me today to pray . . .

March 15 March Meanings - A Sunday Fit for a King

What comes to mind when you think of the month of March? The Ides of March? March Madness? St. Patrick's Day? Mardi Gras? Texas Independence Day? Spring Break? Time Change Sunday? My grandfather, mother and grandson were born in March. If you were born in March, your flower is the daffodil. Sometimes we celebrate Good Friday and Easter in March, occasionally early April. The Sunday before Easter is Palm Sunday, which represents the beginning of the last week of Jesus' earthly life. Palm Sunday is a Sunday fit for a King. Hundreds of years before Jesus, Zechariah, in the midst of his future visions, prophesied, "Rejoice greatly, O daughter of Zion! Shout, O daughter of Jerusalem! Behold, your King is coming to you; He is just and having salvation, lowly and riding on a donkey" (Zechariah 9:9). The time had arrived. The vision was complete. The prophecy was fulfilled. The King was coming! It was a common custom in many lands to cover the path of someone thought worthy of the highest honor. 2 Kings 9:13 reports that Jehu, son of Jehoshaphat, was treated this way. John specifically mentions "branches of palm trees" being placed on the road before

Jesus (John 12:12). The palm branch was a symbol of triumph and of victory in Jewish tradition (Leviticus 23:40; Revelation 7:9). Because of this, the scene of the crowd greeting Jesus by waving palms and carpeting his path with them has given the Christian day its name. It was and is a Sunday fit for a King. Why not take what's left of March to celebrate our Lord's victory. That would make Easter a real Super Sunday.

Today's prayer to continue: Lord, it's time to celebrate Your victory won during the Triumphant Entry in Jerusalem on Palm Sunday and I do so today. I also want to celebrate . . .

March 16 3/16

Today is 3/16. A few years ago 3/16 hit on Palm Sunday. That won't happen again in our lifetime – unless you live another 200+ years. The merging of Roman calendar date and biblical reference caused more than one church to emphasize John 3:16 on Palm Sunday, leading up to Easter. No real connection there, except that John 3:16 is true every Sunday (and Monday through Saturday as well). It made me curious as to what other thoughts appear in 3:16. In my search I discovered 1 Corinthians 3:16 which reads, "Do you not know that you are the temple of God and that the Spirit of God dwells in you?" How's that for an Easter verse? Because He lives, the Spirit lives. Where does the Spirit live? In the temple! Where is the temple, in Jerusalem? There were three temples there, but there is no more. The new temple is in believers. So whatever scripture text is preached where you worship on Palm Sunday and Easter, the post-Palm Sunday/Easter sermon is to be preached through you and me. He lives! Where? He lives in believers. So, I hope your Easter celebration doesn't end at noon on Easter Sunday. The celebration continues in us . . . and through us. Now that Palm Sunday and Easter Sunday are near, this might be a good day to re-cleanse the temple, don't you think?

Today's prayer to continue: Lord, cleanse the temple again, the one in me. I especially need cleansing related to . . .

March 17 Choosing Correctly

The last few days have afforded us an interesting study in human nature. The lottery hit multi-millions and people went wild. Faced with an infinitesimally small chance of winning, folks who had never played the lottery previously, defied all odds, rushed to convenience stores, and asked how to select their numbers. The nightly news carried interviews of such risk-takers. One man confessed, "I'd waste this $5 somewhere else, I might as well take a chance on winning something with it." Another said, "If I don't buy a lottery ticket, I won't have anything to talk about with my friends." Appropriate to the timing – nearby Palm Sunday - one church countered with the following message on their sign: "Place your bets on the man riding the Donkey." Indeed, as Jesus rode into Jerusalem that Sunday, palm branches were waved and hosannas were shouted. Against all odds, people were "betting" this man riding on a donkey was the Messiah. Of course, five days later, many of the same people were shouting "Crucify!" Such is human nature. Life, at best, is a bit of a gamble, made up of choices. Make the wrong choice and you pay for it. Make the correct choice and you "win." I don't know about you, but as we move toward celebrating the resurrection on Easter, I'm sure glad I chose the Man on the donkey (Zechariah 9:9) who won the victory, just like it was predicted. Hallelujah what a Savior!

Today's prayer to continue: Today Lord, I want to place all my options on . . .

March 18 Twitter de, twitter dumb!

It was a long time before I tweeted. I surfed, googled, texted, cellphoned and facebooked, but I didn't tweet. A guy has to draw the line somewhere. So I didn't tweet – at least not for a long time.

Finally I gave in to yet another form of hi-tech communication. According to their web site, Twitter is a service for friends, family, and co–workers to communicate and stay connected through the exchange of quick, frequent answers (tweet) to one simple question: What are you doing? The face of communication has changed. Face-to-face conversation is fast becoming a lost art. At a baseball game recently I saw two teenagers sitting next to each other sending text messages back and forth and laughing together. Thanks to the latest means of communication I now know what friends are doing across the world: what they are having for dinner, what time they are going to bed, what they scored on some internet game, and what the names of their newest friends are. We talk less, but know more. So is there a word from God for this technological generation? How about, "Let your speech (tweet, text, facebook) be with grace, seasoned with salt" (Colossians 4:6). I've already deleted a few social media friends who refused to abide by these words. Hi tech communication? Yes! Hi tech seasoning? Please!

Today's prayer to continue: Whatever the means of communications, today, Lord, I need to tell others that . . .

March 19 Disciplined Silence

While teaching a class on prayer at the Hong Kong Baptist Seminary, I quoted Isaiah 30:15 to illustrate prayerful meditation, "In quietness and confidence shall be your strength." The blank look of the faces of the students told me I needed to stay on this subject a bit longer. Facing me was a classroom of Chinese students who lived in a city where "quietness" was non-existent. So if a source of strength is silence, and you live in 24/7 noise, how can you be strong? I went back to my apartment following class that evening, certain that I had failed to adequately answer the blank stares of my students. By the next class meeting, I had concluded that "quietness" does not always mean the absence of noise. Sometimes, it means the disciplined focus of the mind. Who has not lived in the midst of noise, near a railroad track, by a busy freeway, adjacent to an airport runway, or just in the midst of loud people, without learning how to block out the noisy? Familiarity with noise often breeds inner silence. So whether you are in a quiet place or a noisy place, be confident of this one thing: strength is available to you, at the price of self-discipline.

Today's prayer to continue: Help me to focus so completely on You today Lord that I block out all the noise around me, especially the noise from . . .

March 20 Keep on!

For twenty-two years, my annual assignment was to coordinate the training and placement of approximately 100 Seminary students, hope-to-be preachers into small churches located outside of the Bible-belt for the purpose of conducting spring-break revival meetings. The most difficult part was not the training of the students; it was knowing where to place them. So I fasted, prayed and read the Bible, sometimes for several days, waiting on God to give me a "Go" word, before making any assignments. I was not going to match student preacher and small church without the assurance that God was with me in the process. I'm not sure where in the Bible I started reading one year but I had made it all the way to 3 John and was beginning to wonder if God was going to give me my needed "Go" word. After all, only Jude and Revelation remained in the Bible. Then I read 3 John 5-6, "You do faithfully whatever you do for the brethren . . . if you send them forward on their journey in a manner worthy of God." With that "Go" word given, I proceeded to "send them forward on their journey." Lesson learned and now passed on to you: Keep reading your Bible and praying. God is sometimes slow but never late.

Today's prayer to continue: Lord, I would appreciate a "Go" word from you today, and I'll start reading my Bible in the book of . . .

March 21 Reclaim and Return

"What one generation tolerates, the next generation will embrace." So said John Wesley, the founder of the Methodist movement. Years later, a sociologist enlarged the statement by saying, "What one generation despises, the next generation tolerates, and the third generation accepts as the norm." Without citing illustrations, of which there are many, let me just say that I've lived long enough to see that become a reality. While some would call it progress, and others would call it deterioration, the Bible speaks of a generation where, "everyone did what was right in his own eyes" (Judges 17:6; 21:25). May I remind you that historians also labeled that time, "The Dark Ages of Hebrew History." Our post-modern, new age society says there are no absolutes, no right, nor wrong; if it works for you, it is OK. I spoke to nearly 100 student, wannabe preachers last week as they began their course of study that will culminate in them preaching a revival meeting as a part of a program entitled, "Reclaiming This Nation." While everything around us moves us away from God, it is time to reclaim old truths and "return to the Lord your God, for He is gracious and merciful, slow to anger, and of great kindness" (Joel 2:13).

Today's prayer to continue: Lord, today I want to reclaim the following old truth . . .

March 22 Sunday Tears

I know a few people who weep on Sunday: preachers whose sermons could have used a few more hours of preparation before delivery; homebound folks who would love to be in a worship service but cannot; workers who, by no choice of their own, must be on the job during times of Sunday worship. But the most significant tears ever shed on Sunday were those of Jesus. The day has been labeled by scholars as, "The Triumphant Entry" and by modern holiday-makers as "Palm Sunday." Traveling with His disciples toward Jerusalem, Jesus paused on the top of the Mt. of Olives, "saw the city and wept over it" (Luke 19:41). What He heard and saw was worship. People were waving palm branches, a practice reserved for one of great esteem and respect. They were shouting "Hosanna" meaning "Save us we pray." Jesus didn't weep over the worship but over what would follow, for many of these same people shouting, "Hosanna" on Sunday would be shouting, "Crucify" on Friday. I wonder if Jesus still weeps on Sunday, as He observes our worship – not because it is unplanned or unpolished, but because it is insincere. Often, the intensity of our Sunday worship fails to translate into the consistency of our weekday activities. I want to change that, and be able to say to Jesus, "Don't cry, Lord. It's going to be OK."

Today's prayer to continue: Lord, I'm sorry if I ever made You cry, but today, I want to worship You and I will do so by . . .

March 23 Because He Lives

The questions were posed in a Canadian coffee shop. It could have been anywhere. "Why do you Christians send missionaries to convert people? Why do you proclaim that yours is the only religion? Why don't you just worship your god and leave everyone else alone? Where do you get the audacity to imply I'm wrong?" Good questions. Is it because we Christians are better morally and ethically? Is it because we are more organized? Is it because we're just arrogant? Or is it because we have a commission from our living Lord to "make disciples of the nations" (Matthew 28:19)? Confucius was born around 551 B.C and died in 479 B.C. Buddha was born around 557 B.C. and died in 483 B.C. Mohammed was born in 570 A.D. and died in 632 A.D. Not only is Jesus the only one without a permanent death date, but all the others establish their birth and death dates from His birth. Today is the earliest calendar day that Christians can celebrate Easter Sunday! Given opportunity, I will share, albeit with sensitivity and integrity, that which I am commissioned to share, because He lives! Join me?

Today's prayer to continue: Today, Lord, I want to thank You that You are alive and well, and I want to share that good news with . . .

March 24 Passing by

Never were soldiers, in any army, in any time of history, given a more useless command than that given by Pontius Pilate to unnamed Roman soldiers, posted at the door of a borrowed tomb, outside the city of Jerusalem. These poor soldiers were commanded to secure the tomb. No one was to get in and no one was to get out (Matthew 27:64-66). Two thousand years later Christians are still celebrating the fact that Jesus Christ, who was entombed there, got out. I have often wondered about those soldiers. While we have no details, it is assumed that the soldiers thought so little of their assignment, they fell asleep and Jesus passed by them on His way out of the tomb. Awakened by the earthquake, they "became like dead men" (Matthew 28:4). Willie Nelson sang a song a few years ago that had nothing to do with the resurrection of Jesus, but the title must have been close to what the soldiers felt that morning – "The Last Thing I Needed, First Thing This Morning, Was to Have You Walk Out on Me." It may be the last thing you think you need, but when the living Lord, passes by you today, what will you feel?

Today's prayer to continue: When You pass by me today, Lord, don't let me be asleep, but awake and aware, so that I can . . .

March 25 Worshipping a Listening God

After recent visits I am more convinced than ever that people are desperate to communicate with deity. I visited a Hindu Center and watched as people bowed to statues of animals and flowers, worshipping the created, but not the Creator. I visited a Buddhist Temple and watched people light incense to burn in tribute to overweight images of their deity. I visited a Sikh Temple and watched them put their sacred writing to bed so it could rest. I visited the Muslim Mosque and watched them bow toward Mecca in hopes someone in that direction would hear and respond. One thing I saw in common. Each "worshipper" had some means of attracting the attention of their deity, a bell, a drum, a call, a chant - "waking them up to get their attention" as one adherent explained. I walked away from each with mixed feelings – sorrow for those who walk in darkness and joy that I do not have to awaken my God for worship, for He "neither slumbers nor sleeps" (Psalm 121:4) I also felt that I and those traveling with me were the only ones in the various places of worship talking to a deity that was actually listening.

Today's prayer to continue: Thank You for being awake and listening to my prayer today because I really need for You to hear me say . . .

March 26 God's Heart-beat

Various sources tell us that a normal heart beat is between 60 to 100 beats per minute. When the heart beats faster it tells us we are excited; slower and we are relaxed. What does the heart-beat of God tell us? One day, a disciple of Jesus was, "leaning on Jesus' bosom" (John 13:23). This disciple, "whom Jesus loved" was most likely John, the same disciple who wrote so much about God's love. He laid his head on the heart of God. What an enviable position. How often I long to hear the heart of God and yet how often I simply hear distracting noise, unable to turn down the volume around me. For instance, I've read this passage many times. It is about Peter asking Jesus which disciple will betray Him. Right? Well, mostly right! Until now, I've missed this ear-to-the-heart-of-God portion of the passage. We are allowed, as was a young Jew, to recline on the bosom of our Lord and listen to the heartbeat of our God. I'm going to try that today. Join me?

Today's prayer to continue: Heart to heart, today Lord, what would You like to say to me? Heart to heart, this is what I would like to say to You today . . .

March 27 Servanthood and the Lack Thereof

Every so often I run across a Christian leader who has lost the concept of servanthood. I try to picture this person taking a bowl of water and a towel and washing someone's feet. That's what Jesus did to demonstrate His servanthood (John 13:4-5). Most of the time, my mental image does not work. Some people are just not servants. Servanthood is downward mobility in an upward mobility world. Servanthood is a "me last" concept in a "me first" culture. Servanthood is "I've got to be like Jesus" in an "I've got to be me" society. When servanthood is divorced from leadership, you get selfishness. When servanthood is divorced from divine calling, you get human busy-work. When servanthood is divorced from ministry, you get . . . well, I think I'll let you fill in that blank. Hint: It's a substitute for washing dirty feet and cleaning up messy lives.

Today's prayer to continue: Servanthood is what You demonstrated Lord. I want to be like You, so help me demonstrate servanthood today as I . . .

March 28 Answered Prayer or Coincidence?

The bumper sticker read, "Life is fragile – handle with prayer." There is no argument related to the fragileness of life. Read any church prayer list and see the results of fragile lives. We are fragile physically, mentally, emotionally and spiritually. So Christians pray – for Divine intervention, for strength, for wisdom, for discernment, for guidance and a hundred other categories of prayer requests. We believe the Biblical promise of God, who said, "Call to Me, and I will answer you" (Jeremiah 33:3). When God responds, the cynics say it is mere coincidence. Former Archbishop of Canterbury, William Temple, had the best reply to that logic when he wrote, "When I pray, coincidences happen, and when I don't, they don't." Life is indeed fragile, but when we pray, human-perceived, heaven-sent, coincidences happen. So continue to pray through the fragileness of life.

Today's prayer to continue: Thank You Lord for responding to the fragile areas of life. The most fragile part of my life today is . . .

March 29 Cat Nap or Prayer Partner

I've preached to people who wanted to be a cool cat, but I've never preached to a cool cat that wanted to hear me preach. I received a note and picture from a lady who watched me preach on television at the church where I was serving as Interim Pastor. It read, "My cat Bitsy loves you very much. When I watch your program at home, he runs through the house when he hears your voice and sits close to you. When the service ends, he returns to his usual haunts." The only reference I know of cats in the Bible is when Noah was instructed to take two of each animal on to the ark (Genesis 7:2). I'm not sure how far back Bitsy traces his lineage, but I'm fairly positive he has a Baptist heritage since he appears to be asleep in the picture. Then again, he may be praying.

Today's prayer to continue: Lord, someone in my circle of relationships needs a prayer partner today. Lead me to them and then help me . . .

March 30 The Priority of a Good Start

Breakfast is widely acknowledged as the most important meal of the day. I like it so much I sometimes eat breakfast food for lunch and even dinner. One morning, Jesus invited His disciples to join Him for a breakfast of fish and bread, cooked over open coals on the shore of the Sea of Tiberias (John 21:12). So perfectly prepared was this meal that no one complained of having no catsup or tartar sauce. Only ten times did Jesus appear between His resurrection and His ascension, yet one appearance was reserved for breakfast, the morning meal, an absolute necessity for a healthy day. No doubt the Lord had been up early praying, as was His custom, modeling for His disciples how to get a good spiritual start to the day. Now He teaches them how to get a good physical start to the day. May we be likewise balanced as we begin each day.

Today's prayer to continue: Thank You Lord for Your examples of how to begin the day. Today I want to begin with . . .

March 31 Faith that Releases Power

What is released by your faith? Do you remember the story of the woman who had been ill for twelve years and in faith reached out to touch the hem of Jesus' robe (Mark 5:25-34)? In the midst of the crowd, Jesus asked, "Who touched My clothes?" The disciples chided Him. "You see the multitude thronging around You and You say, 'Who touched me'?" But Jesus had felt the faith-touch and likewise felt power going out of Him. He was touched lightly by a need and affected drastically by the touch. The untouched disciples questioned both the touched one and the touchable One. The woman was healed and helped by a faith-touch. Oh to have the kind of faith that releases divine power.

Today's prayer to continue: My faith sometimes falters, Lord. Help me today to have enough faith to . . .

April 1 April Fools

Today is April Fools Day. For many people it is no big deal. They have three hundred sixty-five of them each year. The Bible cautions us to "walk carefully, not as fools (Ephesians 5:15)." Some folks think they can do whatever they choose to do whenever they choose to do it. We used to call this "doing your own thing." While this may work for a while, ultimately, one must do God's thing or perish. Some say it doesn't matter what you believe as long as you believe something. Right! Pour gasoline over ice cubes into your tea glass and believe it is really iced tea. It looks like iced tea . . . same color . . . same texture . . . You can choose to believe it is tea because it doesn't matter what you believe and see how long you stay out of the Emergency Room. Ultimately it does matter what you believe. Still others believe that they can come to Jesus Christ when they get ready. Beginning in the garden with God looking for Adam, it has always been God's initiative, not ours. You come to Jesus when He is ready or you do not come at all. April Fools! If you are a believer, enjoy hearing that phrase for one day each year. If you are not a believer, get ready to hear it for eternity.

Today's prayer to continue: Lord, I want to walk as the wise do today, "not as fools," so with Your guidance, I can . . .

April 2 The Road Goes on Forever

I love the line from a country song – "The road goes on forever and the party never ends." In spite of the not-so-spiritual story included in the song's lyrics, I've long wanted to make that line biblical. It finally happened. Early in the public ministry of Jesus, he attended a wedding feast in Cana of Galilee. The host ran out of wine. I guess even back then, you never knew how many friends you had until your daughter got married. Nevertheless, the party was over whether the fat lady had sung or not. No more wine, no more party. Then Jesus took water and miraculously turned it into wine (John 2:1-11). I've preached all over that miracle story, but never realized that what Jesus actually did was keep the party going. Next time you're having fun at a Jesus party, rejoice. That road goes on forever and that party never ends.

Today's prayer to continue: Thank You, Lord that life with You is one big forever party, so as I enjoy myself today, I want to . . .

April 3 A Worthy Model

I will never forget the first time I met him. He walked into my office and introduced himself as the new Director of Missions for our Association. He was wearing blue jeans and boots – not drug-store cowboy boots, but work boots. He was on his way to deliver boxes of Bibles to pastors – in his pick-up truck. Not only had I never seen a Director of Missions in blue jeans, I'd never known one who drove a truck. He could work in an office, but he was much more comfortable working out of an office. I was green-as-a-gourd, fresh-out-of-seminary, and struggling. An instant partnership was formed that day. He taught me that "Whatever your hand finds to do, do it with your might" (Ecclesiastes 9:10). I would later preach his funeral. Fifty-two years in the ministry – always working hard, always mentoring younger ministers, always a worthy model. What have you modeled today for a younger person?

Today's prayer to continue: Today Lord, I need Your wisdom so I can pass it on to . . .

April 4 Opening Day and Worship Day

Opening Day of baseball season is one of my favorite days of the year. I've been attending since my Dad used to get me out of school and take me to the opening day game of the Houston Buffaloes 1950's Texas League. I go to watch baseball, but sometimes find myself watching fans as much as baseball. A recent game saw a couple of thirty-somethings, seated in front of me. They had obviously had a few drinks before their arrival for the afternoon game. During the game, they consumed at least one beer per inning. They got loud, then quiet, then obnoxious. A couple of times, they yelled at the wrong time, high-fiving everyone around them who would oblige their inebriated attempt at colleagueship. It made me wonder why they spent good money to attend a game they never watched. I left early so as not to encounter them on the parking lot as they tried to maneuver a motor vehicle through an alcoholic fog. The whole scenario carried over to the following Sunday morning. I found myself wondering why folks attend church. -Certainly not to drink but why attend? Many were there to sincerely worship God. Others were there for friendship and fellowship. So why do you attend a worship service? Why do I? In the midst of instructions to re-build the house of worship, God twice told the prophet Haggai, "Consider your ways" (Haggai 1:5, 7). There are multiple reasons why people attend baseball games, likewise worship services. Consider your ways.

Today's prayer to continue: Next time I attend a worship service, Lord, I need to consider . . .

April 5 Adoration

"Ad" means "to." "Ora" means "mouth." Thus the literal meaning of adoration is "to one's mouth." Romans performed the act of adoration by raising the hand to the mouth, kissing it and then waving it in the direction of the adored object. The word adoration came to mean, homage paid to one held in high esteem, as in worship. The early church felt that adoration was for God alone; feeling that adoration for any one or thing other than God was idolatry. However, controversy arose, distinguishing adoration for God alone, from veneration which was accorded to the saints. In 787A.D. the Second Council of Nicaea concluded adoration was for the worship of God alone, ruling the practice was not to be applied to earthly rulers, angels or saints. Seems to me we have reverted to the early church controversy. It was written of the disciples of Jesus, "When they saw Him, they worshiped Him" (Matthew 28:17). To earthly leaders, pastors, evangelists, counselors, ministers, helpers, etc, let us respect, honor, admire, and follow when such is due. But let us worship and adore Jesus only.

Today's prayer to continue: Lord, it is You and You alone that I adore, primarily because You . . .

April 6 Lifestyle

What does it mean to live a Christian lifestyle? For the Christian, lifestyle is a way of living life with Jesus Christ at the very center. This is easier said than done. One cannot put Christ at the very center without denying self, family and close relations. Jesus issued strong warnings about putting self, family and others ahead of God. Are there guidelines that constitute a Christian lifestyle? From theologian to theologian, any "lifestyle" list would differ and would consist of various listings of rules and prohibitions found in the Bible as well as a list of positive promises. But they would all conclude with the fact that a Christian lifestyle is Christ's life, lived out in human style. It is not Christ's life lived out in His style for He has already accomplished that. It is not mankind's life lived out in human style for that would be secular, perhaps even agnostic or atheistic. It is His life, lived out in human style. It is perhaps best seen in Paul's statement, "I have been crucified with Christ; it is no longer I who live, but Christ lives in me; and the life which I now live in the flesh I live by faith in the Son of God, who loved me and gave Himself for me" (Galatians 2:20). So, live the Christ-life today.

Today's prayer to continue: Not my style Lord, but Your style – that's the kind of life I want to live. Today I need to major on living . . .

April 7 Lifestyle, Continued

The word "lifestyle" was originally coined in 1929 by a psychologist named Alfred Adler but the modern usage of the word seems to come from around 1961. Lifestyle refers to the manner in which a person lives, which may include habits, conduct, language, dress, responses to others, interpersonal relationships and a host of other factors. Beyond self, the Christian lifestyle is one that envisions each believer as a brother or sister in Christ and each non-believer as created by and for God, in God's image. At least three factors shape the Christian lifestyle. The first is other people. "As iron sharpens iron, so one person sharpens another" (Proverbs 27:16). The second factor is circumstances. "And we know that in all things God works for the good of those who love him, who have been called according to his purpose." (Rom. 8:28). The third factor is discipline. "Train yourself to be godly" (1 Timothy 4:7). The Christian lifestyle is one selected by choice. Confronted with multiple options each day, one must decide how to live. Otherwise, one falls unintentionally into some other lifestyle, perhaps the one of current culture or that demonstrated by close associates. Live the Christ-life today!

Today's prayer to continue: Today, Lord I need to discipline myself to be more godly, and for me that means . . .

April 8 Too Busy to Pray?

The Christian form of unceasing prayer may have been preceded by the Psalmist David who wrote, "I have set the Lord always before me" (Psalm 16:8). The Apostle Paul encouraged believers in Thessalonica to "pray without ceasing" (1 Thessalonians 5:17). Never has this method of prayer been more appropriate than in our fast-lane lifestyles. Need a model? In church history, the Celtic people believed that God was with them every moment of the day, so they used short prayers to communicate with God as they performed their chores. Celtic writer, Ester de Waal, explained, "They were the prayers of a people who were so busy from dawn to dusk, from dark to dark, that they had little time for long, formal prayers. Instead throughout the day they did whatever had to be done carefully, giving it their full attention, yet at the same time making it the occasion for prayer." Next time you are too busy to stop for prayer, try this method.

Today's prayer to continue: Forgive me Lord, for not praying without ceasing, not "always" setting You before me. Today, I will try to be sensitive to every opportunity to communicate with You, especially as I . . .

April 9 Leading with Eyes Wide Open

Is it really more spiritual to close one's eyes while leading worship music or does it just feel that way to the leader? I asked one worship leader how he could lead with his eyes closed. His reply was, "My job is to worship. If I worship, they will follow." Last time I checked, preaching was still a part of the worship experience. What if I closed my eyes as I preached? (I know, some worshippers do – as I preach) What if my preaching logic was, "my job is to worship (with my eyes closed), if I worship (at my own preaching), they will follow." That appears to be a bit egotistical. Is it really all about me? Whether leading worship through music or preaching, let's remember, worship is not about us. It's about God. And leadership is about leading, as well as feeling. I'm so glad the Psalmist said, "I will lift up my eyes to the hills" (Psalm 121:1) rather than "I will close my eyes to all that is around me." Granted, one can experience God with eyes open or shut, but leadership carries with it responsibility. Open your eyes and look around. If no one is following, you're not really leading, no matter how you feel. God give us responsible worship leaders who lead with their eyes wide open.

Today's prayer to continue: Open my eyes Lord, so that I can be a responsible leader, especially when I . . .

April 10 Leading With Eyes Wide Open, Continued

The issue is leadership of worship music. Name one biblical character that led with eyes closed and don't name someone who led through prayer. There is not one verse in the Bible that says anyone closed their eyes when they prayed. There are ten biblical postures for prayer. Eyes closed is not one of them. Name one person – politics, sports, business, education, etc. – that leads effectively with their eyes closed. Worshipping with eyes closed in the congregation? I'm all for it. In worship leadership? Less than effective. Can one lead without communication? Bottom line: communicate with those whom you are leading and lead. If one can do that with eyes closed, so be it. In the long run, that may say more about the congregation than the about the leader. And while I'm thinking about, I like to "sing a new song" (Psalm 144:9) every now and then. How can I learn the words with my eyes closed? I appreciate those who disagree with me and I'm sorry for the strong opinion. Every day, I'm getting more like my grandfather, who was, in the language of his day, "sot in his ways" and violently opposed the "High-church, German music" sung by the choir at his church each Sunday.

Today's prayer to continue: Even if I don't have the ability, I'd like to "sing a new song" today, Lord, and may my "singing" be a blessing to . . .

April 11 A Time to Laugh

When circumstances are beyond our control, we have a choice of responses. One of my favorite responses is laughter. As I was being introduced as the preacher for a recent revival meeting, the pastor got his words confused and introduced me as "Dr. Revival who is here to preach for us." I was not sure how many people caught the mistake until afterwards when it became the subject of discussion at a post-service meal. Still, when it was mentioned, everyone looked at me to see how I would respond. I could have showed anger, frustration, irritability, etc. However, I simply passed off the mistake by laughing and saying, "Lord, may it ever be so." In difficult circumstances, Paul encouraged the Christians at Philippi to, "Rejoice in the Lord" and as if they may have misunderstood, he repeated. "Again, I will say, rejoice" (Philippians 4:4). How will you respond the circumstances of this day? Understanding that there are some circumstances where humor is not appropriate, may I nevertheless, recommend laughter as a possibility.

Today's prayer to continue: So many times, Lord, I just need to laugh. In fact, today, I need to laugh at . . .

April 12 Vapor View

I attended two recent funerals neither of which was expected. Both were younger than me. It reminded me that the value of a life is not determined by the years accumulated. It also reminded me of what James wrote, "You do not know what will happen tomorrow. For what is your life? It is even a vapor that appears for a little time and then vanishes away" (James 4:14). I doubt if you have this verse cutely painted on a magnet, displayed on your refrigerator. It really doesn't lend itself to that. Besides most of us are so in love with tomorrow that we can hardly think of not experiencing it. That's why unexpected deaths are such a shock to our system. It's hard to think about life as a vapor, a vanishing mist. It has long since disappeared, but I can still see it – that faded blue cardboard poster, the sliver glitter, worn off of the lettering. Given to me by my parents, the poster hung on my wall for many years. The quote on the poster was attributed to English missionary, C.T. Studd who said on his deathbed, "Only one life, 'twill soon be past. Only what's done for Christ will last." Indeed.

Today's prayer to continue: Lord, I have no idea how many days I have left on this earth, but I sincerely desire to live all of them for You. Especially today, I want to . . .

April 13 Silence: Unbroken and Broken

With the kind of friends Job had, he probably needed no additional enemies. When these three friends heard of Satan's attack on Job's character, property, children, and health, they made a visit to him. The first week of the visit was most interesting. "They sat down with him on the ground seven days and seven nights, and no one spoke a word to him, for they saw that his grief was very great" (Job 2:13). I confess that I have often not known what to say in the face of grief, but seven days of silence is a bit much, especially from friends. Again, it is sometimes enough to simply be present without speaking. But seven days? And when they spoke, Job must have wished for another seven days of silence from them. What shall we make of this? How about this: there is a time to visit and a time to end visitation; there is a time for silence and a time to speak; it is better to remain silent than say the wrong thing. And what shall we do when friends grieve? Pray! Pray for sensitivity; for the right time to visit, and the right time to leave; for the proper words to speak, for the right time to speak them; for the ministry of silence that is not interrupted with inappropriate words.

Today's prayer to continue: I sometimes say the wrong thing, Lord. Today, I want to say the right thing at the right time, so help me to . . .

April 14 Ego-buster or God's Selection Process?

The pastor was relieved that I agreed to preach in his absence because he said he had been turned down by seven others before asking me. Ordinarily that would be classified as an ego-buster.

I'm not sure I've ever been the eighth choice before. However I was encouraged by the reminder that David's seven brothers passed before Samuel and the Lord said "No" to each one. When the eighth son of Jesse was brought before Samuel, "The Lord said, 'Arise, anoint him; for this is the one'" (1 Samuel 16:12). The Lord's choice was number eight, David. Nor was this the first time I had not be the first choice. I have held five different full-time ministry positions (not counting Interim Pastorates). I know for a fact that I was not the first choice in three of them. So next time you are not the first choice by someone or for some assignment or position, be encouraged. While you may not be the first choice on the human level, you may be God's choice

Today's prayer to continue: I have no idea, Lord, where I stand in the human pecking order, but I am thankful that I am chosen by You, so today I want to act in appreciation of that by . . .

April 15 Post-Easter Heartburn

The second most exciting event of that first Easter was a case of heartburn. Early that Sunday morning, Jesus, dead since Friday afternoon, came out of the grave, alive forevermore. That was the best Good News of the day. However, later that same day, a believer named Cleopas and his friend, were walking home from Jerusalem to Emmaus. As they walked and talked of the events of earlier that day, Jesus began to walk with them. The scripture says their "eyes were restrained so that they did not know Him" (Luke 24:16). After all, when you've just come from a death and burial, you least expect to see the one who was buried, walking beside you. Once in Emmaus, Jesus blessed bread and gave it to them. Then "their eyes were opened and they knew Him; and He vanished from their sight" (Luke 24:31). Then came the heartburn as they reflected on the event saying to each other, "Did not our heart burn within us while He talked with us on the road, and while He opened the Scriptures to us?" (Luke 24:32). Perhaps this was the same heartburn felt by Jeremiah, "His word was in my heart like a burning fire" (Jeremiah 20:9) and by David, "My heart was hot within me; while I was musing, the fire burned" (Psalm 39:3) and by all believers who successfully hear the Good News explained, applied, and illustrated. As you reflect on the events of Easter, may you experience post-Easter heartburn. Oh; and one thing more. As soon as the Emmaus walkers felt the divine heartburn, they, "rose up that very hour and returned to Jerusalem" (Luke 24:33-35) in order to share the Good News with others. Go and do likewise.

Today's prayer to continue: Lord, I confess that my heart has burned for many things, but today I want it to burn for you in a way that motivates me to share Your Good News with . . .

April 16 With and Without Form

I'm glad man was not created until the sixth day of the creative week. Imagine how life would have been when "the earth was without form, and void (Genesis 1:2). I'm having trouble even imagining that as I write this in the midst of beautiful, snow-covered mountains. While there is God-created beauty in the flatlands (I was in the desert last weekend.) somehow "form" demonstrates itself more dramatically in the mountains. I love the beauty of both because they remind me of mankind. That which God created in nature, he duplicated in human beings. There are those folks whose life is like the mountains: bold, dramatic, highly-visible, etc. Then there are those whose life is like the flatland: plain, simple, non-assuming, etc. It would be a boring, monotonous existence if life was all mountains or all flatlands and if friends, were "without form, and void." Would you like to join me today in celebrating God's creative diversity?

Today's prayer to continue: Thank You God for Your diverse creation. Today I would like to affirm someone who is not like me, and I'm thinking of . . .

April 17 Home: Place or People?

My parents moved to another city the morning after I graduated from high school. During my college days, when my friends went "home" it was to a place. For me, going "home" was to a place I'd never been before. Going "home" was going to people. I've reached the age where a significant number of my long-time friends are going to their heavenly home. Each day the obituary columns of my newspaper carry pictures of people my age. I know heaven is a place. Jesus said it was in John 14:2. I also know that when folks arrive in that heavenly home they are overwhelmed by the beauty of the place. I'm wondering if they are not just as thrilled by the reunion with people. I guess my age is showing through and my apologies to my younger readers, but I'm beginning to get a little homesick – not just for a place I've never been before, but for people I miss.

Today's prayer to continue: Lord, I have many friends on earth, but I miss those who have gone before and are now with You in heavenly places, I am especially thinking today and thankful for . . .

April 18 A Lesson from my Cell Phone

Before it becomes obsolete, let me say that my cell phone is a lot like the Christian life. When I tried to use it the other day the signal was low and when someone did answer on the other end, I would quickly lose them. Then I remembered! I forgot to re-charge the battery. At least once a day, sometimes more, I need to plug my cell phone into the power source and re-charge it. Otherwise, it becomes weaker and weaker and eventually useless. My spiritual power comes from God. It's how I do what I do. The Bible says, "As your days, so shall your strength be" (Deuteronomy 33:25). If I try to go too long without a spiritual re-charge, I become weak, powerless, and eventually useless. Slow me down Lord, at least long enough to re-charge, lest I become powerless in my ministry and useless to You.

Today's prayer to continue: Some days I feel powerless, Lord. Today, I ask for enough power to accomplish what You have for me to do. I specifically, hope to . . .

April 19 Precious Memories

"Precious memories . . . how they ever flood my soul." An old hymn. My Grandfather's favorite; one of mine also. Recently I was back on the campus of my alma mater, Howard Payne University for the inauguration of the new president. Sitting on the platform in the newly renovated Mims Auditorium – "the spiritual center of the campus" – I had a memory rush, a "flood" so to speak. So many significant things happened in that auditorium during chapel services and campus gatherings. The times I heard from God in that old 1920s building cannot be counted. I even gave an engagement ring to my future wife on the back row during a talent show one Friday night. The seats and the furnishings had been replaced, but the presence of God was still there. Buildings are renovated or replaced. Circumstances and environments change. Memory keeps us connected and balanced. Surely memory is one of God's best gifts. That's why the writer of Proverbs could say, "The memory of the just is blessed" (Proverbs 10:7). Take a few minutes today to stop and remember the past. It will put the present and the future into better perspective. It sure did for me.

Today's prayer to continue: I remember so many things Lord, but today, I want to reflect on spiritual memories like . . .

April 20 Play it where it Lies

My golf ball looks exactly like the one the pros use. It's round and white and has dimples. It is even the right brand name. However, while the ball is similar, the similarity between my golf game and that of a professional ends there. There is a major difference. It is called "lie" but does not relate to untruth (at least it is not supposed to relate). A "lie" in golf is where the ball stops rolling. A common golf term is "play it where it lies" meaning you can't improve the location of the ball (unless of course it is in a hazard). Most of the time, the pros hit the ball in the fairway and on the green. Much of the time, my ball "lies" in the trees or sand. From that unfavorable location, I must play my next shot. The origin of the game of golf is uncertain. A few golf historians actually trace the game back to the Roman game of paganica, in which participants used a bent stick to hit a stuffed leather ball. So perhaps the Apostle Paul played golf. Whether he did on not, he did understand a principle of golf and life. Paul wrote, "I have learned in whatever state ("lie") I am, to be content." (Philippians 4:11). The truth is I can't always control my circumstances ("lie") but I can control how I respond to them. How will you respond to your "lie" today?

Today's prayer to continue: My circumstances have been better and worse than today, so Lord, help me to respond well to this day's circumstances, such as . . .

April 21 The Fireworks were on Key

I was at my seat in time for the national anthem at a baseball game to be followed by a fireworks display. National anthem singers have to audition but some slip through the cracks, or in this case, the music staff. It most definitely was the situation on that night. I'm sure the singer's resume was filled with amateur contests entered but probably no mention of any 1st place finishes or even 2nd or 3rd place finishes. With a country twang and nasal voice that could have come from any rural area, this American Idol wannabe started off key and never found it. The notes wobbled as the singer performed a personal rendition of "The Star Spangled Banner." I wanted to yell, "Just sing it like it's written!" but I kept my mouth shut. My ears were not so fortunate. In retrospect, the only thing that was on key that night was the fireworks that went off during "bombs bursting in air." We've all had nights like that. Peter messed-up three times and then was haunted by an on-key rooster (Matthew 26:69-75). So, put past failures behind you and try until you get it right. Then strive for excellence.

Today's prayer to continue: Lord, off key mistakes dot my past, but today, with Your help, I want to be on key, when I . . .

April 22 Earth Day Every Day

Today is Earth Day - a day designed to inspire awareness and appreciation for the earth's environment. On the celebration of the first Earth Day, American Heritage Magazine-proclaimed, ". . . on April 22, 1970, Earth Day was held, one of the most remarkable happenings in the history of democracy. . ." Sometimes we celebrate the right things for the wrong reasons. Long before the modern Earth Day was celebrated, the Bible had a lot to say about the earth:

• In the beginning God created the heavens and the earth. Genesis 1:1-3.

• The earth is the Lord's, and the fullness thereof. Psalm 24:1.

• O earth, earth, earth, Hear the word of the Lord. Jeremiah 22:29.

• Blessed are the meek, for they shall inherit the earth. Matthew 5:4-6

• At the name of Jesus every knee should bow, of those in heaven, and of those on earth. Philippians 2:9-11

• Now I saw a new heaven and a new earth, for the first heaven and the first earth had passed away. Revelation 21:1-3

Hmmmm! Seems to me we ought to celebrate Earth Day every day and Christians ought to lead the celebration. Happy Earth Day!

Today's prayer to continue: Thank You Lord for creating such an amazing earth and allowing me to live on it. I am specifically thankful for . . .

April 23 "When Your Prayers are Unanswered"

"Why didn't God answer my prayer?" That was the question posed by the new Christian, although the question is not unique to new Christians. First of all, there is no such thing as unanswered prayer, in spite of the old hymn text by B.B. McKinney. Sometimes, God says "No" or "Wait" but those are answers. When it seems God is not answering we tend to look for reasons. We blame God – "God doesn't care about me!" We blame others. In "My Utmost for His Highest", Oswald Chambers wrote, "When prayer seems to be unanswered, beware of trying to fix the blame on someone else." We blame self – "I must not be living right!" We even blame circumstances – "That's just the way things are right now!" Understanding that God is also present in apparent silence, what ought we to do? Three suggestions: (1) Listen more intently; (2) Walk more closely; (3) Wait more patiently. In Matthew 7:7, Jesus said to "ask," "seek," and "knock." While each of those actions promised response, none of them implied the response would be immediate.

Today's prayer to continue: For answering all of my prayers, Lord, I am grateful. For waiting times, I am appreciative. I continue to ask . . .

April 24 Now Abides Faith and Hope

The speaker at a recent law enforcement graduation said, "Hope is not a survival strategy." Christians talk much of hope but usually not in a negative context. His statement got my attention so I thought through it again. Paul wrote, "Hope that is seen is not hope" (Romans 8:24). The writer of Hebrews added, "Faith is the substance of things hoped for, the evidence of things not seen" (Hebrews 11:1). While we hope in the unseen, we prepare within the context of the visible. That's why a visible profession of faith in Christ is necessary for eternal life in heaven (also called "the blessed hope" in Titus 2:13). You can't simply "hope" to go to heaven. You've got to prepare by taking a step of visible faith. You can't simply hope to live a Christian life. You've got to employ discipline. If hope is not a survival strategy, what is? Faith is; faith in your preparation, your plan of survival. For the Christian, it's our faith in Jesus Christ, who has done for us all that we cannot do for ourselves.

Today's prayer to continue: Lord, my faith is in You and You alone, and with that foundation, I hope for . . .

April 25 Real, Relevant or Both?

Recent studies have shown that as high as 70% of young Protestant adults between the ages of 18 and 22 have stopped attending church regularly. How could this happen? We tried so hard to reach them with slick slogans, casual clothing, shorter sermons, power point presentations, video clips, live praise bands, no awkward welcoming of visitors, creating a theater atmosphere with low lights and spot lights, etc. While there is nothing inherently wrong with any of the above methods, the relevant must be matched with the real. Young adults have been raised in a culture of distrust, dysfunction, and distaste. They are looking for something and someone that is real. The wrappings can be flashy or faded, but the content must be authentic and genuine. Paul asked, "Do you look at things according to the outward appearance" (2 Corinthians 10:7)? Could it be that we focus on the outward to the exclusion of the inward and in our zealous attempt to be relevant, we fail to be real?

Today's prayer to continue: Lord, I know that Your message is real. May I be more interested in reality, than I am in the relevance of . . .

April 26 Shipwrecked Faith

Does your faith ever falter? Apparently Timothy's faith was on the verge of doing just that. Paul wrote to young Timothy concerning faith and said some, in "good conscience", had rejected the faith and thus had "suffered shipwreck" (1 Timothy 1:19). It is important to understand that a shipwreck is not necessarily fatal. One can survive a shipwreck without being drowned or lost. In fact, Paul had done so three times (2 Corinthians 11:25). So this is not about losing one's faith. It is about losing one's grip on faith. And it has to do with conscience. Conscience, like a computer, is programmed with the will of God. A clear conscience allows God's will to direct. A violated conscience sets off a warning signal – the computer is under attack, a virus is attempting to invade, faith is in trouble. So how do you keep the faith? I saw a piece of graffiti once that had been altered. Originally it read, "Keep the faith baby!" Someone had added one word, making it read, "Keep sharing the faith baby!" We are channels of faith, not reservoirs. One way to avoid shipwrecked faith is to keep sharing it.

Today's prayer to continue: Today, Lord I ask for Your strength and wisdom as I share the faith with . . .

April 27 Called to Worship

What does it mean to be "called to worship?" Following a week to be forgotten, a pastor stepped to the pulpit at the beginning of the Sunday worship service and proclaimed, "I've had a terrible week and I don't feel like calling you to worship, so why don't you call yourselves to worship." After a stunned silence, someone shared a passage of scripture, another prayed. Finally someone began singing a familiar song. Others joined in. Eventually, they were worshipping. Are you called to worship because someone with authority announces it; or because you enter a place of worship; or because it is the appointed time for worship? What constitutes a "call to worship"? Jesus told a well-side woman, "The hour is coming . . . when true worshippers will worship the Father in spirit and truth; for the Father is seeking such to worship Him" (John 4:23). Bottom line: the Lord is calling to worship, those who sincerely desire to worship the Father with integrity. Times, places and methods are secondary.

Today's prayer to continue: Lord, I sincerely want to worship You today. I will try my best to accomplish that by . . .

April 28 Watching and Waiting

There is a difference in watching "for" and watching "with". Most of the time we are watching "for" God to reply, respond, act, etc. In the midst of Gethsemane grief, Jesus asked His disciples to "watch with" Him (Matthew 26:40). Unable to do so, they opted instead for a few moments of sleep, watching and waiting only for Him to finish praying. While we may not opt for sleep, seldom do we "watch with" Him. We conclude that we are far too busy for such passive activity. We've got things to do, places to go, people to see. How could we possibly spend time simply "watching?" When will we learn that quiet time is never wasted time when it is spent with Him? The disciples would later learn not only to "watch with" Him on one occasion, but for the rest of their lives. Fanny Crosby, who could not "watch" as most of us can, wrote, "Watching and waiting, looking above, filled with his goodness, lost in His love." May He never have to ask of us, "Could you not watch with me" (Matthew 26:40)?

Today's prayer to continue: "With" is such a key word in discipleship. Lord, I will try my best to "watch with" You today, as I . . .

April 29 Ministry by Paranoia

Paranoia is a thought process heavily influenced by anxiety or fear. Many people minister by paranoia – fearful of what someone might think or say. In my younger days, working hard to be liked and fearing rejection, I practiced ministry through paranoia. Basically I liked to be liked and I feared failure. Jesus, on the other hand, was never anxious or intimidated by what others thought. After He called Zacchaeus down from the tree, He walked with him through the streets of Jericho, unafraid of the watching crowd or the wagging tongues. He was intent on going to the home of a rather notorious sinner where not only Zacchaeus, but the entire household would be saved. Deuteronomy 31:6 says, "Be strong and of good courage, do not fear nor be afraid of them; for the Lord your God, He is the One who goes with you. He will not leave you nor forsake you." Lord, deliver my friends and me from ministry by paranoia.

Today's prayer to continue: I am too often afraid and intimidated, Lord. But I don't want to be that way. Give me courage today as I . . .

April 30 Today and Tomorrow

It was one of those weeks; early morning to late night for five days and a four hour flight on Saturday that turned into six hours due to storms. Then three sermons preached on Sunday plus leading a break-out session. I was physically, emotionally, mentally, and spiritually exhausted. In an attempt to ease the pain of my private pity party, I posted my feelings on Facebook. I know, I know, but at least I wasn't boring readers with what I had for dinner or the latest traffic jam, or my farm animals. I received a significant response, mostly encouraging, some humorous. I have the funniest friends on Facebook. As I was I scrolling through the responses, I came to one that simply said, "Strength for today and bright hope for tomorrow, right?" Even though I recognized the idea from the old hymn, "Great is Thy Faithfulness" based on Lamentations 3:22-23, it was a fresh word; a much needed word and a word worth sharing. So, if you are tired – physically, emotionally, mentally or spiritually – I pray that you find strength for today and bright hope for tomorrow. Right? Right!

Today's prayer to continue: Lord, I pray that for myself – strength for today, and bright hope for tomorrow, because today I need to . . .

May 1 Let the Children Come

One of my favorite worship services is the one when the children's choirs share their spring music concert. Last Sunday was no exception. Children sang. Parents smiled. Grandparents smiled broader. Cameras flashed. It's no wonder Jesus loved children and rebuked His disciples when they tried to keep the kids away from Him. "Let the little children come to Me, and do not forbid them; for of such is the kingdom of heaven (Matthew 19:14; Mark 10:14; Luke 18:16)," He said. I've never understood why some churches consistently have difficulty recruiting volunteer children's workers. I'm often tempted to say on a given Sunday, "Someone else preach. I'm going to work with the kids today." In fact, I said that in one church where I was serving as Interim Pastor and immediately had a host of volunteers. Seems no one wanted to preach. In the midst of all our slick strategies to grow churches, let's not forget that if we miss the children, we create the possibility for a dead church in two generations. Let the children come.

Today's prayer to continue: Thank You Lord for those who ministered to me when I was a child, especially do I remember . . .

May 2 Good, Better, Best

The quote was on the back of a T-shirt, three rows in front of me at a baseball game. "Good, better, best...never let it rest, until your good is better and your better is your best" but it was attributed to a professional basketball player who was not born until the mid-1970s. So what's the problem, you ask? The problem I was having with quote being attributed to the basketball player was related to the fact that on my first school day at Miss Baker's Little Kindergarten in Paris, Texas, my mother saw me out of the front door by reminding me of that quote, and that was a long time before the mid-70s. A little research informed me that the basketball player said the quote came from his mother who made him memorize it and say it every night before his bedtime. A little more research informed me that the actual quote, "Good better, best, never let it rest until the good is better, and the better is best" came from St. Jerome, a Catholic priest, born in 347 A.D. and best known for his translation of the Bible into Latin (the Vulgate), as well as his extensive writings. Not sure where Jerome got the idea for the quote, unless it was from the author of Hebrews who wrote, "Therefore, leaving the discussion of the elementary principles of Christ, let us go on to perfection" (Hebrews 6:1). Wherever it started, it is a worthy goal. So this week, let's work on making our good, better and our better, best.

Today's prayer to continue: My good is never enough for You Lord. Today help me to make my good, better, and my better, best.

May 3 Reunion Anxiety

There's a lot of anxiety involved in attending a reunion. I'm coming up on my 50th high school class reunion. I'm anxious that others will have changed so much they might not recognize me. I'm anxious someone might look at me and ask, "What happened to you?" I'm anxious someone might remember that I owe them money. I'm anxious someone might ask, "Didn't you date my wife?" Psychologist Joyce Brothers once wrote, "Ninety-nine and nine-tenths percent of people have some anxiety about going to a reunion. The rest are people who are so secure and have done so well they have no intention of going back." I've done fairly well, but I'm going back. I haven't been to one since the 35th year reunion. The anxiety of the reunion makes me extra glad that my heavenly reunion holds no such emotion. The Bible is clear that, "He who began a good work in you will complete it" (Philippians 1:6). Stay tuned for my "Reunion Attended" report.

Today's prayer to continue: While earthly reunions carry a bit of anxiety, Lord, I rejoice in the possibility of an anxiety-free reunion in heaven with . . .

May 4 Progressive Dinner

Have you been to a progressive dinner lately? You remember - appetizers are at the first house, salad at the second house, the main course at the third house, and desert at the fourth house. According to the Food Channel on television, there is a street with restaurants from forty-two countries on it. Now that's where I want to have a progressive dinner – and then likely suffer from international indigestion. For the believer the progressive dinner began in the Upper Room when Jesus, "Took bread, blessed and broke it, and gave it to the disciples and said, 'Take eat; this is my body.' (Matthew 26:26)" Then He said the same concerning the cup. We missed the first part of the progressive dinner, but we're on the journey now and will ultimately arrive in heaven in time for dessert (the "marriage supper of the Lamb", Revelation 19:9). I'm glad to be on the journey with you.

Today's prayer to continue: Lord, I'm so glad to be on this progressive dinner with my friends . . .

May 5 Travail

While not a biblical word, "travail" is a biblical idea. The first known usage of the word was in the 13th century and it described work of a painful or laborious nature. Synonyms were agony, torment, distress, tribulation, woe. Some modern translations of

Galatians 4:19 and Romans 8:22 describe "the pains of childbirth" by using the word "travail." Not sure when Christians first began to use the word related to prayer, but we have ceased to use it with the same frequency as our forefathers. While most prayer is joyful, some prayer includes exhausting work. Hezekiah and Isaiah "cried out to heaven" (2 Chronicles 32:20). The sons of Israel "cried out" to God in confession of sin (Nehemiah 9:28). Hannah was "in bitterness" and "wept in anguish" in her prayer (1 Samuel 1:10). According to the writer of Hebrews, Jesus prayed with "vehement cries and tears" (Hebrews 5:7). Indeed our Lord prayed with such intensity in Gethsemane that "His sweat became like great drops of blood" (Luke 22:44). Paul asked believers in Rome to "strive together" with him in prayer (Romans 15:30). Epaphras was "always laboring fervently" in his prayers (Colossians 4:12). Our forefathers in the faith spoke of "importunity" in prayer. Today, we speak of "agonizing" or "wrestling" in prayer. It is all a form of travail. Serious prayer warrior, I ask you a question. How long has it been since you travailed in prayer? When was the last time your sweat appeared as blood? Pray on!

Today's prayer to continue: Lord, I confess that "travail" is not often enough a part of my prayer life, but it needs to be, so today, I want to pray in anguish for . . .

May 6 Keep on Keeping On

In his attempt to convince the graduates that there was more to life than attaining an academic degree the commencement speaker quoted a tombstone inscription, "Here lies Flo. G.P.A. 4.0." After congratulating the graduates with high grade point averages, the speaker shared how tragic it would be to get to the end of life with nothing more to show than a high G.P.A. He was right on target! The fact, that within a year, most graduates do not remember what their commencement speaker said is beside the point. Until the day we die and some meaningful inscription is carved on our tombstone, there is still more to life. Edwin Louis Cole, founder of the Christian Men's Network, wrote a book entitled, "Never Quit" with a subtitle, "Winners are not those who never fail but those who never quit." So persevere. Keep on keeping on. Whatever tribulation comes your way today, remember the words of the Apostle Paul, "Tribulation produces perseverance; and perseverance, character; and character hope" (Romans 5:3). A 4.0 is not bad, neither is a perfect personality, or a successful career, unless you quit before the finish line.

Today's prayer to continue: Lord, I'm not anxious to finish, but I do want to finish well, so my tombstone will reflect a life . . .

May 7 Re-proving Truth

The key to happiness among religious people is close friendships with fellow church-goers. That was the conclusion of a recent study led by a professor from the University of Wisconsin and a researcher from Harvard University and released in an issue of the "American Sociological Review." I never cease to be amazed at how large sums of money and great expenditures of time are spent trying to prove what the Bible has already proclaimed as truth. In Romans 12:5, Paul states that believers, "being many, are one body in Christ, and individually members of one another" and in 1 John 1:7, John instructs believers to "have fellowship with one another." This study reminded me of an earlier study reported by a now defunct scientific magazine, which proved man needs at least one day of rest out of every seven. It made me want to ask, "So how far did you get in your attempt to read through the Bible, maybe Genesis?" My suggestion? Read the Bible as God's authoritative word and save yourself time and money trying to re-prove what is already stated as truth.

Today's prayer to continue: Thank You Lord, for revealing truth so simple that it confounds the wise. I'm thinking today of another such truth . . .

May 8 Two Heavenly Mansions; Two Earthly Saints

Funerals were held for two men last week. One was a common man, who for many years worked with children at his church on Sundays and assisted with the meal on Wednesday evenings. The other was a well-known dignitary, a public servant, a man of great prestige. The common man had an obituary of less than half a newspaper column, while the other's obituary covered all six columns of one page in the same newspaper. Both men were greatly loved and both made significant contributions. One was widely known and had a large, elaborate funeral. The other man was known mostly by members of his church, children who were rocked by him in the church nursery and to whom he gave candy on Sunday and widows whose yard he mowed. Both were men of faith, and may well have met by now. It is easy to picture them meeting in heaven, walking on the same golden street, breathing the same heavenly air, enjoying their heavenly reward, and then separating, each going to their mansion, neither mansion larger or more special than the other (John 14:2).

Today's prayer to continue: Thank you Lord for those who serve without public applause or recognition. I'm thinking today of . . .

May 9 Praying in Sleepless Weakness

It was one of those Saturday nights. The events of the week had created a scenario wherein my body was too tired and weak to sleep. Nor was my mind in very good shape either. I tossed and I turned but I did not sleep. To make matters worse, I had to preach twice the next morning. I kept praying to God that I really needed to sleep so I could be at my best on Sunday morning – for God's glory of course. Still no sleep. My prayer slowly evolved to a request to be clear and focused in spite of the lack of sleep. I reminded God that I would be delivering sermons in sleepless weakness. I may have slept a couple of hours, but I eventually got up, got dressed, drove to church and preached twice – with clarity and focus. During the invitation, people came to the front to pray. More than the normal number of folks made positive comments on the sermon. So what happened between my late night/early morning sleepless prayer and the delivery of the sermons? Oh, that's the good part of the story. As I often do, I awoke that Sunday morning with a song on my mind. That morning it was the old hymn, "Guide me, O Thou great Jehovah, pilgrim through this barren land; I am weak, but Thou art mighty; hold me with Thy powerful hand." Almost immediately, the verse came to mind from 2 Corinthians 12:9, "My strength is made perfect in weakness." Then I went to my computer where a new Scripture verse greets me each morning. The verse for that day was from 1 Samuel 30:6, "David strengthened himself in the Lord his God." Need I say more?

Today's prayer to continue: For strength in the midst of my weakness, I am grateful Lord. Today I need Your strength for . . . .

May 10 Reunion Attended

Well my 50th High School class reunion is history. It was similar to the stock market with gains and losses: weight gained, hair lost. Few looked the same. In fact when I entered I thought I had the wrong group. It looked more like a Branson, Missouri tour group than my classmates. Thanks to Facebook, and the fact that a sizable number of my classmates had become religious over the years, I was more popular at the reunion than I was in my student days. As a minister, I was reminded of a few life lessons. People change: the quiet, shy ones are no longer that way; the athletes are no longer in shape. There are exceptions to that "change" factor: some teen-age drunks are now senior adult drunks. Teachers, coaches, and counselors die even though some of them seemed to be bullet-proof. Long-time friends are gone: Out of our senior class of 693, 79 were known to be deceased, another 164 are missing. A person needs something steadfast in an ever-changing world: Jesus is "the same yesterday, today and forever" (Heb. 13:8). I'm more pleased with that today than I was before last the recent reunion.

Today's prayer to continue: Thank You Lord for being unchanging, even as everything around me is changing. Today, I'm noticing change related to . . .

May 11 Coincidence

What a coincidence - at least for me. This week was both Mother's Day and the Global Day of Prayer. Among many things my mother taught me was the need to pray for the world and those who had been called by God to minister cross-culturally. Her missionary heart led her to be a prayer warrior extra-ordinary, claiming Psalm 2:8. "Ask of Me and I will give you the nations as your inheritance, and the ends of the earth for your possession." Even though my mother has gone on to her heavenly reward, you would honor her memory and my memory of her, by praying for the nations today.

Today's prayer to continue: Lord of all nations, I pray today for those nations, specially the nation of . . .

May 12 Mother Love

Mother's Day always reminds me that mothers love things that no one else loves. My grandson told his mother he wanted to rent, "The Muppet Movie." When she asked why, he explained that Miss Piggy and his mother were a lot alike. Other than admitting she had indeed kissed a few toad frogs in her life, she was speechless. Only love kept her from having a violent reaction. Only a mother could love being compared to Miss Piggy. I remember a night, many, many years ago, when my best friend was staying at my house and we were running wildly through the house shooting our plastic guns at each other. My mother was no doubt irritated by the noise, but rather than yell at us to be quiet, she simply found another plastic gun, hid behind a chair in the living room, and waited. On our next trip through the living room, she jumped out and yelled, "Pow! Pow! Pow!" I thought my friend had suffered an early cardiac arrest and I was in no shape to assist him. Only a loving mother could love two loud boys that way. The Bible is filled with stories of mother love, from Eve, the original mother, to Sarah, the mother of Isaac, to Rebekah, the mother of Esau and Jacob, to Jochebed, the mother of Moses, to Mary the mother of Jesus. In every case, and to this day, it is said of loving mothers, "Her children rise up and call her blessed" (Proverbs 31:28). I am indebted to my mother's love and I miss her greatly, especially Mother's Day.

Today's prayer to continue: Thank You Lord for Mothers and especially today, I give thanks for my own mother and the time she . . .

May 13 What Would Mother Say?

May is the month that we honor Mothers. Even though my mother re-located to heaven years ago, she fits the description of Able of Old Testament days, "he being dead still speaks" (Hebrews 11:4). Although she had many memorable lines, her most remembered statement, reflecting her always-positive attitude, even in the midst of difficult circumstances, was "It will all be better tomorrow." No matter what my aches and pains were, I got no sympathy from my mother, only this statement! Even into my adult years, when I would call home and share some stressful situation, I would hear the same predictable statement, about tomorrow being better. Looking back, she was correct, is still correct, and will ultimately be correct. Today, facing the aging process with all its challenges, I know exactly what my mother would say, if I could talk with her – "It will all be better tomorrow." I envision meeting her some day on heaven's golden streets, surrounded by beautiful mansions, reveling in God's glory, and hearing my mother say, "Didn't I tell you it would all be better tomorrow?"

Today's prayer to continue: Tomorrow is always better with You, Lord. One of the better things that I anticipate is . . .

May 14 Jesus and Humor

We know that Jesus wept – over Jerusalem (Luke 19:41) and over Lazarus (John 11:35) – but did he ever laugh, smile, display a sense of humor? The Scriptures never say so directly, but it is often implied. How could he have wept in times of sorrow and not laughed in times of joy? Can you imagine Jesus not smiling when children crawled over Him as the disciples had a fit or when the host of a wedding feast in Cana, suddenly went from lots of water, but no wine to 600 gallons of wine and no water? Surely Jesus laughed at Simon Peter on several occasions. What about the spectacle of Zacchaeus out on a limb, desperately trying to see Jesus, as the wind blew through the branches? I believe Jesus had a great sense of humor. I also believe you and I ought to have the same. It's part of being Christ-like. Laugh at something today.

Today's prayer to continue: While I give thanks for God's gift of laughter today, I'm laughing at . . .

May 15 When Knowledge Trumps Action

It's not what you know but who you know that makes a difference. I don't know how many times I've heard that advice repeated. Still, how many times have you and I seen that proven to be true – in business, education, athletics, military, church, etc. The Old Testament people knew what to do to please God, or so they thought. One could please God by doing the right things – like making the correct offering. So they worked hard at doing the right things, making the correct sacrifices. And they prided themselves in knowing "what" to do. However God said, "I desire . . . the knowledge of God more than burnt offerings" (Hosea 6:6). I spent most of a career trying to do the right things. It has only been in recent years that I have decided that as important as it is to do the right things, it is extremely more important to know God the right way. Action is important. It gets the job done. But action without adequate knowledge is simply busy-work.

Today's prayer to continue: Too much busy-work Lord. Today, I want to know more of You. Please reveal . . .

May 16 God's Requirements

Requirements are easy to identify in the world of education. Teachers make assignments. Students understand what is required. They are fairly easy to identify in the medical world. Doctors examine you and tell you what is required for you to do or take or undergo. In the athletic world coaches develop a game plan and show you what is required to do in order to win. In the business world, you study the growth charts and determine what is required to turn a profit. What about in the spiritual world? What does God require? That is the very same question that was posed in Micah's day, and then answered in Micah 6:8: "What does the Lord require of you, but to do justly, to love mercy, and to walk humbly with your God." It is required that we do justly before God, before others and before self. Not only what the law requires, but we are to love mercy, kindness, compassion, benevolence. How are we to carry out these requirements? We respond by walking humbly, under submission, in fellowship with God. Pretty heavy assignment for today!

Today's prayer to continue: Lord, the part of these requirements that I'm going to need the most help with is . . .

May 17 The Cost of Love

Someone said, "There's no free lunch." While that may be true, there is free love, at least in a manner of speaking. God's love for us is free, meaning it cost us nothing to receive it and nothing to keep it. God said, "I have loved you with an everlasting love" (Jeremiah 31:3). "Everlasting" means it lasts forever. Free, unchanging, eternal! What a love! The very fact that God's love is based on nothing of our doing makes us all the more secure. We can do nothing to earn it, deserve it, facilitate it, support it, or maintain it. We can only receive it – and respond to it. Ah, there is the cost! Not to purchase, but to reply. We do not serve in order to get God to love us. We serve because God loves us with an everlasting love. In response to God's great love, what service will you render today?

Today's prayer to continue: Today, Lord, I wish to render the following service on Your behalf . . .

May 18 Kindergarten Dreams

I attended my grandson's kindergarten graduation this week. Student answers to three questions were shared with the audience as they received their diplomas. What do you want to be when you grow up? Grandson: "A paleontologist." What's your biggest wish? Grandson: "To own 7 rifles, 2 shotguns and a pistol." What do you hope to learn in the 1st grade? Grandson:" How to fish and how to kill a squirrel." I'm fairly sure when I graduated from kindergarten I had never heard of a paleontologist, nor could I have looked it up, since I would not have been able to spell it. I did desire to own a Daisy Red Ryder BB Gun, at least till my cousin shot me with his. I never much cared for guns after that. And what was my desire for 1st grade? It was probably to get to 2nd grade, since I was never the sharpest student in the class. Who would have dreamed that someday, I'd be "Dr. Dan"? The content of dreams change, yet even with the changing times, the act of dreaming about the future remains constant. So it was meant to be. The Bible says that "Old men shall dream dreams" (Joel 2:28; Acts 2:17) but surely nothing like those dreamed by young men. So dream on kindergarten graduates. The world awaits you.

Today's prayer to continue: Lord, I still dream of becoming, but now my dream includes . . .

May 19 Back of the Line

"Putting on the uniform never gets old." Those were the words of the new Manager of the Fort Worth Cats minor league baseball team, but with an adjustment or two, they could have been my words. I feel that way about my academic regalia. Long ago I lost count of the graduations and convocations in which I marched in my cap and gown. On those occasions, my attention was often drawn to the back of the line where walked the retired professors, those who had given their lives to the training of the called-out ones, my academic heroes, men and women, "of whom the world was not worthy." (Hebrews 11:38). I remember thinking, "the last will be first."(Matthew 20:16). I also remember thinking how honored I would someday be to walk at the back of the line, retired, accomplished, proud. But times change and traditions die. Once retired, I was never once asked to walk in graduation or convocation again. It's OK! There is a great line in an old spiritual that says, "All of God's chillun got a robe." My reservation is secure in a place where time never overrules tradition; my eternal robe has been fitted; my place in line has been assigned. Someday, I'll put on the heavenly uniform (celestial cap and gown) and it will never, ever get old again, even if I'm at the back of the line.

Today's prayer to continue: Lord, it matters little to me where I am in the eternal line, as long as I'm in, but today, I'm concerned about . . .

May 20 Why so Many Intercessors?

Why does one seek ever increasing numbers of persons to pray on their behalf? Do we think that by getting our prayer request listed on as many prayer lists as possible and sharing it via social networks with folks we hardly know, the sheer numbers will impress God and thus win favor and produce a positive response? God is no more impressed with our numbers than He was with the efforts of many people to build a tower in His honor at Babel (Genesis 11:1-9). While God did respond to the prayers of the multitudes in the Bible, He more often responded to the prayers of a faithful few or even to the intercession of a single saint. It is not then necessary to secure ever increasing numbers of prayer partners for the purpose of impressing God. Understanding that there are some prayer concerns that are so personal they should be shared with only a select few, why then should we add up intercessors for other concerns? Because prayer is ministry. The more people we can involve in a ministry of intercession, the more people will grow spiritually and be blessed by the results. In addition, I don't know who God desires to use as part of His response to my prayer concern. If only a few are informed, only a few are blessed and we limit God on who He can use as a channel of blessing and response. So share prayer concerns with sensitivity, not to impress God, but to provide an opportunity for ministry and blessing to others.

Today's prayer to continue: OK, so I need to share my prayer concerns with more than just a few. Today, Lord, I will try to share my concerns with . . .

May 21 The End is not Yet, but Could Be

Six p.m. on a particular Saturday came and went without the world ending. It could have ended, but not because of the predictions of a California radio preacher. The Bible is clear that "of that day and hour no one knows, not even the angels of heaven, but My Father only" (Matthew 24:36). So it could have ended Saturday. It could end today. Then again, it may not end in your lifetime. Predictions of the end are not new. Before the Bible was even fully recorded, the Thessalonians confronted Paul with a rumor that the day of the Lord was at hand, and they had missed the rapture. Since then, there have been over 240 end-of-the-world predictions. In 1555, the most famous doomsday prophet, Nostradamus wrote in his book, "The Prophecies", "The year 1999, seventh month, from the sky will come a great King of Terror" and would thus end the world. In 1806 the "Christian Science Monitor" reported, the "Prophet Hen of Leeds," a domesticated fowl in England, began laying eggs that bore the message "Christ is coming" leading locals to believe the end of the world was at hand. Religious broadcaster Pat Robertson told followers: "I guarantee you by the end of 1982 there is going to be a judgment on the world." The book "88 Reasons Why the Rapture is in 1988" proposed that the rapture would occur during a three-day window from Sept 11 to13. I remember Seminary students asking me if they came to class on those days and I had been raptured, what should they do? I told them to check with the Dean's Office. The proponent of Saturdays' end of the world theory, had already miscalculated once, predicting that the world would end in Sept., 1994. Nor do these predictions end. Several scientists and speculators have observed numerous astronomical alignments hinting at the planet's demise, based on the view that the calendar of the ancient Mayan civilization would end on Dec. 21, 2012. It didn't. So when will the world end? I don't know. I've not been assigned to the Time & Place Committee, but rather to the Preparation Committee. "Therefore . . . be ready, for the Son of Man is coming at an hour you do not expect" (Matthew 24:44). The end is not yet, but it could be.

Today's prayer to continue: Lord, I don't know when You are returning, but I want to be ready, and I want to help everyone I know be ready. Today, I am thinking of helping . . .

May 22 Standing in Need of (Saturday Night) Prayer

Pastors need the intercessory prayer of their people, perhaps never more strongly than on Saturday night. I don't know how it is at your church, but the folks who hear me preach on Sunday mornings, seldom hear a sermon preached on a full night's sleep. Saturday nights are filled with off-and-on sleep mixed with human anxieties, emotional roller coaster feelings, Satan motivated questions and doubts, worries about physical inadequacies. For me, sleep only returns as I pray my way through the problems. Then, I am often awakened by another set of concerns. I'm fortunate if I preach on four or five hours of sleep. When I was young, I wondered why my pastor-father always took a nap on Sunday afternoons. Now I know. A verse that I can quote better than I can live is Philippians 4:6: "Be anxious for nothing, but in everything by prayer and supplication, with thanksgiving, let your requests be made known to God." I am not usually anxious, but I confess that Saturday nights are different, at least for me. I'm sure there are others, more spiritual ones to be sure, who sleep like a baby on Saturday night, but not me. Anxiety often rules the night. It is an awesome thing to stand before God's people (and some who are not yet God's people) and deliver God's message. I have served as pastor of two churches and interim pastor of over twenty churches. Every church is different and preaching in every church has similarities and differences. The churches where God seems to bless my preaching the most are the churches where I know some church members are interceding on my behalf – starting on Saturday night. So, check with your pastor. You may need to be praying on Saturday night.

Today's prayer to continue: Lord, from now on, I plan on interceding for my Pastor (or for fellow-pastors) on Saturday night, beginning with . . .

May 23 Just in Case

I walk to keep my doctor happy. The younger man at the track, had a much more serious purpose. I was doing my casual mile and a half at the school track near my house. He was earnestly sprinting, jumping, stretching. On my last lap I inquired of him,

"Football or track?" "Football and Basketball" he replied. "Where do you go to school?" I asked. "Oh, I don't go to school anywhere. I'm just staying in shape in case anyone calls." I walked on, thinking, "That's it!" That's what Paul was telling Timothy when he wrote, "Exercise yourself toward godliness for bodily exercise profits a little, but godliness is profitable for all things" (I Timothy 4:7-8). We are called to stay in spiritual shape, just in case God calls. What does that mean for you today? What spiritual disciplines, what exercises, will you need to continue or implement, in order to be in shape when God calls?

Today's prayer to continue: Lord, if You call today, I want to be in good spiritual shape, beginning with . . .

May 24 Just Live the Golden Rule, or Not

A television talk-show guest was asked to share his thirty-second advice with the audience. "Live the Golden Rule" he said. Then he added (to fill up his thirty seconds), "If everyone just lived the Golden Rule, it'd be a better world." No doubt. But my question is, can "everyone" live the Golden Rule? For those who don't remember, the Golden Rule comes from Jesus' Sermon on the Mount, "whatever you want men to do to you, do also to them" (Matthew 7:12). It also has some background in Obadiah 1:15, "As you have done, it shall be done to you." Whether the words come from the prophet's preaching on the judgment to come or from the Messiah's standard of discipleship, they are given to believers. Is it then possible for a non-believer to live the Golden Rule of believers? How can one treat others right if they themselves are not right? How can one who does not accept the grace-treatment of our God, treat others with grace? Some days my manna comes in a nice, warm, fuzzy thought designed to jump-start your day. Today, it is something to think about, reflect on, and digest for a while. And while you're at it, what would you share if you had thirty seconds with an audience?

Today's prayer to continue: If I had thirty seconds with an audience, Lord (and I'm sure I will today), I would share . . .

May 25 When God Does Not Answer Immediately

Have you ever asked God for something and received no immediate answer? Saul asked God for counsel but God, "did not answer him that day" (1 Samuel 14:37). In many Seminary classrooms and in conferences too numerous to count, I have taught that there is no such thing as unanswered prayer for believers. Sometimes God says "yes," sometimes "no," occasionally "wait," perhaps "how about this" (when the answer is different from the request), maybe even "you've got to be joking." But there is no such thing as God refusing to answer a believer's prayer request. So what do we make of this apparent non-answer from God to Saul? There are several possibilities. Perhaps Saul asked "amiss" (James 4:3). Maybe Saul had unconfessed sin in his life that blocked his communication with God. Then again, it could have been the sin of someone else, like Jonathan that prevented an immediate answer. A human father must always consider the good of the family over the good of any individual member of the family. It could be that God had a larger plan for the family, than would be reflected in Saul's request for personal "counsel." When God does not respond to our "asking," what are we to do? Try "seeking" and if that doesn't work, try "knocking" (Matthew 7:7). While God may not respond immediately, He will eventually respond. Walk on – not by sight, but by faith. Pray on – not occasionally but without ceasing. Listen on – to God and all whom God might use in the answer. Remember, it only took eight verses (1 Samuel 14:45) for God to eventually answer Saul's prayer and He did so, not with His own words as Saul was expecting, but through the actions of the people.

Today's prayer to continue: Lord, the answer to prayer that I've been looking for has not yet come, therefore I think I should . . .

May 26 His Way in the Storms

As I am writing this there is a storm brewing outside my window. I can hear the thunder. The radar shows wind and rain only a few miles away. Only a few hours ago the sun was shining brightly and the weather was warm and clear. Funny how life is like that. We go from clear, quiet days to storms and turbulence. As Nahum prophesized to God's Old Testament people, he spoke of God having, "His way in the whirlwind and in the storm" (Nahum 1:3), nor is this the only time in the Bible that we find such a reference. God spoke to Job out of the whirlwind and descended on Mount Sinai in a storm and tempest. The Bible speaks of the clouds being God's chariots. In one sense, as soon as God reveals Himself, He disturbs the whole atmosphere, and excites storms and tempests, yet in other places He is described as lovely and gracious. From the original Hebrew language, this verse literally says, "the LORD, in the whirlwind and in the storm is His way." It is easy to experience God on clear days of lovely weather and favorable circumstances. It is not so easy to experience God in the storms of life. The comforting thing to know is that, not only does God have His way in the smooth ways of life, He also, "has His way in the whirlwind and in the storm."

Today's prayer to continue: Remind me, Lord, that You are near and active in the current circumstances of my life, which are best described as . . .

May 27 Putters and Plumb Lines

This week, I saw a golfer hold up his putter and dangle it downward, lining up a putt. The announcer described it as a "Golfer's plumb line." The plumb line is an instrument that has been used since at least the time of ancient Egypt to ensure that constructions are "plumb", or vertical. It is usually a string with a weight, providing a vertical reference line. For the golfer it helps determine the break of the green. In the days of Amos the prophet, The Lord used a "plumb line," to determine how upright His people were, saying to Amos, "Behold, I am setting a plumb line in the midst of My people" (Amos 7:8). God still uses a plumb line today. Neither how upright we think we are, nor how upright others think we are, means anything to God. He is only interested in how upright we are measured by His standards of measurement. If God were to set His plumb line of measurement next to you, how would you measure up?

Today's prayer to continue: I sincerely desire to measure correctly on Your plumb line Lord. So for today, that means . . .

May 28 Memorial Day Meaning

This week is Memorial Day. Americans have been celebrating this day long enough that we should know its meaning by now. The fourth Monday in May is supposed to be a day when we remember and honor those who died at war, fighting for our country. Formerly known as Decoration Day, it originated after the American Civil War to commemorate the fallen Union soldiers of the Civil War. By the early 20th century, the last Monday in May had become an occasion for more general expressions of memory, as people visited the graves of their deceased relatives in church cemeteries. More recently the American flag is annually raised to the top of the staff and then solemnly lowered to the half-staff position, where it remains only until noon. At noon their memory is raised by the living, who resolves not to let their sacrifice be in vain, but to continue the fight for liberty and justice for all. Sadly, Memorial Day now looks more like a day to party hearty, eat hot dogs at a ball game or barbecue in a back yard, lift a drink or two, watch a race on TV, and end the day with fireworks. So let's remind ourselves why our federal government gives us a long weekend. It is because men and women laid down their lives for us in the midst of a battle over freedom. "Greater love has no one than this, than to lay down one's life for his friends" (John 15:13).

Today's prayer to continue: On this year's Memorial Day, Lord, I remember with thanksgiving . . .

May 29 Another Soldier has Gone Home

God doesn't lie. That's why not everyone who arrives in heaven will hear "Well done, good and faithful servant" (Matthew 25:21, 23). Those who receive that welcome will be those who have done well; those who have served faithfully and good. As sure as I am of this truth, I am likewise sure that on a recent day, Jasper heard those words when he arrived at his eternal reward. Reader's Digest used to have a regular column entitled, "The Most Unforgettable Character I've Ever Met." Jasper could have been one of those "characters" for me. He was every pastor or interim pastor's dream deacon. I was doubly privileged to serve as his interim pastor twice. Career military, long-time Sunday School teacher, father of two wonderful friends of mine, confidant and critic, I miss him. But he has now answered heaven's muster, passed inspection, and assumed his rightful place in the King's eternal army. Janet Paschal graciously allowed me to use the words of one of her songs in a book I wrote. They were also quoted at my father's funeral. They are appropriate again. "Strike up the band; assemble the choir; another soldier's coming home. Another warrior hears the call; he's waited so long; he'll battle no more; but he's won his wars. Make sure heaven's table has room for one more. Sing a welcome song. Another soldier's coming home."

Today's prayer to continue: Lord, I want to hear, "well done" when I arrive in heaven, so that means for today, I need to . . .

May 30 The Windows of Heaven

Some windows are large, others small. Some are cute but have limited benefit. A few have spiritual significance. There are round windows, rectangular windows, storm windows, solar windows, stained glass windows. Regardless of the size, shape, or significance, all windows do at least three things: (1) They shut out – wind, dust, heat, bugs, etc., (2) They admit – air, light, etc., and (3) They release – whatever is poured or thrown out. The Bible says God will "open" the "windows of heaven" and "pour out" a "blessing" that we will not have room to receive (Malachi 3:10). Wow! How do I take advantage of all these godly "blessings"? Oh, that's the tough part! I've got to give in order to receive. Just like I must insert my cash card into the ATM in order to get cash out of the ATM, likewise I must put blessing into the heavenly window, before receiving any blessing from same window. You can't draw money out of the bank unless you've put money into the bank. The same scripture passage in Malachi instructs me to "bring all the tithes into the storehouse." Simple formula: tithe in, blessings out. What does your checkbook tell you about your faith?

Today's prayer to continue: Please Lord, don't let me get behind in my giving, my "putting in" so today (or very soon) I need to give . . .

May 31 Remembrance

One of God's greatest gifts is memory. This month we've had a day devoted to memory – Memorial Day. When we remember, we sometimes sit in a recliner and reflect. Other times we DO something to in response to memory. This month people placed flowers at gravesites and memorials of those who paid the ultimate sacrifice for our country. People attended ceremonies in cemeteries and at national monuments. We acted out our remembrance. That is exactly what Jesus asked us to do related to Him – act on the memory of His life, death, and resurrection. In Luke 22:19, as

Jesus instituted the memorial supper, He said, "do this in remembrance of Me." Note that Jesus did not say "think about this in remembrance of me." He told us to DO something in memory. Remembrance is something we do, not just something we feel. Thank God for memory and memories this month . . . and DO something about it.

Today's prayer to continue: What can I do today for You, Lord? How about . . .

June 1 Sorry, but You Can't Come In

Answering the doorbell, I was greeted by total strangers who offered to give me some printed material about their beliefs. When I respectfully declined, they asked if they could come in and talk with me about what they believed. When I again declined, they asked if they could make an appointment to return at a more convenient time to talk with me. Three strikes and you're out. Shouldn't I have invited them in for the purpose of sharing my beliefs with them? Wasn't this a perfect opportunity for spiritual dialogue? Maybe, but not when they made their fourth offer by assuring me that my neighbors had invited them into their houses for the purpose of sharing "truth" – a statement that I knew for a fact was untrue, since one neighbor had already called me about the visitors. I believe in sharing my faith with my neighbors and beyond. What I don't believe in is allowing someone from another belief system to assure my neighbors that I am open to their version of "truth." I firmly believe Jesus Christ is the only way to "truth." That's what He said, "I am the way, the truth, and the life. No one comes to the Father except through Me" (John 14:6). Concerning "the doctrine of Christ" the apostle John wrote, "If anyone comes to you and does not bring this doctrine, do not receive them into your house nor greet him" (2 John 10). Tough call!

Today's prayer to continue: Lord, help me to be sensitive to opportunities to share my faith while at the same time being cautious of false teachers, especially . . .

June 2 A New Song

A young mother and her daughter were sitting nearby in a restaurant where I was eating breakfast. As they waited for their order, the little girl was singing a song - not a recognizable song, but her own song. She would grow up and learn to sing the songs of others, both good and bad, but in her innocent child-years, she was singing her own song. I watched, listened, reflected, and dreamed a bit of earlier days and earlier songs. But this was a new day and I had a new song taught to me by a little girl, as yet unaffected by the songs of the world. David, the great song-writer of the Bible wrote, "Sing unto the Lord a new song! Sing to the Lord, all the earth" (Psalm. 96:1). Ultimately, all believers will sing a new heavenly melody (Revelation 5:9), but for this day, try singing a fresh, new, child-like song.

Today's prayer to continue: Lord, the new song in my heart today is about . . .

June 3 Agreement and Disagreement

I have a long-time friend whose ideas seldom mesh with mine. In fact, over the years, there have been more subjects on which we disagreed than those on which we agreed. Yet I have learned from him, and I think he has learned from me. What a shame to think that we can only learn from those with whom we agree. It was Winston Churchill who reportedly said, "If two people agree on everything, one of them is unnecessary." When was the last time you read a book or an article by someone with whom you disagreed? When was the last time you listened to a sermon or lecture, delivered by someone with whom you differed? When was the last time you entertained an idea that, at least initially, seemed to be out of sync with your own thinking? If the truth we hold is not strong enough to stand the test of disagreement, we need stronger faith. So don't panic when your beliefs are challenged by those whose thoughts differ from yours. Agree to disagree and move on. The greatest lesson I ever learned on the writing and recording of my thoughts was from a man whose thoughts differed greatly from mine on most subjects. The Bible says we are "members of one another" (Romans 12:5). It does not say we are one another.

Today's prayer to continue: Today, Lord, I am thinking of one with whom I disagree, and my prayer for them is . . .

June 4 Passing a New Way

I just completed a long interim pastorate. What I tried to say to the people on my last Sunday with them, about the future of their church, is a good thought today to individuals about their own future. Joshua was 40 years old when the Israelites left Egypt. When Moses went up on Mt. Sinai, Joshua went part of the way with him. Later, Joshua was one of the spies who went to see Canaan. The other spies gave a bad report. But Joshua and Caleb said that the Israelites should trust God and move into Canaan. Forty years later, Joshua and Caleb were the only two Egypt-born Israelites to move into Canaan. Having heard from God, Joshua spoke to the people, "You have not passed this way before" (Joshua 3:4). There was no attempt to move the people by things familiar to them. Just the opposite was true. This was a new way. It is so different for us. We try hard to assure people that the future will not change much. It will be comfortable, known. But the future will be different. So, Joshua says, "Sanctify yourselves" (Joshua 3:5). Sanctify means to set apart, in this case, for service to God. It is the only way to effectively serve God. God needed no half-hearted, wishy-washy, semi-committed followers. The same is true today. God needs totally committed, sold-out followers, separated from worldliness, and sanctified to Godliness. And the result? "The Lord will do wonders among you" (Joshua 3:5). This was God's promise delivered by God's messenger to God's people. Once sanctified, they would experience the "wonders" of God. And so it was: they wondrously overthrew powerful Jericho - and then they forgot and were defeated at tiny Ai. The "wonders" of God are done among us, not for us. How excited would you be over your future if you knew the Lord would do "wonders" with you? So, "sanctify yourself" and see.

Today's prayer to continue: If I understand sanctifying myself correctly, Lord, today, I need to . . .

June 5 The Wind Beneath my Wings

I've said it repeatedly that the heart and soul of my ministry abides in my prayer partners. To use a line from a not-so-recent, popular song, they are the "wind beneath my wings." A large percentage of the prayers in the Bible, where we know what God's answer was, were intercessory prayers – prayers for others. Praying for self is biblical. Jesus prayed for Himself. Paul did likewise for himself. But praying for others is clearly a major teaching of the Bible. I don't actively recruit more prayer partners because I think God is impressed with my numbers, nor because I think sheer numbers will win some favor with God. I recruit prayer partners so they can be blessed by being a part of what God does in and through me and because I need all the "wind" I can get "beneath my wings." Strangely, "wind" is often used in the Bible as a symbol of the presence of God. Ezekiel stood over a valley full of dry bones and was told to call for the "wind" to breathe life into the bones (Ezekiel 37:9). When Jesus was trying to help Nicodemus understand God he used the wind as a symbol (John 3:8). When God's presence filled the place where the disciples were gathered, it was described as "a rushing mighty wind" (Acts 2:2). So thanks to my prayer partners, who assist me in understanding God's presence, directions, blessings, and favor in my ministry. The last line of the song says, "Thank you, thank you, thank God for you, the wind beneath my wings."

Today's prayer to continue: Lord, I both need "wind beneath my wings" and I need to be "wind" beneath the wings of others. Today, I pray for . . .

June 6 Working on Becoming Young

I know I'm getting older since I now choose my cereal for the fiber, not the toy, and I've discovered that the volume knob on my radio also turns to the left. Some days I feel older than on other days. Working with university students for 18 years, then teaching seminary students for 26 years, kept me young. But now I am fully retired from both of those callings and it's more difficult to feel young. The Psalmist (who knows how old he was when he wrote these words?) proclaimed, "They shall still bear fruit in old age; they shall be fresh and flourishing" (Psalm 92:14). I sincerely desire to remain productive as long as possible. Seems to me, remaining productive (if not "fresh and flourishing") helps one to reduce the fear of growing older. After all, aging is a reality as well as a privilege denied to many far better than ourselves. I understand my call to ministry as being life-long, not simply until some man-made retirement age. However, as circumstances change, callings must be re-evaluated and adjusted. I'm not a big fan of Pablo Picasso, but I love his quote. Asked after a show of his works why his earliest works were the dullest and the last ones were so alive, colorful, and youthful, he reportedly replied, "It takes a long time to become young." Or to express it another way from the sayings of Casey Stengel (of whom I am a huge fan), "The trick is growing up without growing old." I'm still growing up; working on becoming young – again.

Today's prayer to continue: If I am going to remain productive Lord, I need to . . .

June 7 Deceiving Looks

At first glance, I thought he was a Seminary student, sitting in one of the soft mall chairs, usually occupied by not-so-patient husbands waiting on their wives to shop in one more store. He was even reading his Bible. When I completed my daily walk, I sat down next to him and asked, "Are you a seminary student?" His answer surprised me. "No" he said, "I'm homeless." Long story made short: he had worked in a restaurant that closed and thus, he had lost his job. Unable to find another job, he had eventually run out of money and was evicted from his apartment. He had come in the mall to escape the three-digit temperatures outside. I looked at his Bible, got his name off the front, and called a restaurant manager friend. Within a few days, the homeless, seminary student look-alike, had a new job, and a new outlook on life. I knew I had only stopped to talk with him because he looked like a seminary student. How many homeless, hurting people have I passed by because they looked like what they were? You really can't tell some people by their appearance. One day the disciples asked Jesus, "'Lord, when did we see You hungry or thirsty or a stranger or naked or sick or in prison, and did not minister to You?" His answer convicts me. "Assuredly, I say to you, inasmuch as you did not do it to one of the least of these, you did not do it to Me" (Matthew 25: 43-45).

Today's prayer to continue: Please don't let me pass by a hurting person today, Lord, judging them by their looks only. Help me to . . .

June 8 However You Pronounce It

During my seminary student years, I was a very young pastor of a very small rural church in deep East Texas. Even though I was the pastor there was a head deacon who was the real leader of the church. He also taught the adult Sunday School class, in which I sat each Sunday prior to the worship service. One Sunday, he taught the lesson out of the Old Testament book of Habakkuk, but gave the prophet a deep East Texas pronunciation of running the first two syllables together and hitting the third syllable hard, Haba-KKUK, rather than the traditional first syllable emphasis (and heretofore correct HA-bakkuk). I did not correct him. I would have been fired on the spot for correcting the head deacon, adult Sunday school teacher, and resident theologian. Although I was proud of my seminary training, to them I was only a student wannabe preacher, serving for a few months as their pastor (student-pastoral tenures are often short in rural, deep East Texas churches). I did learn a valuable lesson from Habakkuk that Sunday. "Behold the proud, his soul is not upright in him" (Habakkuk 2:4). Better to leave some things alone, than to proudly display one's knowledge.

Today's prayer to continue: Lord, I know a lot more things today than I probably need to share. Help me to know when to speak and when to . . .

June 9 Praying for the Pastor

The highly successful London pastor, Charles Haddon Spurgeon was once asked, "What is the secret of your great influence?" Spurgeon replied, "My congregation prays for me." How often do you pray for your pastor? How specifically do you pray for your pastor? Do you pray for his spiritual growth? Do you pray for his time management? Do you pray for his sermon preparation and delivery? Do you pray for his counseling sessions? Do you pray for his hospital visits? Do you pray for his community relationships and influence? Do you pray for his family? Do you pray for his accountability? Do you pray for his resistance of satan? The list goes on. The Internet is full of articles on "How to" pray for your pastor, including scriptures to use. My question is, do you? Knowing how is not enough. In his Pastoral letters, Paul asked for prayer (Ephesians 6:18-19 and elsewhere). So when should you pray for your pastor: Saturday nights when satan attempts to rob sleep; Sunday mornings when the congregation must be faced and fed; Monday mornings when the adrenalin rush is over and vulnerability sets in; any other time God brings the pastor to your mind. It was Spurgeon who also said, "A prayerless church member is a hindrance. He is in the body like a rotting bone or a decayed tooth. Before long, since he does not contribute to the benefit of his brethren, he will become a danger and a sorrow to them. Neglect of private prayer is the locust which devours the strength of the church." So get busy this week, praying for your pastor.

Today's prayer to continue: Lord, I want to pray for my pastor (or fellow pastors) today in the following ways . . .

June 10 Faith in Action – Intensity or Consistency?

Recently I preached at a church that was observing "Faith in Action" Sunday. Theirs was an intentional effort to minister to the community and they did it well with over one thousand church members ministering in thirty-five locations. Intensity is to be applauded, especially when it applies to the acting out of faith. However, consistency must reside along-side intensity. While the intense activation of faith on special occasions is good, the consistent living-out of faith is also to be desired. Faith, by its very nature must be active. James writes, "Faith without works (He could just as easily used the word 'action.') is dead" (James 2:20). William Booth, founder of The Salvation Army, wrote, "Faith and works should travel side by side, step answering to step, like the legs of men walking. First faith, and then works; and then faith again, and then works again — until they can scarcely distinguish which is the one and which is the other." If faith is only activated on special occasions, it gives off the appearance of being "dead" on all other days. If faith is only day-by-day consistent, with no special occasions for intensified action, it gives off the appearance of being routine. When you can have both the consistency of day-to-day faith in action and the intensity of special occasions like "Faith in Action" Sunday, you are indeed acting out living, biblical faith.

Today's prayer to continue: Today, Lord, I want to act out my faith in the following ways . . .

June 11 Second Chance to Follow

Many American fathers want their sons to grow up to be NFL quarterbacks, or All-Star pitchers, or successful attorneys, doctors or businessmen. Jewish fathers wanted their sons to grow up to be rabbis. At the age of twelve, young Jewish boys faced their first test. By this age they were expected to have memorized the first five books of the Bible and sit before the rabbi to recite. If they passed the test they could begin to follow the rabbi, with the possibility of eventually becoming one them self. If they failed the test they were told to go back into the family business, which for many was fishing. That's why Peter and Andrew were fishing when Jesus walked by and said, "Follow Me" (Matthew 4:19; Mark 1:17). They had most likely been rejected earlier as rabbi candidates, thus they were now fishermen. The offer of Jesus was a second chance to follow – this time, to follow a different kind of rabbi (John 1:38; 3:2). There is good news for all who have been rejected at some point in life – Jesus never rejects anyone. In fact, Jesus said, "Come to Me, all of you . . ." (Matthew 11:28). Occasionally, I meet people who feel they are not worthy to be selected by Jesus. It is my chance, and yours, to assure them, it's not about worthiness, it's about privilege. Jesus calls all to follow Him. We who do so are blessed.

Today's prayer to continue: Thank You Lord for affording me multiple chances to follow You, I want to share that possibility today with . . .

June 12 Necessary Edification

Two post-sermon comments are lodged in my memory. The first: "Your sermons have meant so much to my husband since he developed dementia." The second; "Every sermon you preach is better than the next one." How does one respond to such comments? Anger would be inappropriate. Laughter would be insensitive. Silence would be unacceptable. Correction would be needed but how? Paul must have had a few such responses to his messages. In Ephesians 4:29, he wrote, "Let no corrupt word proceed out of your mouth, but what is good for necessary edification, that it may impart grace to the hearers." What is "necessary edification"? One translation reads, "talk . . . as fits the occasion." Another reads, "talk . . . as meeting the need of the moment." One commentary says, "edifying; according as the occasion and present needs of the hearers require, now censure, at another time consolation. Even words good in themselves must be introduced seasonably. Not vague generalities, which would suit a thousand other cases equally well, and probably equally ill: our words should be as nails fastened in a sure place." Nails? That's so tempting, especially as I now remember a third post-sermon response, this one from a rough, uneducated, redneck, from deep East Texas: "When they introduced you as a seminary professor and all, I thought we was in trouble, but after hearin' you, well, you jus like us." Necessary edification!

Today's prayer to continue: Lord, may my words today be edifying to all of those I meet, especially . . .

June 13 What it takes to be Happy

Sophocles, an early Greek playwright, said, "When a man has lost all happiness, he's not alive. Call him a breathing corpse." He must have been correct. By the thirteenth century Thomas Aquinas, an Italian philosopher and scholar said, "There is within every soul a thirst for happiness." So, we do need something to make us happy. What does it take for you to be happy? Albert Einstein said, "A table, a chair, a bowl of fruit and a violin; what else does a man need to be happy?" Well, Albert, I can't speak for my readers, but I think I'm going to need a little more than what you propose. So somewhere between "a breathing corpse" and a "bowl of fruit and a violin" we find that for which we thirst; that which makes us happy. Is it a warm puppy, a heavy blanket on a cold night, a beautiful sunset, enough money to pay the bills, an inter-personal relationship? While any or all of these might be a part of our happiness, the heart and soul of genuine happiness lies in being right with God. The Psalmist worded it this way: "Happy are the people whose God is the Lord (Psalm 144:15)!" If you're happy and you know it, shout "Amen

Today's prayer to continue: Lord, I know so many unhappy people. Thank You for offering genuine happiness. Today, I hope to share that happiness with . . .

June 14 Remember and Recommit

Not long ago, I spoke briefly to graduates at my own Alma Mater, my last official function as President of the Alumni Associations' Board of Directors. I'm not sure how much graduates actually hear at commencement services, but should some have been listening, I told them that from this day forward, their University days will be the subject of memories. Future conversations with fellow classmates, such as at Homecoming events, will likely begin with, "Do you remember . . ." or "Remember when . . ." I shared a couple of my memories of student days (I always hated that when alumni returned to speak in Chapel), then challenged them to file away memories for future years. Memory is one of God's greatest gifts, and one of life's greatest losses when it leaves us. My prayer for these young graduates was that when they look back it will be true of them, even as the Lord said to His people long ago, "You shall remember that the Lord your God led you all the way" (Deuteronomy 8:2).

Why not spend a few moments reflecting on how God has led you in the past, and as you remember, give thanks. Then recommit yourself to continued following of God's leadership in your life.

Today's prayer to continue: Your leadership in the past is something for which I am eternally grateful, Lord. Continue to lead me today as I . . .

June 15 Fading Desires

"It is possible to work in a bakery and lose one's appetite for bread" said Vance Havner. I guess that explains why I no longer have a desire for some of the ministry things that I used to do with gusto. I'm currently reading Billy Graham's latest book, "Nearing Home" and it's reassuring to know that I'm not the first person to face this loss of interest in previously exciting things. It's nothing serious. My faith is not fading. It's just little things. I'm fast losing interest in such as anything that has the word "committee" in it. Red-eye flights no longer seem exciting. All night lock-ins lost all appeal years ago. My new idea of "roughing it" is a hotel with a hard mattress. I'm also not really interested anymore in what's on my resume. I don't have to go anywhere or perform any ministry or pay tribute to any human, to pad the resume. I've done what I've done. I'm not through, but I seem to be pickier these days. "I am who I am" is the response God used in the Bible when Moses asked for His name (Exodus 3:14). Maybe Popeye's version is a better fit for me: "I 'yams whats I ams, and dats all that I 'yams." I'd hate to think I'm the only one feeling this way. Now if any of you young readers feel this way, don't tell anyone. It won't look good on your resume.

Today's prayer to continue: Thank You Lord for making me the way I am. May who I am, afford someone a blessing today. I'm thinking particularly of . . .

June 16 A Symphony of Prayer

A recent study of a major symphony revealed how orchestra members perceived each other. Percussionists were seen as insensitive, yet fun-loving. String players were perceived as arrogant and stuffy. Brass players were judged as loud. Woodwind players were described as quiet, though a bit egotistical. With this diversity of feeling for each other, members of the orchestra arrive for the concert. Each tunes his or her own instrument, often oblivious to those around them. The combination of sounds creates discord, not harmony. So how does such a group with such diverse feelings for each other, and such individualistic sounds of preparation, play beautiful music together? The answer is simple: regardless of feelings for each other, regardless of warm-up chaos, orchestra members subordinate their biases and their uniqueness to the leadership of the conductor. When Jesus spoke of His followers agreeing in prayer under His direction (Matthew 18:19-20), He used the Greek word, "sumphoneo," a word normally used for diverse musical instruments harmonizing together under the Maestro. So, which prayer is God most likely to hear, the discord-like prayers of our individual wants and desires or the united prayers of a group, under the direction of the Master?

Today's prayer to continue: Lord, for the purpose of united and harmonious prayer today, I am joining with . . . .

June 17 Truth or Fiction?

I was reminded recently of an old but interesting quote. The great 19th century English actor William Charles Macready was addressed by an eminent preacher: "I wish you would explain to me something." "Well, what is it? I don't know that I can explain anything to a preacher." "What is the reason for the difference between you and me? You are appearing before crowds night after night with fiction, and the crowds come wherever you go. I am preaching the essential and unchangeable truth, and I am not getting any crowd at all." Macready's answer was this: "This is quite simple. I can tell you the difference between us. I present my fiction as though it were truth; you present your truth as though it were fiction." May God help those of us who present God's truth – whether from behind a pulpit, over a lectern, across a breakfast table, or in informal settings – to do so as essential and unchanging truth in which we strongly and sincerely believe. "Speak each man the truth to his neighbor" (Zechariah 8:16).

Today's prayer to continue: As I have opportunity today, Lord, may I speak the truth as the truth to . . .

June 18 Keep Your Eye on the Ball

This month we celebrate Father's Day. For sixty-one years I was blessed with a wonderful, earthly father. It's hard to believe that he died so many years ago. In many ways, he was my best friend – certainly when it came to talking church or sports. In fact, one of my most remembered quotes came rather consistently after my baseball games when he would say, "How many times do I have to tell you to keep your eye on the ball." As the years passed I began to realize that he was teaching me a lesson that surpassed baseball. Perhaps that one quote is why I have experienced extra skill in setting and keeping priorities, staying focused, and getting the job done. He was my sports confidant and my best life adviser. I learned early to "Listen to your father who gave you life" (Proverbs 23:22). I still miss him. But the next time I see him, I will never again have to say "Good-bye." For all eternity, we are going to talk about whatever folks talk about in heaven. I hope you are able to celebrate Father's Day this month with great respect and/or wonderful memories.

Today's prayer to continue: Thank You Lord, for wonderful fathers who offer such good advice like . . .

June 19 Polishing the Parts

These words haunted me when I was a young believer: "Therefore you shall be perfect, just as your Father in heaven is perfect" (Matthew 5:48). It was difficult enough setting an example as a pastor's kid but being perfect was an ominous challenge. I continued struggling with this idea as a seminary student and week-end pastor of a small rural church. Then a godly Missions professor quoted someone in class one day (and I cannot document the quote or even assure I have it exactly correct). The quote, as I remember it, was, "Released from the necessity of being perfect, I am now free to be good." It was a hallelujah moment. I would have shouted, but in those days, one could get dismissed from seminary for such action. Then I did what I should have done years earlier, a word study. The word means "finished, complete, pure, holy." Originally, it was applied to a machine that was complete in its parts. Applied to people, it refers to completeness of parts, where no part is defective or wanting. The word implies full development, growth into maturity of godliness, not sinless perfection. Ever since that day, I have tried to polish my parts, so the whole of me can represent godliness. As the country song says, I am a work in progress. So let's see. What parts do I need to work on today?

Today's prayer to continue: Lord, help me today as I try to polish my parts. The part that needs to most attention is . . .

June 20 God's Will and Boldness

When it comes to God's will, there are three types of believers: (1) those who know the will of God and try to live it; (2) those who know the will of God and don't live it; (3) those who don't know the will of God and therefore do not live it. There are relatively few in the first category. In fact British Revivalist Henry Varley, said to D.L. Moody, "The world has yet to see what God can do through one man totally committed to Him." The third category is full of believers, attributed to everything from spiritual immaturity to apathy to disobedience. It is the second category to which Paul writes in Ephesians 5:17: "Therefore, do not be unwise (foolish), but understand what the will of the Lord is." This group has an idea what God's will is, they just do not believe that they understand it fully enough to do it, thus Paul calls them "unwise" or "foolish." My observation of this group is that in their inability or unwillingness to fully know God's will, they are hesitant to take a step in the direction of living it. Thus the problem with group two is not so much a lack of understanding or even ignorance, as it is a lack of boldness. Francis Bacon said, "boldness is a child of ignorance." So, be bold, do what you believe to be God's will. If it turns out to be God's will, you win. If it turns out not to be God's will, get up, brush yourself off, and try again. I really think God is more impressed with failed boldness than He is with inactive faith.

Today's prayer to continue: Today Lord, I want to be bold, especially in the area of . . .

June 21 The E's of Teaching

In more than 35 years of teaching at the university and seminary levels, I've noticed four types of teachers. One type is highly educated, skilled in teaching methodology, polished in presentations, with great teaching EXPERTISE. They may have gone straight from the academic arena as a student to the academic arena as a teacher, bypassing the field of experiential learning. A second group is filled with stories of how it is when their teaching field encounters reality, equipping their student for real-life experiences. They may have spent less time in academic preparation and more time in practical service. They teach largely out of EXPERIENCE. A sad third, but gratefully small group has neither proper EXPERTISE, nor adequate EXPERIENCE, yet they teach. Blessed is the student who sits under the fourth type of teacher, one with both EXPERTISE AND EXPERIENCE. These are the EXPERT teachers. They share out of their own academic preparation as well as from their on-field activities. So here's a formula for the want-to-be teacher: EXPERTISE + EXPERIENCE = EXPERT. The formula is a biblical one. Jesus was both the formal teacher in the synagogues and the practical teacher in the midst of life's activities. "Jesus went about all the cities and villages, teaching in their synagogues, preaching the gospel of the kingdom, and healing every sickness and every disease among the people" (Matthew 9:35). Learn from those who teach from head knowledge. Likewise, learn from those who teach from hand knowledge. Especially, learn from those who successfully blend the two into expert teaching.

Today's prayer to continue: Lord, I seem to be short on one and long on another. Help me today, to seek a better balance in my teaching/mentoring relationships, especially with . . .

June 22 Honk or Pray?

The vehicle in front of me had a bumper sticker that read, "If you love God, pray. Anyone can honk." The humor of it was lost on me since I was having one of those dreaded days when I not only felt bad physically, but everything was going wrong. I actually felt more like honking than talking to God. Maybe you've never had one of those days. Nevertheless, I resisted the urge to honk, mostly fearing that the driver might be someone who knew me. Then I prayed and asked God to forgive me for not wanting a conversation with Him at that time. Then I remembered what I had taught for many years, namely that prayer is not dependent on our feelings, but on God's desire to hear from us. Just as earthly parents love hearing from their children, even in bad times, so God loves to hear from His children, however we are feeling at the time. I figure since God made everything, He made those things that make for bad days, and thus He understands why I sometimes have a bad day. But bad days are no excuse for failing to communicate with the God who had Paul encourage us to, "Pray without ceasing" (1 Thessalonians 5:17). Since I can't drive around with eyes closed, or writing in a prayer journal, or concentrating on some prayer acrostic, this verse must mean to be in a continual attitude of prayer . . . even when you feel like honking.

Today's prayer to continue: I confess that some days, I feel more like honking than communicating with You Lord. But today, I want to communicate with You related to . . .

June 23 Helping with Holiness

I confess it is a challenge for me to find many exciting verses in the book of Leviticus. However, one caught my full attention this week. How does God show holiness? There are other answers, but one answer is found in Leviticus 10:3, "This is what the Lord spoke, saying: 'By those who come near Me, I must be regarded as holy; and before all the people I must be glorified'." Two things hit me. First: our responsibility. If we do not "come near" to God, holiness cannot be "regarded" as God wishes, thus we must continually "come near" to God. Second: God's follow-up. When we do our part, God is glorified before all people. Now, I'm sure God could do all of this without us, but that is not God's method. God chooses to use people like us. What an honor to be able to help with holiness

Today's prayer to continue: I am honored today Lord to be used in the area of holiness, but before that, I need to . . .

June 24 An Unmarked Grave

Elbert Lafayette Crawford was my great grandfather, whom I never knew. He was from Mississippi as was his wife. They married in Ft. Smith, Arkansas and moved to central Texas where she died at the age of 38. He was a farmer in Bell County, Texas where he died and was buried in the Wilson Valley Cemetery of Little River, Texas. Here is the sad part. For some strange reason I decided to find his grave. I was told by a cemetery historian, "We do not have a grave with a Crawford headstone. We have so many graves in our old section of the cemetery without a headstone, we know they are there because we have found death information that states they were buried in Wilson Valley Cemetery and E.L. Crawford is one of those." My great grandfather, buried in an unmarked grave, known only to God. What was he like? Would we have enjoyed each other? Did I inherit any of his characteristics? Was he a believer? Is he in heaven today? Jesus spoke of what my great grandfather and I have in common: "The hour is coming in which all who are in the graves (I might add: marked and unmarked graves) will hear His voice" (John 5:28). Someday, I'll know more. For now it's an unmarked grave in a central Texas cemetery.

Today's prayer to continue: Thank you Lord for the reminder that the memory is more important than the marker. May I so live today that my decedents will remember ...

June 25 Night-time Aroma

I remember the sweet smelling aroma just outside my bedroom window as I was growing up. I knew it as the night-blooming jasmine, although it was officially known as Cestrum nocturnum, a species of Cestrum in the plant family Solanaceae, native to the West Indies. All I knew was that a powerful, sweet perfume was released at night. I would later learn of the night-blooming cereus, the common name referring to a large number of flowering Cereus cacti that bloom at night in the desert. "The night seasons" is a phrase used by the Psalmist (Psalm 22:2) and the 19th century hymn writer, George Young ("God Leads us Along") referring to times of difficulty. I have often taught the greatest witness borne by the believer is in times of difficulty. The truth is that the non-believing world knows that we believers do well in the good times, the bright sunshine times. What they are waiting to see is how our faith holds up in the bad times, "the night seasons." –A popular saying is, "Bloom where you are planted." Let the sweet aroma of our blooming be not just in the daytime, but also in "the night seasons." The Apostle Paul said it this way, "Now thanks be to God who always leads us in triumph in Christ, and through us diffuses the fragrance of His knowledge in every place" (2 Corinthians 2:14).

Today's prayer to continue: Lord, may the aroma of my faith be released today in the presence of . . .

June 26 God's Slow Response to our Prayer for Revival

A child desperately wanted a new high-tech gadget. He had heard about it from older friends. He begged and pleaded his parents for the gadget to no avail. He cried for it, promised he be good forever if he got it, and offered to give up other possessions if necessary. Still the parents did not yield. Why? Were they mean? Unloving? Hateful? Unresponsive? Insensitive to his requests? No. The truth was that the child was not yet mature enough to properly benefit from the gadget. Sound familiar? We hear of revival and we pray to God to let us experience it. Sometimes we beg and plead for revival. We make promises to God if we can just experience revival. We offer to give up things if revival will just happen. And yet no revival comes. Why? Is God mean, unloving, hateful, unresponsive, and insensitive? No. The problem is not with God, who longs to send revival. The problem is often with believers whose stewardship level is not yet mature enough to properly handle the blessings and responsibilities of heaven-sent revival. If we don't know what to do with revival when it comes, God will not send it, just because we want it and ask for it. We continue to pray with the Psalmist, "Will You not revive us again, that Your people may rejoice in You" (Psalm 85:6).

Today's prayer to continue: Lord, help us to understand the stewardship of revival, so we will be ready when You decide to send it. Being ready for heaven-sent revival means . . .

June 27 You Never Know . . .

You never know who is watching you. For several months I have been doing my early morning walking at a nearby shopping mall. Since the stores do not open until later, the only people in the mall are walkers and there are a good number of them. Fast walkers pass slower walkers and slow walkers are passed by faster walkers. Greetings are exchanged, but few conversations are held. Walkers come and go. I often wish one of the coffee shops would open early so I could fellowship with fellow walkers, but it hasn't happened. So I continue to walk anonymously, or so I was thinking. One particular couple always seemed extra friendly. Last week, as I walked past them, he asked, "How's your ministry in Vancouver going?" Long story short, they are members of a nearby church where I have shared the story of my Vancouver ministry. Until that revelation, I thought no one in the mall knew me. I remember a word passed on to me by my late Pastor-Father – "The most dangerous place to be is where you think no one knows who you are." I came home and re-read the second half of 1 Timothy 4:12, "Be an example to the believers in word, in conduct, in love, in spirit, in faith, in purity" and thanked God that I had not done or said anything at the mall to tarnish my "example". Be careful today. You never know who is watching you.

Today's prayer to continue: I'll try to be careful today, Lord, so that I do not tarnish my example, but I will especially need help with . . .

June 28 Pilgrims on the Earth

John Wayne was not the only one who called people "pilgrims." The writer of Hebrews referred to early believers as "strangers and pilgrims" on the earth (Hebrews 11:13). Likewise Peter wrote, "Beloved, I beg you as sojourners and pilgrims. . . " (1 Peter 2:11) If we are pilgrims, it follows that we are on a pilgrimage. Given opportunities for rest and retreat, it also follows that if we are not on a pilgrimage, we are not really pilgrims. We are not called to a position or a standing, but to a path and a progression. Is this pilgrimage geographical? Possibly, but it is more. It is a spiritual journey, moving ever upward toward Christ-likeness. John Bunyan was in the midst of a twelve year prison sentence for refusing to conform to the state sponsored church, when he wrote, "There's no discouragement shall make him once relent his first avowed intent to be a Pilgrim." Happy trails!

Today's prayer to continue: Lord, my pilgrimage has been interesting and I am thankful for that, but today, I need . . .

June 29 Excellence is also in the Striving

Always strive for excellence. A well-known professional golfer, after not winning a major golf tournament, was reported to have said, "I'm not good enough . . . in 13 years, I've come to the conclusion that I need to play for second or third place." I'll give him the benefit of the doubt and hope that he spoke in frustration, as we all have done when we finish lower than our expectations. But if he was serious, you won't find me pulling for him in any future tournament. Whether it's golf or some other endeavor, you should always strive to be the best you can be. Never settle for second best. You were created for more. You may never achieve excellence, many people do not, but as long as you are striving for it, I'll be your cheerleader. The Apostle Paul said it this way, "Not that I have already attained, or am already perfected; but I press on . . . forgetting those things which are behind and reaching forward to those things which are ahead, I press toward the goal for the prize of the upward call of God in Christ Jesus" (Philippians 3:12-14). Seems to me, excellence is as much a part of the striving as it is a part of the goal.

Today's prayer to continue: I'll keep striving for excellence Lord, but today I will need Your assistance with . . .

June 30 The Mystery of the Gospel from two Perspectives

"What can we do for you?" That was the question asked of ten church planters in an area where less than 2% of the population claim to be a part of evangelical Christian churches. All but one responded with the same first answer – "pray for us." There were other answers with expressed needs, but prayer was most-often first on the need list. The truth is - prayer is much more of a felt-need on the front lines of ministry being carried out on satan's turf, than in areas where Christian churches are populated and Christian resources are plentiful. Unfortunately, when we can provide for ourselves, we become less dependent on God to provide, and thus our need for intercessory prayer diminishes in our minds. Seeing God's response to intercession for these unreached areas and the pioneers who serve there, makes me wonder what God would do if folks in the Bible-belt, with ample human and financial resources, would take prayer seriously. Yes, there are exceptions, but they are far too few. The Apostle Paul, who often served in areas heavily populated with unreached people, requested of the believers in Ephesus, "Pray for me, that utterance may be given to me, that I may open my mouth boldly to make known the mystery of the gospel" (Ephesians 6:19). In satan's strongholds, the "mystery" is what God can do in a life. In the Bible-belt, the "mystery" is often, what God would do if properly asked.

Today's prayer to continue: Lord, I'm not sure if I ask properly or not, but I sincerely desire to be used by You to accomplish . . .

July 1 National Pride and Intercessory Prayer

As a Citizen on Patrol (COPS), I drove through my neighborhood, and noticed a small American flag on the curb of every home. It was, after all, the 4th of July week. So, you ask, "Do you live in a neighborhood of all red-blooded Americans?" No, actually we have neighbors who were born in other lands, and in fact, may not even have U.S. citizenship yet. In fact, like me, they may be upset with this country occasionally. But this week, at this time of our independence, they allowed the Neighborhood Association to place a flag on their property as we all celebrated. Some of us followed the exhortation of the Apostle Paul to Timothy: "Therefore I exhort first of all that supplications, prayers, intercessions, and giving of thanks be made for all men, for kings and all who are in authority" (1 Timothy 2:1-2). I wonder what America would be like if we prayed more and criticized less. Oh, I've got my list of issues, as we all do, but this I know: (and I have only been in fifty-seven other nations, so I am by no means of measurement, an expert on the conditions of the world), every time I'm on an airplane that lands on American soil from another country, I breathe a deep sigh - Home! So, this week I will have barbecue, beans, and sweet tea for lunch; wear red, white & blue; place my hat over my heart for The National Anthem at a baseball game; eat a hot dog; enjoy a root beer float; watch fireworks; and feel pride. So, my fellow Americans, whether you were born here, enjoy the privilege of living here, or live in another country with an American citizenship, I hope you feel pride this week. And I hope you'll intercede for our leaders today.

Today's prayer to continue: Thank You Lord for the benefits I enjoy because of America. I pray for the country's leaders today, especially . . .

July 2 Celebrating from a Distance

This will not be the first time I've been out of the country on the 4th of July. In fact, I've been away several times. It never gets easier. It's like missing the birthday of a loved-one. In fact it is missing the birthday of a loved-one – my beloved home-country. Home. Now there's an interesting subject and a difficult one for me to discuss. In my lifetime, I've lived at twenty-eight different addresses in twelve American towns, plus spent extended time in four foreign countries. I really can't go home again. It would take too long and some of the places are not even there anymore. What I can do is celebrate my home in Christ. "The Message" translates Jesus saying in John 15:4 "Make your home in me just as I do in you." While others celebrate Independence Day in their home-country, I will spend July 4th celebrating my dependence on the Lord, my home away from home.

Today's prayer to continue: For being my true home, Lord, I give thanks and specifically today . . .

July 3 Birthday Losses

Birthdays are usually about gifts and gains and growth. They can also be about losses. Shortly after Jesus' twelfth birthday, his parents took Him to Jerusalem and lost Him. In the midst of the return caravan, they discovered Him missing and hurried back to Jerusalem to look for Him. They found Him in the Temple, among the people of God (Luke 2:41-52). This month Americans celebrate a national birthday – 4th of July, we call it. There will be gifts and gains and growth, but perhaps there are losses as well. Maybe we've lost a little more of Jesus in the past year. As we journey along, it may become more apparent that Jesus is no longer with as He once was. What will we do then? Hopefully, we will return to where we last experienced Him and find Him there among the people of God. Have we lost Jesus as a nation? Time will tell. If so, it is time to seek Him again.

Today's prayer to continue: To the extent that I have lost touch with You, Lord, I apologize and ask . . .

July 4 Happy Birthday America

Today - with flags and fireworks, parades and picnics, back-yard cook-outs and ballgame tailgates, water sports and watermelon, patriotic church services and patriotic goose bumps - we will celebrate our nation's birthday one more time. Make no mistake about it, I am proud to be an American. I am glad I live in a country where I can celebrate my nation's birthday with fellow Christians in a church service. However, I have worshipped with enough people groups in other countries, to not want to wrap up the Gospel in red, white and blue. If we sincerely pray for God's will, "on earth as it is in heaven (Luke 11:2)" we need to remember that heaven is populated with people from every tongue, tribe, nation, and people. Red, white and blue will be only three of the colors in the heavenly mosaic. While I'm proud to claim them here on earth, the eternal perspective is different. Nevertheless, happy birthday, America - one more time!

Today's prayer to continue: Thank You once more, Lord, for America. But thank you also for my friends who live and serve elsewhere, like in …

July 5 Celebrating a Specific Freedom

More than physically tiring, the prayer journey around the world, was emotionally draining and spiritually challenging. Having worshipped with underground believers in China, met on a dirt road around a campfire in India, posted a guard nearby so we could have a prayer meeting in Yemen, it was good to be back home. I reflect on that three-week trip during special occasions. One of those occasions is July 4, Independence Day for Americans. Among other things, we celebrate the freedom to worship without fear of governmental interference, without what the Apostle Paul calls, "a yoke of bondage". In Galatians 4 it is shown that the gospel is freedom, but the Mosaic law is the covenant of bondage. Hence Paul bids his readers to, "Stand fast therefore in the liberty by which Christ has made us free, and do not be entangled again with a yoke of bondage" (Galatians 5:1). Having worshipped and prayed with people who live in such a yoke, I am grateful without limits, to live where I can worship without fear. Americans celebrated the 4th of July yesterday with fireworks, parades, and barbecue along with various other means of festivity. Even as I join in these types of freedom celebrations, I give thanks for being free from bondage.

Today's prayer to continue: Today, Lord, I am thankful to be free from the bondage of . . .

July 6 Which Way to Go

Faced with a dilemma: which way to go? Do you take the high road or the low? Do you turn right or left? Isaiah understood: "Your ears shall hear a word behind you saying, 'This is the way, walk in it.' Whenever you turn to the right hand or whenever you turn to the left" (Isaiah 30:21). This "word behind" is thought by some to be an illustration of teachers, who stand behind their students, to guide, teach, and instruct; by others, of shepherds following their flocks, who, when they observe any of the sheep going out of the way, call them back; or to travelers, who, coming to a place where there are several ways, and inclining to turn to the right or left, are called to by persons behind them, directed in the right way. The voice behind the "word" is obviously the voice of God. Sometimes, an answer simply poses an additional question. Yes, God will tell you which way to go, but how do you hear from God? Basically God speaks through His Word, the Bible, not in contrast to what He has already said, but in harmony. God speaks through other people, trusted friends who walk with Him. God speaks through circumstances. In fact, sometimes the only way God can communicate with us is by allowing something to happen in our lives, that gets our attention. Finally, God speaks through what the Bible calls, "a still, small voice" (1 Kings 19:12), a reference to God's voice inside of us that gives us peace in decision making. So, listen. God is speaking. Which way do you go?

Today's prayer to continue: Sometimes Lord, the decisions are tough, and I need to hear from You so I can know which way to go and . . .

July 7 Moving On

Sometimes you just have to move on. I'm not talking only of geography, but also of moving emotionally, mentally, or spiritually. Life was good in Capernaum. The people were loving, and accepting of Jesus. In fact on one occasion, Mark writes, "The whole city was gathered together at the door" (Mark 1:33) and again, "Everyone is looking for You" (Mark 1:37). Jesus was so popular that He could have stayed in Capernaum, built a mega-church, had a multi-media ministry, and never been crucified. But that is not why God sent Him to earth. So the response of Jesus, "Let us go . . ." (Mark 1:38) is not surprising. The purpose for which we are called often pulls us onward, much to the amazement of our friends. Simply, there are things we must do. Mark Twain wrote, "Twenty years from now you will be more disappointed by the things you didn't do than by the ones you did do. So throw off the bowlines. Sail away from the safe harbor. Catch the trade winds in your sails. Explore. Dream. Discover." Are you where you need to be today or is it time to move on?

Today's prayer to continue: Is it time, Lord, to move on? If so, please show me how and where and . . .

July 8 One Caffeinated Blue Jay

While I was sitting on my front porch, a blue jay landed by my coffee cup and took a sip. My first ministerial thought was surely there is a sermon illustration in this somewhere. (I confess to an earlier thought that was not ministerial. In fact I gave this bird a different name than that given to the "birds of the air" by Adam in Genesis 2:20.) Desiring to share my experience and opportunity with others I posted this on Facebook, anticipating creative replies from my Facebook "friends." I received a variety of replies, some serious, others humorous. Then came the poem. While I occasionally share a quote from someone else in this, I'm not sure I've ever shared someone else's poem. But with the permission of my good friend, Randal Whitt, enjoy:

I sat down this morning with coffee by my side, On the quietness of my porch, in my Lord to confide, Startled a bit I turned to see The eyes of a blue jay staring at me.

He had swooped down from its perch to check things out. I wondered...what exactly was this unusual encounter about?

In an instant I saw him peek, Then just as quick he dipped his beak Into my cup and took a small sip, Then flew away with a song on his lips.

I did not understand what he had to say, But I do know this: he was now one caffeinated blue jay.

So what did I learn from this visit today? What message from God was being conveyed? Perhaps it's as simple as this little phrase:

Even on your porch, God can amaze.

Today's prayer to continue: For the amazing things I have seen and will see today, Lord, I give You thanks, especially for . . .

July 9 Tireless Praying

Have you ever wondered how you can "Pray without ceasing" (1 Thess. 5.17)? Those of us who grew up in a church learned this verse early. But how do we follow it? We can't walk around with our heads bowed and our eyes closed. Other responsibilities call for our attention. You can't pray all the time. Or can you? A look at the original Greek translation offers little help when it instructs us to "pray continuously, without interruption." A missionary friend tells of his discovery in a Swahili Bible, which translates this verse literally as, "pray without getting tired to the point of wanting to give up." So we are to continue praying, even if we feel we are not successful in our efforts, even if we grow weary in the same intercessions, even when no answer is apparent, even when circumstances seem hopeless. Keep knocking at midnight even when no one seems to respond (Luke 11:5-8). Keep pleading before the Judge when no immediate response is offered (Luke 18:1-8). Hang in there! Pray on!

Today's prayer to continue: Give me endurance Lord so that I can keep on praying tirelessly for . . .

July 10 Feeble Knees and Facing Life

The surgery was minor, out-patient type, and rehabilitation began the afternoon of the morning procedure, but I nevertheless sent an advanced notice to my prayer partners concerning the orthoscopic procedure on my knee. Among the replies was a reminder that I should be comforted since on two occasions the Bible mentions "feeble knees" (Isaiah 35:3; Hebrews 12:12). I had been needing comfort. As I was trying to think of an old athletic injury with which to glorify this surgery, the surgeon reminded me that older people recover slowly. Reality check! Why is it that we look in the mirror and often see a much younger, slimmer, more athletic figure than the one standing in front of the reflection? Two quotes may help clarify this. Satchel Paige, who became famous pitching in both the old Negro Leagues and in Major League Baseball and pitched his last professional game two weeks before his sixtieth birthday, asked, "How old would you be if you didn't know how old you was?" The ancient play-write, Sophocles, said, "A man growing old becomes a child again." Now any writing that quotes both Satchel Paige and Sophocles should be valued. Seriously, life is both a challenge and a treasure at any age. Face life today with respect and adventure.

Today's prayer to continue: Lord, the knees are getting feebler each day, but You continue to bless my every endeavor performed for You, such as . . .

July 11 Praying Outside of God's Will

What happens when your prayer is not in sync with God's will? It matters little whether you are praying for recovery of relationship, removal of pain, or revival of spirit, if the prayer is outside of God's will, the answer is different from the request. James wrote, "You ask and do not receive, because you ask amiss" (James 4:3). Did that ever happen in Scripture? Sure it did. A prime example would be Paul asking God to remove his thorn in the flesh (2 Corinthians 12:7-9). The response was, "My grace is sufficient for you, for My strength is made perfect in weakness." How do we respond when our prayer has proven to be outside of God's will? Some act like an immature child whose parent has said no to a request. They whine, and cry, and fuss, and make threats, all to no avail. Nor is God a wishy-washy parent who can be manipulated with such actions. Others become reclusive, pouting, and feeling sorry for themselves that they should be denied, again to no avail. Nor is God one on whom a display of human emotions can necessarily bring about change. The most mature response is to join Paul, living in the sufficiency of God's grace. Meanwhile keep praying until you get it right.

Today's prayer to continue: I've lost count, Lord, in the times I've prayed amiss, so today, help me get it right as I pray for . . .

July 12 Re-connecting with Facebook Friends

In recent days, I've lost a few of my Facebook friends. No, they didn't "un-friend" me nor I them. God called them home. As much fun as Facebook is and as rewarding as it is to re-connect with long-lost friends via Facebook, there is within the social network a subtle reminder that as precious as life is, it comes to an end on this earth. I doubt if God cares much for Facebook, other than enjoying his children having fun. God does understand enjoyment, even to the point of death. The Psalmist records, "Precious in the sight of the Lord is the death of His saints" (Psalm 116:15). "Un-friending" a friend on Facebook, while not nearly as difficult as saying good-bye at the graveside, is nonetheless, sorrowful. However, the majority of my Facebook friends are believers, and as such, we grieve, but not "as others who have no hope" (I Thessalonians 4:13). We will be friends again and the heavenly re-connection will be ten thousand times ten thousand more glorious and enjoyable than Facebook.

Today's prayer to continue: Thank You Lord for friendships and for the promise of the believing ones being eternal. I am especially thankful today for my friendship with . . .

July 13 Glory Up and Blessings Down

The American Olympic gold medal winning gymnast expressed thanks to God for the ability to compete. -Nothing much different from what many athletes say to reporters these days but then she added, "It's kind of a win-win situation. The glory goes up to Him and the blessings fall down on me." Winning a gold medal is a reward for faithful commitment, disciplined preparation, and determined effort. But in life, there is more than gold. The Apostle Peter wrote, "The genuineness of your faith, being much more precious than gold that perishes, though it is tested by fire, may be found to praise, honor, and glory at the revelation of Jesus Christ" (1 Peter 1:5-7). Through genuine faith in God, we obtain that which is more valuable than Olympic gold and through the exercising of that faith we offer praise, honor, and glory back to God. Thanks Olympian, for using your new found platform to share your faith. Enjoy your gold medal and keep sending the glory up.

Today's prayer to continue: May I be quick today to share that which I have that is worth more than gold. Lord, today, I need to share with . . .

July 14 Memorizing with Meaning

I never knew why Psalm 121 was scripture we had to memorize as boys involved in Royal Ambassadors at our church. No one told us what it meant, so I grew thinking it meant "I will lift up my eyes to the hills from whence comes my help." Meaning the help comes from the hills. Not so. I didn't memorize the question mark. Correct meaning: "I will lift up my eyes to the hills – From whence comes my help?" Then the answer comes in verse two that I never connected to verse one. "My help comes from the Lord . . ." It seems that I was led/forced to memorize Scripture just for the sake of memorizing Scripture. I'm glad I did, and I wish I had memorized more when I was young and had the capability to do so. I had a 12th grade English teacher who made us answer the roll call by quoting a verse of English poetry. As much as I hated that assignment, I still remember many of those verses. Her motive was clear: English poetry committed to memory is part of a balanced education. My Royal Ambassador leader's motive seemed to be to memorize Scripture because the manual said to do so. I wish the motive would have been different and the biblical meaning taught along with the emphasis on memorizing. So memorize if you can. Hide the Word in your heart (Psalm 119:11), but memorize it with meaning.

Today's prayer to continue: Lord, that Word that You hid in my heart needs to be shared today. I remember it as . . .

July 15 Breathless or God-breathed?

I'm a sucker for catchy quotations. They stick to the shelves around my desk. There is one that I keep seeing on cards, in videos, on T-shirts, in frames, quoted by politicians and ministers alike. Supposedly, in the mid to late 1970's a university student wrote a line for Carleton Cards, a Canadian card company. These unknown authors were paid a pittance to write cute sayings for greeting cards, copyright included. The quote has been attributed to many people over the years, but it is anonymous because Carleton never realized that so many would find the quote significant. Today, the author is well aware of the irony of his words.... thousands of dollars have been made off of this quote. He made a quarter. The quote? "Life is not measured by the number of breaths we take, but by the moments that take our breath away." Actually the quote could have originated from a spiritual experience in Genesis 2:7 where God allowed man to have a pre-creation, breathless moment followed by a God-breathed moment. "The Lord God formed man of the dust of the ground, and breathed into his nostrils the breath of life; and man became a living being." God has been re-breathing life into us ever since. In the words of Edwin Hatch from a hymn written in the late 1800s, "Breathe on me, breath of God, fill me with life anew, that I may love what thou dost love, and do what thou wouldst do."

Today's prayer to continue: Thank You, Lord for the breath-taking experience of . . .

July 16 Aging: Praying or Pouting?

Aging is both a blessing and a barrier. (I confess to a different "b" word when I first had this thought, but for this means of communication, I'll go with "barrier.") Having passed the biblical standard of "three score and ten" (Psalm 90:10, KJV) I feel qualified to comment on this subject. One blessing of aging is the obvious additional years that God has purposely given. Obviously, God is not finished if we are still here. Additional years allow for ministries that, for whatever reason, we didn't perform earlier. My mother is a good example. Homebound the last twelve years of her life, she developed a rather extensive prayer ministry. In her pre-internet, email, Facebook, Twitter world, she used her telephone to call through the church directory repeatedly to see what matters she could include in her prayer for that day, often singing a hymn or chorus to the person on the other end of the line. The barrier created by aging is likewise obvious – physical, emotional, mental, limitations. An unnamed friend is a good example. He pouts about everything. "If it works, it hurts!" he exclaims. "This young generation . . ." and he continues with a list of complaints about youth. As one who now attends more funerals than weddings, I want my aging years to be a blessing, not a barrier.

Today's prayer to continue: Lord, make me a blessing today to . . .

July 17 When God Whispers

I'm always challenged (if not always happy) when someone invites me to speak, then, after I've accepted, gives me the subject of my presentation. A friend recently invited me to preach in his absence at the church where he is Pastor and assigned me a theme, for which I was both happily challenged and appreciative. The theme for the month was, "Power of a Whisper." We decided I would preach on the subject, "When God Whispers." Robert Browning raised the fact of God whispering when he wrote (Abt Vogler): "God has a few of us whom He whispers in the ear. . ." But do you know of any occasion in the Bible where God ever whispered to anyone? Granted, it's an assumption, but I've recently been to two funerals and was reminded how, in the presence of death, people talk low, like in a whisper, unlike at normal worship services, where Americans, at least, enter and depart rather loudly. The Old Testament book of Joshua begins with the words, "After the death of Moses, the servant of the Lord, it came to pass that the Lord spoke to Joshua . . ." (Joshua 1:1). Could these words from the Lord have been spoken to Joshua in a whisper? There's no way of knowing for sure, but its close enough for a sermon text. Has God ever whispered to you?

Today's prayer to continue: Lord, if I "whisper a prayer" to You, will You whisper a response to me? If so, I whisper to You today . . .

July 18 What We Leave Behind

An administrator said to me, "When you're gone, the only thing you leave behind is what you've written." My reply: "With all due respect sir, I disagree with you 100%. I've got books in the Library whose pages are turning yellow, and whose check-out record is empty. On the other hand, I've got former students all around the globe, in whose lives, at least some of my influence lives on." Well, I'm gone, at least from that place of ministry. The pages of the books are getting more yellow with each day. Hundreds, yea thousands, of my former students, the pride of my life, are making significant impact for the Kingdom of God all around the globe, some in places I cannot even pronounce, much less spell. Am I alone in that feeling? No. As early as 495 – 429 BC, Pericles, a prominent and influential Greek statesman, orator, and general of Athens during the city's Golden Age, said, "What you leave behind is not what is engraved in stone monuments, but what is woven into the lives of others." Even before Pericles, the Old Testament tells of Jonathan's influence in the life of David that ultimately spared the life of the future king (1 Samuel 19:1-6). A few years after Pericles, the Apostle Paul instructed young Timothy concerning investments in people, "The things that you have heard from me among many witnesses, commit these to faithful men who will be able to teach others also" (2 Timothy 2:2). I know that what I write is important, a God-given ability, and that many people are blessed, but it is the investment of time and perhaps wisdom, in the lives of others that keeps me going. It's what I will someday leave behind. How about you? What are you planning on leaving behind?

Today's prayer to continue: Lord, when I'm gone, I especially want to leave behind . . .

July 19 Warnings

The bumper sticker of a pick-up truck on a rural road testified to the driver's intentions: "Due to the rising cost of ammo, do not expect a warning shot." When you earn negative consequences, how many warnings do you think you deserve? Fortunately, for those like Paul's readers in Colossae, teaching accompanied warning. "Him we preach, warning every man and teaching every man in all wisdom, that we may present every man perfect in Christ Jesus." (Colossians 1:28). "Warning" relates to repentance, to one's conduct, and is addressed primarily to the heart. "Teaching" relates to faith, refers to doctrines, and is addressed primarily to the intellect. The Bible teaches us what to do and then warns us of the consequences of not obeying the teaching. So how are you doing today with what you have been taught? How many warnings do you deserve?

Today's prayer to continue: I pray Lord that You do not have to warn me more than once, especially in the area of …

July 20 Left Behind

Have you ever been left behind? I remember a childhood experience when my father was leaving the house to attend a sporting event and not taking me with him. I almost always went with him to such events. This time someone else had offered him a ticket and there was no ticket for me, but I didn't understand that at the time. My only emotion was that of being left behind. Although that emotion re-occurred through the years, it was likely never felt more deeply than that night many years ago. Maybe that's why I've always had an affinity for Titus. We don't know much about Titus. He was a young pastor, an occasional traveling companion of Paul. From the tone of Paul's pastoral letter to him, it appears that Titus wanted to travel on with the great missionary. Early in the letter, Paul says, "For this reason, I left you in Crete" (Titus 1:5) as if Titus was requesting or perhaps demanding a reason for being left behind. The reason, spelled out in the letter, was to "set in order" or organize, the churches in Crete. For some unknown reason, Paul was unable to finish his business there. Since Crete was one of the largest islands in the Mediterranean, this was no small assignment. Nevertheless, Titus was left behind, and we hear no more about him in the Scripture. So what do you do when you get left behind? You faithfully finish what you have been given to do.

Today's prayer to continue: Lord, I still need to finish . . .

July 21 Will and Willingness

I was fifteen years old, laying in a hospital bed with a broken second vertebra of my neck, when I first began to understand that God had a will for my life. According to the doctors, it was a miracle that I was alive, having survived a violent automobile accident. I reasoned that if God had spared my life, there must be purpose, a divine will. It was later that I discovered that God has a will for every life. No one is created minus a purpose, or a divine will for their life. Paul summed up his understanding of God's will for his life by stating, "For to me, to live is Christ" (Philippians 1:21). The specifics of God's will for Paul included serving as missionary, preacher, teacher, writer, prisoner, etc. Still later, I discovered that not everyone is willing to do God's will. Since God has a will, we must have a willingness, or the divine will is thwarted, de-railed, short-circuited. Do we ever reach an age, when God no longer has a will for our life? My answer, at my age and experience, is, "Not yet." As long as Christ has a will for my life, I must have willingness for His life. I affirm with Paul, for me to live is Christ. Indeed, the Christ-like lifestyle is simply, my life, lived out in His style. Are you living your life in His style, willing to live according to His will?

Today's prayer to continue: Today, Lord I interpret Your will for me to be . . .

July 22 Ordinary and Encouraged

It was an interesting title for a conference, especially when most of the conferences these days are related to mega-churches. This one was named the "Ordinary Pastor's Conference." The stated purpose was, "to encourage, instruct and bless the ordinary, average, vanilla flavored, mega-nuthin' pastor and his wife." The instruction was given early in the day that the one thing that was illegal was to ask another pastor how many he had attending his church. This conference was not about numbers, but about encouragement. For a first year conference it was well attended. Invited to lead a break-out session on "When All Else Fails . . . Pray," I was unsure who might attend. Would I have a room full of ordinary pastors, or would I have less than ordinary pastors striving to become ordinary, or would it be extraordinary pastors fearful of becoming ordinary? All in all, it was a wonderful day, filled with affirmation. This much I re-learned: All pastors are ordinary. In fact Peter and John were described in Acts 4:13 as "ordinary men" (NIV). As ordinary pastors enjoy the prayer support of ordinary friends, they are empowered by an extraordinary God to be more than ordinary. Now that's encouraging.

Today's prayer to continue: Since I am ordinary and You, Lord, are extraordinary, please make me more like You, especially in the area of . . .

July 23 How Much is Enough?

How much is enough when it comes to following God's will? I remember as a teen-ager, feeling called by God to the ministry yet trying to rationalize in my own mind how I could follow that calling, yet still fulfill the personal plans I had for my life. That experience taught me that God has little interest in part time followers. Have you had an experience like mine – maybe for a life calling, maybe for a less lengthy calling, perhaps for a simple decision of complete or partial following? If God graded on the curve, you might get by. However, God doesn't grade on the curve. So, how much is enough? What if Noah had built the arc up to 90% of God's specifications? What if he had taken only half of his family on to the arc with him? What if he had decided not to take doves on the arc? For Noah, it was 100%. "Thus Noah did; according to all that God commanded him, so he did" (Genesis 6:22). Whatever God tells you to do, do it all.

Today's prayer to continue: If I am missing any part of Your will for my life, Lord, please share it with me now . . .

July 24 Belonging

Apart from a few loners, everyone wants to belong. Children long to be chosen for a team. Teen-agers search for a group, occasionally choosing the wrong group, just so they can belong. Those of us who served on university campuses observed that students needed a group, or they suffered from an aloneness that affected their entire academic life. Adults of all ages join various kinds of groups to keep from being alone. Numerous studies have shown that the need to belong is one of the strongest human needs. In his book "Nearing Home" Billy Graham concludes, "We are not meant to be isolated from and independent of each other, either as human beings or as Christians. . . A solitary Christian is inevitably a weak Christian because he or she is failing to draw strength from what God is doing in the lives of fellow brothers and sisters in Christ." Paul spoke to this need as follows "All things belong to you, and you belong to Christ; and Christ belongs to God" (1 Corinthians 3:22-23 NAS). The appeal of Christianity is a belonging relationship with a personal Savior, and more. In my global travels, I learned that as soon as I found a group of accepting believers, I found a "koinonia" fellowship to which I could belong. Give thanks today for belonging.

Today's prayer to continue: Thank you Lord for allowing me to belong to . . .

July 25 Living the Jesus Way

Living the Jesus way includes running with the lame one, jumping with the paralyzed one, celebrating with the restored one, listening with the deaf one, shouting with the mute one, observing with the blind one, rejoicing with the healed one. If you don't understand any of this, you can ask the once demon possessed one who, having met Jesus found himself, "in his right mind" (Mark 5:15; Luke 8:35). What does all this mean? It means that those who live with and for Jesus live with the daily possibility of miracles. Life with the Lord is one potential surprise party after another. And even when a miracle is requested and denied, God gives us the sufficient grace to deal with its absence. Trust me. I've been the recipient of both miracle and grace and I've observed that those who choose to live without Jesus, experience neither. What an awesome God we serve!

Today's prayer to continue: Lord, I could use a miracle today, but I desperately need grace. Grant me Your grace related to . . .

July 26 Tracks Left Behind

"We will be known forever by the tracks we leave" said the American Indian proverb that I read recently. As accurate as is this proverb, the idea is not original with the American Indians. Years before, it was said of Jesus, "Christ also suffered for us, leaving us an example, that you should follow His steps" (1 Peter 2:21). Likewise it was passed on as advice to young Timothy by the aging apostle Paul, "be an example to the believers in word, in conduct, in love, in spirit, in faith, in purity" (1 Timothy 4:12). How are you doing with your attempt to be a good example, to leave positive tracks for others? Maybe we could use Paul's six categories as a test. How well have you been an example this week in word? How about in conduct? What kind of steps have you left behind this week in love? How about in spirit? What tracks are there behind you this week through activities regarding faith? How about through purity? I will be forever grateful to those who went before me and left good tracks, steps I could follow. I wonder how grateful those are who are following my example . . . and yours?

Today's prayer to continue: I am grateful Lord for those who left good tracks for me to follow and today I need to leave good tracks for . . .

July 27 A Displeasing Voice

When God impresses upon our minds some pleasing thought, everyone is happy. What about when God sends a displeasing word? What about when we pray for health and illness lingers? What about when we ask God to send us to a particular place and God sends us elsewhere? What about when we intercede for God to perform some specific act and God does just the opposite? What about when we petition God for rain and no rain falls? Can we follow God when the response we get from our prayers is a response that is not to our liking? One day, the captains of the remnant forces came to Jeremiah with a request for prayer and guidance. When the prophet agreed to pray and then to tell them what God said, they replied, "Whether it is pleasing or displeasing we will obey the voice of the Lord our God" (Jeremiah 42:6). Nowhere in Scripture or in human experience, are we promised that God will answer our every prayer with pleasing responses, no matter how hard or long we pray, nor how many people we enlist to join us in our requests. Sometimes, in spite of our efforts, God's answer is displeasing to us. Following God when directions are displeasing surely is a mark of spiritual maturity.

Today's prayer to continue: Help me Lord to follow You whether Your directions are pleasing or displeasing. I especially remember the following directions . . .

July 28 Playing the Part

I took a drama class in high school, only because the Principal came to our Advanced Speech class and asked for volunteers to switch to the drama class while looking straight at me. The drama teacher, Mr. Wyman, told us to observe people so we'd know how to portray them when we were assigned their part in a play. He especially spoke of elderly people. "Watch how long it takes them to sit down and get up". He continued, "Observe how slowly they move at times." I never played the part of an elderly person until recently and only now because I am getting elderly. It takes longer to sit down and longer to get up. I move slower at times. The elderly lady I helped step off a curb recently turned out to be my wife. A friend advised me that if I woke up some morning and nothing ached, to check the obituaries. Yet the Bible declares, "Wisdom is with aged men, and with length of days, understanding" (Job 12:12). Aging is a challenge and takes all the "wisdom" that accompanies it and for sure, has its own drama inherent within. So, be kind to older people. If you live long enough, you'll be one yourself. And whatever your age, follow another of Mr. Wyman's sayings and "Play your part well today."

Today's prayer to continue: Thank You Lord for allowing me to have a part in Your divine drama. As I play my part today, may in influence . . .

July 29 A Home Where We've Never Lived

I took the ferry from Vancouver to Vancouver Island and back again last week. I first took this ride in 1980, in bright sunshine one way, and heavy snow on the return. I fell in love on that trip -

with the lower mainland and islands of British Columbia, Canada. I've lost count of the number of times I've been back in the following years and now God crowns my calling by allowing me to serve more fully in such a beautiful place. Every time I return, it's like coming home, yet I've never lived in the Vancouver area for more than a month at a time. For Jesus, it was Bethany. He never lived there, but often visited there with his friends, Mary, Martha, and Lazarus (John 11:1). Anyone else have a place like that? Thanks be to God who allows us to have a home away from home. Perhaps, this is a preview of how it will be when we arrive in our heavenly home, having never lived there before.

Today's prayer to continue: For the refreshment and renewal that comes from visiting a home away from home, Lord, I am thankful. I am especially thankful for . . .

July 30 No Autocorrect with God

The church bulletin was explaining the plan of salvation but instead of the word "sin" it encouraged readers to "ask God to forgive your sings." Even though I personally need forgiveness for my singing, I knew it was a mistake. Spell check would have done no good. The church could have used autocorrect. The Urban Dictionary defines autocorrect as, "a feature built into many modern phones, which automatically changes unrecognized words to their closest matches, if any exist. Of course, on occasion it will select the wrong word, usually changing the original meaning of the sentence completely," such as the man who texted his wife that the result of his doctor's visit was a sinus infection, but the autocorrect changed it to "dinosaur infection." Most of the other well-known autocorrect mistakes can't be printed here. When it comes to sin, we have something similar to autocorrect. The Holy Spirit within us convicts us of sin, but God does not automatically correct our sinful mistakes. We must do the correcting ourselves. While "all have sinned" (Romans 3:23), not all have corrected their sinful mistakes. As the Spirit of God convicts of wrong, we must do the correcting. There is no autocorrect with God.

Today's prayer to continue: Thanks You Lord for Your willingness to forgive our sins, and for some of us, our "sings" as well. I ask for Your forgiveness today in the area of . . .

July 31 Mountain Top Encounters or Flatland Ministry?

Which do you like better – mountain top excitement or flatland routine? One day Jesus, along with His disciples, Peter, James and John, were on the mountain experiencing divine encounters. As the disciples were looking at Jesus, "His clothes became shining, exceedingly white, like snow, such as no launderer on earth (could) whiten" (Mark 9:3). Furthermore, Moses and Elijah arrived. Considering they had both been dead for many years, it had to be an unexpected and exciting shock to the disciples. As if that was not enough excitement for one day, the voice of God spoke from the heavens, "This is My beloved Son. Hear Him!" (Mark 9:7). By Mark 9:14, Jesus and the three disciples were back in the flatlands with human encounters – a man bringing his son to the disciples for healing from "a mute spirit" (Mark 9:17) followed by Jesus' rebuke to the disciples for their faithless response, and His teaching on prayer and fasting. Had you been one of the disciples, Peter, James or John, which would you have preferred, mountain or flatland? The truth is, life consists of both and a balance is highly desirable. Ministry to people is better when paced with time on the mountain, and time on the mountain is better if it leads directly back to ministry in the flatlands.

Today's prayer to continue: Lord, I realize the need for both mountain top as well as flatland experiences. Today, I mostly need . . .

August 1 Failure is Not Final

How long has it been since your last failure? According to Wikipedia, "Failure is the state or condition of not meeting a desirable or intended objective, and may be viewed as the opposite of success." We've all failed, including Thomas Edison, who said, "I have not failed. I've just found 10,000 ways that won't work." Because Albert Einstein didn't speak until he was four years old, his teachers said he wouldn't amount to much. Walt Disney was fired from a newspaper job because he lacked imagination and had no original ideas. Oprah Winfrey was demoted from news anchor because they concluded, she wasn't fit for television. Michael Jordan was cut from his High School basketball team. The Beatles were rejected by Decca Recording Studios because they reportedly had no future in show business. At age thirty, Steve Jobs was removed from a company he started. From a Biblical perspective, a study of Bible characters reveals that most were men and women who failed at some point, and some of them drastically, but who refused to continue living in their failure. The Psalmist wrote, "The steps of a good man are ordered by the Lord, and He delights in his way. Though he fall, he shall not be utterly cast down; for the Lord upholds him with His hand" (Psalm 37:23-24). The next time you experience failure, know that failure is not final. Trust God, and try again.

Today's prayer to continue: Lord, remind me that there is no finality in my failure of . . .

August 2 Morning Prayer or Night Prayer?

How many times have we heard that Jesus prayed early in the morning and thus we ought to do the same? Granted, early morning prayer is both needed and valuable. But what if I am not a morning person? What if I wake up slowly and don't think very well until a few cups of caffeine? What if I am a night person?

Good news. God hears and responds to prayer in the evening as well as in the morning. The Psalmist said, "The Lord will command His lovingkindness in the daytime, and in the night His song shall be with me—A prayer to the God of my life" (Psalm 42:8). Jesus often prayed at night, even on one occasion, He prayed all night — "Now it came to pass in those days that He went out to the mountain to pray, and continued all night in prayer to God" (Luke 6:12). Nighttime praying is a good time to reflect on the activities of the day, thank God for specifics, praise God for who He revealed Himself to be that day, ask forgiveness for that day's short-comings, and intercede for those who serve God on the other side of the globe where it is day. So, morning prayer or night prayer? It's not either/or, it's both/and.

Today's prayer to continue: Thank You Lord that I can pray at any time and never get an answering machine with You because You are always listening. Today I want to pray . . .

August 3 Self Made or Multi-made?

Most of the time, I enjoy reading what people proclaim on their t-shirts/sweat-shirts. This one announced that the person wearing the shirt was, "Self Made." From a strictly human perspective, and being a third generation Texan, I understand the meaning. In fact, I'd like to think that at least a part of who I am is "Self Made." The trouble with self-made folks is that they tend to worship their supposed creator (self). From a larger perspective, I am not simply "Self Made." I am made of parental and grand-parental influence, plus teacher/professor/coach input, family/friend support, and even enemy resistance. Added to all of this is the over-riding fact that I am made "in the image of God" (Genesis 9:6), saved and called by God, with a divine purpose to become more and more Christ-like. With all of this mixture, I can hardly proclaim myself to be "Self Made." Rather I am a multi-made, work-in-progress, composite. How about you?

Today's prayer to continue: I am so diverse Lord, it's hard to know who I really am. But today, I want to be . . .

August 4 Sometimes there is Crying in Baseball

I wept Thursday night. I'm not sure if it was the little boy in me, or the father in me or the grandfather in me weeping, but I wept. I wept for a little boy who I did not know. He went to the ball game with his Dad, like I did so many times with mine, like my son did with me, like my grandson does with me. In fact, my grandson, went to the local minor league game with me the same night. He came home with me and a foul-ball, his second of the season. Another little boy went home without a ball or a Dad. Father and son had gone to the Texas Ranger game Thursday, stopping on the way to buy the son a new glove, for the purpose of catching a baseball. Seated on the front row of the outfield bleachers, the Dad reached over to catch a ball for the son, and fell to his death, twenty feet below. As a little boy cried for his Daddy, a game stood still. Life (and death) came into perspective. Simon Peter wrote that he lived in the knowledge that, "the laying aside of my earthly dwelling is imminent" (2 Peter 1:14, NAS). Not knowing the time nor circumstances of our earthly death, so must we live, even at a baseball game. I'm reminded of the oft-quoted line from baseball Manager Jimmy Dugan in the movie, "A League of Their Own," - "There's no crying in baseball." Sometimes there is.

Today's prayer to continue: For the ability to cry, I give thanks today. Most recently Lord, I have wept for . . .

August 5 Faith and the Prosperity Gospel

I've always been suspicious of the "Prosperity Gospel," the belief that God wants every believer to prosper and all a believer has to do to prosper is trust God properly. There are two initial problems with that thinking: (1) It's extremely difficult to consistently trust God properly and (2) if God's blessings are delivered solely by our trust, it deletes God's ability to determine how and when to bless. Faith is believing that God can, not that God will. God can bless above and beyond our requests. However, God will bless as He chooses, as He sees and knows the big picture. So relax in faith. If God blesses to your expectations, so be it. If God blesses according to His plan, stop worrying about it. Many years ago, Henry Ward Beecher said, "Every tomorrow has two handles. We can take hold of it with the handle of anxiety or the handle of faith." That is close to the definition offered by the writer of Hebrews, "Faith is the substance of things hoped for, the evidence of things not seen" (Hebrews 11:1). And even closer to a paraphrase in "The Message," "Faith is the firm foundation under everything that makes life worth living. It's our handle on what we can't see" (Hebrews 11:1, MSG). Even closer to this truth is a statement made by Max Lucado, "Faith is not the belief that God will do what you want. It is the belief that God will do what is right." So, don't place your faith in the Prosperity Gospel. Place your faith in God and live with what He gives you.

Today's prayer to continue: Today Lord, let me take what You have given me and use it to ...

August 6 Giving Our Best

Beginning in Kindergarten, and for many years following, my mother said the same thing to me every morning as I left the house. "Do the best you can, with what you have, where you are, for Jesus sake today." Only recently, did I discover that she was paraphrasing a quote from Theodore Roosevelt. I'm not even sure she knew that's what she was doing, but it worked. I've lived with that daily motto for many years. In my teen-age years, I added the words of a then popular song, "Hear ye the Master's call, 'Give Me thy best!' For, be it great or small, that is His test. Do then the best you can, not for reward, not for the praise of men, but for the

Lord." Then came the awareness of a quote by John Wesley, "Do all the good you can, in all the ways you can, to all the souls you can, in every place you can, at all the times you can, with all the zeal you can, as long as ever you can." Still later in life, I came across Numbers 18:29 that speaks of what we give and instructs us to give "our best" offerings to God. All of this reminds me to ask myself (and you), what is the best I (you) have to give to God today? And the follow-up challenge is, "Well then, give Him your best!"

Today's prayer to continue: As well as I can determine, my best today Lord is . . .

August 7 Too Much Vision

When someone shares too much information, they are often met with the initials, TMI. What happens when one shares too much vision? It's an old, but ~~still~~ good, story. Might even be a true story. In the midst of his sermon, a preacher exclaimed, "If this church wants to be great, it needs to walk with God," to which the congregation replied, "Let it walk, Pastor!" Inspired at the response, the preacher continued, "If this church wants to be great, it needs to run with God," to which the congregation replied, "Let it run, Pastor!" Sensing momentum, the preacher said, "If this church wants to be great it needs to fly with God," to which the congregation replied, "Let it fly, Pastor!" On a communication roll, the preacher said, "If this church wants to be great, it needs more money," to which the congregation replied, "Let it walk, Pastor!" The Bible warns, "Where there is no vision, the people perish" (Proverbs 29:18 KJV), but similar results can be expected, if a leader shares too much vision (TMV?) with followers.

Today's prayer to continue: May I see things with Your vision today, Lord, especially as it relates to . . .

August 8 A Wedding Prayer, Many Years Later

On this day, many years ago, we had a rather unusual prayer sung at our wedding. We selected it because we believed that God had called us to ministry and knew there was biblical proof that when God calls, God also accompanies. Moses was dead. Joshua was the new anointed leader. Three times in Chapter 1, God said to Joshua, "Be strong and of good courage" (Joshua 1:6, 7, 9). Why? Because Joshua had been called to lead the people to the promise land, and he had heard God's promise to, "be with you wherever you go" (Joshua 1:9). How would God accompany Joshua? In empowerment and encouragement! It has been our experience, through seven separate ministry locations spanning more than fifty years, that when God leads, God accompanies and when God accompanies, He grants power and courage for the assignment. Changing the words from singular to plural, our wedding soloist sang, "Our heart, our life, our all we bring, to Christ who loves us so; He is our Master, Lord and King, wherever He leads, we'll go." We were willing to go anywhere as long as God empowered and encouraged. Are you feeling God's power and courage today? You may be exactly where God wants you to be.

Today's prayer to continue: With Your power and courage today, Lord I want to . . .

August 9 Settled Before Sleep

Many years ago, on a hot south Texas afternoon, my wife and I both said "I do." Yesterday, we celebrated the fact that, we still "do." In a society that not only allows "no fault divorce" but celebrates it, how can one couple stay together for so long? For one thing, we took our vows seriously. We promised before God, family, and friends, that we would love, honor, and obey (some traditional ceremonies change the word to "cherish"), till death. Specifically, we said we would do that "for better or for worse, for richer, for poorer, in sickness and in health." As if those vows were not enough, my new grandfather-in-law, came through the reception and offered further counsel. This retired minister, with years of counseling behind him, simply said, "Don't ever go to bed mad" and he moved on down the reception line toward the cake and punch. I wish I could say we have always lived by that advice. While we have had some short nights due to long discussions and while there were a few nights of trying to sleep angry, his advice was solid, because it was based on Ephesians 4:26: "Do not let the sun go down on your wrath." What works for marriages, works for all inter-personal relationships: So, settle your grievances before you sleep.

Today's prayer to continue: Before I sleep tonight Lord, I need to settle . . .

August 10 Grieve in Grace

Everyone grieves – some of us at the death of a loved one, some at the loss of a job, some at a medical report, some at the betrayal or even attitude of a friend, some at the circumstances around them, and a multitude of other reasons. Grief is rather normal. It goes with the territory. By definition, grief is a natural response to loss, and we all suffer losses. Grief strikes believers and non-believers alike. However, believers have a resource that helps them cope with grief. God offered to Paul and to us sufficient grace. "My grace is sufficient for you" (2 Corinthians 12:9). Grace is the loving and merciful presence of God with us, because God desires us to have that presence, not because of anything we have done to earn it. Grace doesn't remove grief. But with God's comforting, assuring, affirming-presence, believers can grieve in grace.

Today's prayer to continue: Lord, thank You for your grace. I especially need it today related to . . .

August 11 Precious Memories and Positive Eulogies

Have you noticed that in death, nearly everyone is spoken of in positive terms? Seems we are hesitant to say anything negative about one who is deceased. It reminds me of the rugged cowboy who attended the funeral of a scoundrel friend, one who had broken at least three-fourths of the laws in the Old Testament. As the pastor was waxing eloquent on the positive characteristics of the deceased, the old cowboy got up and went to the casket to look in. Startled, the pastor asked if there was something wrong. "Nope" said the cowboy, "I was just checking to see if I was at the right funeral." And then there were the two brothers, equally notorious in their small town. Just before the start of the older brother's funeral, the younger handed the pastor a $100 bill and said, "Say something nice about my brother." Mid-way through the eulogy, the pastor paused and said, "Now, I'd like to say something nice about our deceased." Into the suddenly silent auditorium, the pastor calmly said, "He was a better man than his younger brother." In contrast, Shakespeare wrote, "The evil that men do lives after them, the good is oft interred with their bones." I've been through a season of tragic deaths of friends and equally positive eulogies, many of them heartfelt and accurate. Whatever we may think of the lifestyle of the deceased or the sincerity of their eulogies, the Bible says, "Precious in the sight of the Lord is the death of His saints" (Psalms 116:15).

Today's prayer to continue: Lord, may I so live that the words spoken about me at my funeral be both positive and accurate and especially . . .

August 12 Some Ships Sail, Others Don't

Most of the time, I succeed at what I plan. However, my preparation occasionally exceeds my performance. Has that ever happened to you? It happened to Jehoshaphat, when he was king of

Judah. On one occasion, he tried to live up to the reputation of Solomon, who, as king of Israel, built ships and sent them to Ophir three times each year for gold. Yet when Jehoshaphat attempted to do the same, the ships never made it out of the harbor. They were safe in the harbor, but ships are never built for the harbor. They are built for the open waters. 1 Kings 22:48 tells the sad result, "Jehoshaphat made merchant ships to go to Ophir for gold; but they never sailed, for the ships were wrecked at Ezion Geber" - the port where they were built. As soon as they sailed, they were broken to pieces against the rocks near the harbor. Oliver Wendell Holmes, Jr. wrote: "We must sail sometimes with the wind and sometimes against it - but sail we must, and not drift, nor lie at anchor." So, make your plans and set sail, praying that your preparation and performance will resemble Solomon more than Jehoshaphat.

Today's prayer to continue: Help me prepare so well Lord that my performance is pleasing to You. I'm thinking specifically of . . .

August 13 An Unbeatable Formula

I had experienced what I determined to be a call from God to the ministry and was offered an opportunity to preach at the Star of Hope Mission in downtown Houston. Since I was still a teen-ager, my grandfather was strongly opposed to me doing so. I did what he may have thought disrespectful; I quoted scripture to him. "I can do all things through Christ who strengthens me" (Philippians 4:13). Granddad mumbled something that sounded like, "Your name is not Paul!" and I declined the invitation out of respect for him. It's been too many years ago to determine who was right, and who was wrong, but since then, I have preached and taught in many a diverse circumstance, including places similar to the Star of Hope Mission and in some places that surely made my grandfather turn over in his grave. I have become a firm believer in Philippians 4:13 as well as a quote from Henry Ford, "Those who believe they can do something and those who believe they can't are both right." I am consistently trying to determine what God is calling me to do, and in God's strength, attempting to do it. What has God called you to do that you have not yet done? What's the cause of the delay? Human opportunity plus divine strength is an unbeatable formula.

Today's prayer to continue: Today Lord, in Your strength, I need to take the opportunity to . . .

August 14 Double Discipleship

Is there ever a good reason to despise someone? Maybe so. There seemed to be a good reason that the Jews despised Roman soldiers. The law said that a Roman soldier could require a Jewish citizen to carry the heavy military backpack for one mile. Many Jewish citizens had markers located one mile from their homes to inform a Roman soldier of the limit of their legal responsibility. Jesus had some hard sayings for His Jewish followers, especially for His disciples in the Sermon on the Mount. Perhaps none of His descriptions of discipleship were more difficult to hear than the one recorded in Matthew 5:41, "whoever compels you to go one mile, go with him two." I enjoy the company of second-mile believers. You know who they are! They're the ones who show up early and stay late to see what else needs to be done. They're the ones who call at just the right time to see if you need anything. They're the ones who pray for you when everyone else has said, "Amen." They're the ones involved in double discipleship – second mile folks. How about being a second mile disciple today.

Today's prayer to continue: As best as I can determine Lord, for me to go a second mile today involves . . .

August 15 Reading about Prayer or Praying?

I read recently an estimate of how many people are reading books on prayer these days and I wondered how many of these readers were actually praying. With one popular website listing 48,000 books on Christian prayer for sale, there is no shortage of reading material, and new books are being published daily. Certainly writing and reading on the subject is needed and valuable, but praying is crucial. There are a few folks who would read a book just out of curiosity, or strictly for information purposes, but most read books to learn and live. The disciples' request of Jesus, "Lord, teach us to pray" (Luke 11:1) did not ask to be taught "how" to pray, indicating they already knew how. What they desired was to actually practice prayer like Jesus did. So, keep reading and learning about prayer, but don't forget to pray. Paul E. Billheimer, author of the classic book on prayer, *Destined for the Throne*, wrote, "Satan does not care how many people read about prayer if only he can keep them from praying." Beloved, let us pray!

Today's prayer to continue: Lord, my simple prayer today is . . .

August 16 Age-related Smiles

I've come to expect the phrase at every doctor and dental visit of these "golden years" and there have been far too many of the visits to suit me. Somehow the diagnosis always includes the term, "age-related." I've learned to live with the term. I know there are things I will never do again – score from second base on a single to right field, teach an I-term class eight hours a day for five straight days, participate in an all-night lock-in, run a marathon (actually I never got around to that the first time.). But there are things I can do now that I could never do before – enjoy grandkids, attend fifty year reunions, reflect on the way things used to be. Did I mention enjoying grandkids? Some anonymous person, who must have been having age-related issues, wisely said, "Don't cry because it's over, smile because it happened." Job, who had his own set of issues, said, "Now my days are swifter than a runner; they flee away . . . I will put off my sad face and wear a smile" (Job 9:25, 27). So, I'm going to smile today and if I smile big enough, you can even see my new dental implants. Onward!

Today's prayer to continue: Every day is a day for smiles, Lord, but today I am smiling because of . . .

August 17 Faith's Landing Place

The African impala can jump to a height of over ten feet and cover a distance of greater than thirty feet. Yet these magnificent creatures can be kept in an enclosure in any zoo with a three-foot wall. Why? The animals will not jump if they cannot see where their feet will land. If they were to be described in biblical terms, we would say they jump by sight, rather than by faith. Faith is the ability to trust what we cannot see. The writer of Hebrews says, "Faith is the substance of things hoped for, the evidence of things not seen" (Hebrews 11:1). Faith is an absolute necessity in the life of the believer. By faith you were saved; by faith you are being justified; cleansed, and look forward to the return of Jesus. What changes have come in your life because of faith, and how is faith growing in your life? Can you jump, trusting God for your landing place?

Today's prayer to continue: Lord, I need to make a leap of faith, but I can't see the landing place. Help me today to jump in faith toward . . .

August 18 Harvest-Field Praying

I've often wondered what prompted the disciples of Jesus to ask Him to teach them to pray (Luke 11:1). Many things happened between their call to follow Him and their request to be taught prayer. According to Luke, just one chapter prior to their request, Jesus described the harvest as "great" and the laborers as "few" and then told them to pray (Luke 10:2). Since He was sending seventy of them into the harvest, two-by-two, they might have been surprised that prayer was included in His outreach strategy. They obviously understood the commands to go, to serve, to share, to minister, to teach, to preach, but the command to pray? This may have been the most confusing command of Jesus. Today, in many circles, it is the forgotten command of Jesus. I have heard, read and been part of the planning of more outreach strategies than I can remember. Those saturated with prayer were in the minority. It must have thrilled Jesus to be asked about prayer, on the heels of His command to go to the harvest field. It would no doubt, thrill Him today, if we made prayer more a part of our harvest-field strategy.

Today's prayer to continue: I know the harvest field is all around me Lord and I see it is ripe for harvest. So today, related to the harvest, I want to pray specifically . . .

August 19 Getting Out or Getting Content

Waiting to board my next flight, I was observing the passengers deplaning from another flight. One man, much older than me, came down the ramp and entered the terminal with the words, "How do I get out of this place!" I suspect many of us have had a similar experience. Your desire to "get out" may have been in emotional, mental, or even spiritual surroundings, but it was none the less felt. When faced with this circumstance, we have two options: to find a way out, which may be both the wanted and needed alternative; or to accept and adjust to the circumstances. Paul's circumstances involved captivity, but whether he lacked bread to eat or clothes to wear, whether he was hungry or thirsty, cold or naked, he wrote, "I have learned in whatever state I am, to be content" (Philippians 4:11). The word for "content" is a common word in Greek philosophy. It means "self-sufficient," "independent." In other words, Paul had adjusted, adapted, to his circumstances and was ready to be used by God in the midst of them. What are your surroundings today? Do you need to "get out of here" or take steps to be "content?"

Today's prayer to continue: Some days, Lord, I don't know if it is better to get out or adjust. Help me today to know the difference and determine the best course of direction especially as it relates to . . .

August 20 Upholding or Upheld?

Some days I uphold people. It's part of my calling. However, on other days, I need to be upheld. Let's start with calling to servanthood. In Isaiah 41:9, God says He has called people from the "ends of the earth" to be His "servants" – that is, to do ministry on His behalf. I first understood that calling at age fourteen, at Palacios Baptist Encampment on the Gulf Coast of South Texas. On a hot July night, in that humid, mosquito infested, foul tasting water place that some thought was ten miles beyond "the ends of the earth," I heard God's call. On days when my priorities are in order, I join the called out ones from around the globe, to do God's work. What is God's work? In Isaiah 41:10, God says, "Fear not, for I am with you; be not dismayed, for I am your God. I will strengthen you. Yes, I will help you. I will uphold you with My righteous right hand." One of God's works is to "uphold" those whom He has called to Himself and I try to do that on His behalf. But on other days, I am the one who needs to be upheld. Not only is God faithful to uphold me, but He sends other called out servants to assist in that upholding. So what about today? Are you upholding others or needing to be upheld?

Today's prayer to continue: I may need to be upheld myself Lord, but today, I'd like to be used in upholding . . .

August 21 Praying for Those for Whom We'd Rather Not Pray

Every day, during my prayer time, I pray for my family, my colleagues, a few friends, folks on my prayer list for that day, those who have requested special prayer, but there is one group that is often missing from my prayer list – my enemies. Frankly, I'd rather not pray for them. It would be far more comfortable to ignore them, maybe even despise them. Apparently, the disciples had a similar problem. In His Sermon of the Mount, considered by many as the most important sermon Jesus ever preached, the disciples heard Him quote Leviticus 19:18, "You have heard that it was said, 'You shall love your neighbor and hate your enemy'" then add, "But I say to you, love your enemies, bless those who curse you, do good to those who hate you, and pray for those who spitefully use you and persecute you" (Matthew 5:44). OK, I have very little problem with the outward acts proposed by Jesus – love, bless, do good, but when it comes to the inward, intimate act of prayer, well, as they say, "He stopped preaching and started meddling." How can I pray for my enemies, when I don't even like them, don't even want to think about them? Seriously, when someone "spitefully" uses me and "persecutes" me, I'm supposed to pray for them? For me at least, this is a sign of maturing discipleship, and it only happens on my more spiritual days. But happen, it must. And I must discipline myself to include this more often in my prayer life. American newscaster David Brinkley once said, "A successful man is one who can lay a firm foundation with the bricks others have thrown at him."

Today's prayer to continue: Lord, today I need to pray for those who have "despitefully" used me beginning with . . .

August 22 When Baby and Body Belong to God

Recently, I prayed with a former student whose wife delivered their planned and expected child very early in her pregnancy. The baby did not live and they were grieving the loss, trying to understand, yet accepting it as God's plan. Then I turned on the TV and heard arguments that a woman's body is her own and does not belong to anyone but herself. The logic further alleges she is therefore free to terminate an unwanted pregnancy. The argument is often seen as strong from a human perspective, but there is a higher fact. A woman's body (and for that matter, a man's body) belongs to God. The apostle Paul said it this way: "Do you not know that your body is the temple of the Holy Spirit who is in you, whom you have from God, and you are not your own? For you were bought at a price; therefore glorify God in your body and in your spirit, which are God's" (1 Corinthians 6:19-20). There is a distinct difference in the two illustrations. In one case God gave and God took away, and God's people tried to understand, accept, and move on. In the other case, God gives, and people take away. The temptation is an old one – to take matters into our own hands and minds; to try to do, and understand for ourselves. Job discovered that it was the Lord, and only the Lord, who gives, the Lord, and only the Lord, who takes away, and then proclaimed, "Blessed be the name of the Lord" (Job 1:21). We would do well to allow God to be God, and His Word to be our Guide.

Today's prayer to continue: The subject is a difficult one Lord and I frequently hear both sides, but thank You that our bodies belong to You. Today I want to re-commit my body to You for the purpose of . . .

August 23 A Barnabas Word

I received word of a new skin cancer surgery in my near future. I was still recovering from the last surgery. The new cancer location is near the first, so there is a possibility that the cancer is spreading. Not good news. I spent an entire day feeling sorry for myself. All I really wanted on that day was to hear an encouraging word. None came. Then God sent a Barnabas. The Apostle Paul needed encouragement on one occasion when the believers in Jerusalem refused to accept him due to their fear of his past. Acts 9:27 begins with "But Barnabas . . ." and continues to relay the account of Barnabas living up to his name – "Son of Encouragement" (Acts 4:36). There are actual and potential readers of this book. Ideally, I would like to minister to every reader, every day. Practically speaking, I'd hope to minister to a few each day. Today, the law of averages says someone reading this needs a word of encouragement. For you, I want to share a Barnabas word, and say, be encouraged. God has a plan and He is good. He will not forsake you. Be faithful. I hope you have a good day.

Today's prayer to continue: Thank You Lord for the encouragement of a Barnabas in my life. May I likewise be an encouraging Barnabas today in the life of . . .

August 24 This, That, and the Other

Every so often, I hear a word or phrase that I haven't heard in years. Last week, I overheard someone say, "This, that, and the other." My grandfather used that phrase often. I assumed it just meant, "Whatever." It was a catch-all phrase, used when nothing else seemed to fit. Google the term and you'll find: "(idiomatic) Particular items belonging to a large, diverse set, but items of the general kind of item indicated." Take for instance, the biblical word "love." Limit your reading to 1 John 4 and you'll find references to God loving us, us loving God, and us loving each other, with an implication that we ought to also love ourselves – diverse, yet of the same kind. A lot of my days seem to consist of diversity, yet sameness - encounters with different personality types, surrounded with a variety of circumstances, confronted with various levels of stress, etc., yet all within God's call and direction in my life. I guess life is like that. So, I wish for you a good day, a week filled with this, that, and the other.

Today's prayer to continue: In the diversities of this day, Lord, help me be a blessing to someone, maybe even . . .

August 25 Sending Prayers Where?

"Sending prayers your way." I'm noticing this comment more and more, especially on Facebook and other social media. I know what the sender intends to say. At least, I sincerely hope they are not actually sending the prayers toward the person in need. If so, they should not expect an answer to their prayer. Only God answers prayer and then likely only prayer offered directly to Him. The direction of our prayer must always be God-ward, not man-ward. The Bible instructs us to "pray for one another" (James 5:16), and to address our prayer to God alone. Prior to Jesus teaching His disciples to pray what we call "The Lord's Prayer" He said, "When you pray . . . pray to your Father" (Matthew 6:6). Paul modeled prayer addressed to the Lord, when he wrote, "Concerning this thing I pleaded with the Lord . . ." (2 Corinthians 12:8). I know, some will say that I'm just a picky professor of prayer, attacking something that is no more than a word game. But prayer is a serious matter, and we will practice it best when we think and speak of it correctly. So today, I'm sending prayer TO God, FOR you.

Today's prayer to continue: Lord, today I'm sending prayer to You on behalf of . . .

August 26 Balancing Service and Rest

One popular author wrote of another, "At an age when he should have been enjoying retirement on a beach in Florida, he kept getting on airplanes and flying to places to proclaim a gospel he believes with all his heart. . ." While there is no beach in Florida calling out to me, I do know the tension of the desire to serve balanced with the need to rest. The older I get, the more rest I need between opportunities of service, but the tension is not limited to those who are aging. Jesus understood and often took His disciples to a quiet place – the mountains, the desert, the sea shore – away from the crowds needing ministry. On one occasion "Jesus no longer walked openly among the Jews, but went from there into the country near the wilderness" (John 11:54). He taught us that the best way to minister to people was to occasionally get away from people. But it is so hard, especially if you are one who never says "no" to an invitation to serve. As one friend said, "The mind writes checks that the body can't cash." But rest we must. Another friend encouraged me to "divert daily, withdraw weekly, and absent myself annually." I'm trying. How about you?

Today's prayer to continue: Help me Lord, to get the rest needed by my body so that I can do what You have for me to do today, which is . . .

August 27 Thank God for God

After sharing thanks for various things, a friend said to me, "And thank God for God." Not being familiar with that phrase, I soon went to my Bible to see if it was there. I found lots of phrases that began with "Thanks to God . . ." and "Thank God for . . ." and "Thanks for God's . . ." but no "Thank God for God." Did anyone in the Bible thank God for God? Best I can tell, they did not, at least not in those exact words. Oh, many thanked God for various things and a few expressed thanksgiving for God's attributes, but was God ever thanked for simply being God? The closest I could get was Psalm 116:17: "I will offer to You the sacrifice of thanksgiving, and will call upon the name of the Lord." Further, I found a few Google references to the phrase, but nothing of specific benefit. So I pondered. When I am thankful for something or someone, I thank God, but when I am thankful for God, whom do I thank? Obviously, I have no one better to thank for God, than

God. So, let me encourage you to join me in beginning today thanking God for God.

Today's prayer to continue: So today, I thank You God, for just being God, but more specifically, I thank You for being . . .

August 28 Legion

I never got into the "Roots" popularity of the 70s – the idea of tracing one's heritage to places of influence. I never lived anywhere long enough for a place to influence me much. My father was a pastor who assisted with the short average tenure of ministers. We changed churches every four to five years. In every church but one, the parsonage was re-located during our tenure, causing me to switch school systems. I attended eight schools in twelve years prior to college. My roots were in people, not places. Yet, everywhere we lived, there were those who impacted my life – family members, Sunday School teachers, Royal Ambassador leaders, school teachers, youth ministers, coaches, professors, collegiate ministers, role models, friends, and colleagues. One day Jesus met a troubled man. "He asked him, 'What is your name?' And he answered, saying, 'My name is Legion; for we are many'" (Mark 5:9). The name of people who have impacted my life is "Legion" for they are many. The ones whom I need to thank the most are already enjoying their heavenly reward. So, is there anyone you need to thank today?

Today's prayer to continue: Lord, I give thanks today for . . .

August 29 A Ninety-One year Old Cadillac

He is a 91 year old friend of mine. I've known him for his many years of teaching prayer and living a prayer life-style. As the occupant of the Chair of Prayer and Spiritual Formation at Southwestern Baptist Seminary, I was responsible for the Prayer

Room bearing his name. He prayed with me and for me, on many occasions. He has recently had some heart-related issues and his son (also my good friend) shared with me the words of the cardiologist to his Dad: "You are like a Cadillac with 400,000 miles on it. You have taken a lot of hits, but still on the road. We can clean you up, and polish you up, but we can't make you like new; can't turn back the odometer. You have some miles left. We all know death is coming, but go ahead and order the Michelin tires." What a great perspective! My own father, who died of cancer at the age of 84, was still preaching within a month of his death. Caleb's life illustrates for us that there is no retirement plan in doing the Lord's work. At the age of eighty-five (several years past normal "retirement"), Caleb returned to the borders of what would be the land of God's people. When the Lord offered him a challenge in his advanced years, Caleb gladly accepted it (Joshua 14:10-12). Join me this week in giving thanks for those who set the pace for us and have gone on to glory, and for the older models that are still among us.

Today's prayer to continue: Thank You Lord for those who have gone before setting the pace and showing the way for the rest of us. Today, I am thinking especially of . . .

August 30 Holy Boldness or Not?

This past week we have had six different sales persons in our home, each making presentations and submitting estimates for a new air conditioner/heater unit. Some were very aggressive and forward. Others were very precise and detailed. One was a healthy mixture of both. We found him to be acceptable. He reminded me of a Greek word in Acts, that is most often translated "boldness." "Now, Lord, grant to Your servants that with all boldness they may speak Your word . . ." (Acts 4:29). When we think of "boldness" we normally think of aggressiveness and hard-sell. But the word has a secondary meaning of "clarity" which implies being precise and understood. In Acts, Luke was asking God for assistance in speaking, assistance that the witness would be both aggressive and clear. People I know whose speech is bold are often misunderstood. Likewise, those I know who are precise and detailed often lack aggressiveness. Perhaps, if we could blend the two meanings of the Greek word, the responses we receive from our witness might be more acceptable to God.

Today's prayer to continue: Help me to be bold today Lord – aggressive and clear – particularly as I witness to . . .

August 31 Sentimental (Prayer) Journey

My last day of full-time employment at Southwestern Baptist Seminary was on this date in 2007. It hardly seems like 22 years ago that I entered my first class room full of seminary students. I remember being filled with a mixture of holy boldness and absolute fear. Come to think of it, those are the same two emotions that I'm feeling as I face the first days of retirement. I arrived on campus early to take a sentimental journey/prayer-walk, through the Rotunda with its presidential portraits, down the hallways lined with pictures of beloved professors and colleagues, past classrooms where I both studied and taught. As I thanked God, precious memories flooded my soul. Back in my retirement office, I read (as I have for years) the daily entry in *My Utmost for His Highest* by Oswald Chambers. The verse was appropriate, "That your joy might be full." (John 15:11) and mine was. Chambers' final line of the devotion was more appropriate, "The lives that have been of most blessing to you are those who were unconscious of it." Unfortunately, most of my heroes never knew they were my heroes. So today, I asked the Lord to just pull them up next to Him and tell them thanks from me. Have you taken a sentimental prayer journey lately, even if only in your mind? Maybe today would be a good time express thanks for some memories and those who helped create them.

Today's prayer to continue: Lord, I have so many wonderful memories of Your servants who ministered to me. Today I give thanks for the memory of . . .

September 1 Gray Headed Declarations

I am officially retired from Southwestern Baptist Seminary after 22 years on the faculty. Since there is no biblical evidence for retirement from God's call to ministry, I prefer to view this as a transition, not a retirement. And I have a new "life verse" to go along with my transition. In my teen-age years, as I was sensing God's call on my life, my verse (we knew nothing of "life verses" back then) was Romans 8:28, "We know that all things work together for good to those who love God, to those who are called according to His purpose." About the time I joined the faculty of Southwestern, I added a new, special passage of scripture, Proverbs 3:5-6, "Trust in the Lord with all your heart, and lean not on your own understanding; in all your ways acknowledge Him, and He will direct your paths." Now, in the midst of this current transition, God has given me yet another "life passage," Psalm 71: 17-18, "O, God, You have taught me from my youth; and to this day I declare Your wondrous works. Now also when I am old and gray headed, O God, do not forsake me, until I declare Your strength to this generation, Your power to everyone who is to come." While, I don't have much gray hair, I do have enough to qualify for this passage. And since I am only retiring from my position, not from my calling, I plan to keep on "declaring." Do you have a special passage?

Today's prayer to continue: Lord make me sensitive for opportunities to "declare Your wondrous works" especially to . . .

September 2 My Retirement Office

My office was moved again last week – this time into a retirement office. It is my seventh office in 22 years on the

Southwestern Baptist Seminary faculty, and my last. My wife won't let me bring all the books and file cabinets and pictures home. So I have two options: keep teaching as an adjunct professor, thereby keeping an office, or die, in which case my entire library will go to someone else. Spiritually, I'm ready to die. Physically, I'd like to teach a few more classes. Speaking of spiritual, I need to draw something spiritual out of this situation or this will cease to fit the purpose of these writings. For me, at least, life has been a series of moves – geographical, vocational, emotional, spiritual. Hopefully, all have been directed or at least, allowed, by God. This last move – to retirement and a retirement office - was a bit more traumatic than I had anticipated. As has been my custom over the years, I looked to God's Word for help. Standing in the midst of the Areopagus in Athens, Paul said, referring to Jesus, "in Him we live and move and have our being" (Acts 17:28). I trust that this last office move was "in Him" and I pray that all of your moves will likewise be "in Him."

Today's prayer to continue: More than anything Lord, I wish to be thought of as being "in" You. Today that means . . .

September 3 Retirement, Promotion, Adjustment, or Transition?

Life is a series of adjustments. I just had another one, but I'm not sure what to call it. I made a big deal about "retirement" not being biblical for those called to vocational ministry, reminding folks that I was only "retiring" from a position, not from a calling. At my "retirement" reception, the secretaries ordered the cake icing to read, "Congratulations Dr. Crawford on your promotion." I was afraid I remembered what that meant and sure enough, from the Salvation Army web site, came these words: "Promotion to Glory: The Salvation Army's description of the death of Salvationists." I'm not a member of the Salvation Army but my great grandmother came from New York to help begin the

Salvation Army in Texas, so I am kind of related – enough that I don't like this "promotion" idea any more than the "retirement" idea. Finally, I decided I would use the word "transition" for this latest adjustment, but when I looked that up in my "Cruden's Complete Concordance" I found only "transgression" and I didn't want any part of that. Back to "promotion" I discovered Proverbs 4:7-8 where wisdom promotes and honors one and I decided to be "promoted." But I refused to eat the part of the cake with that word on it. I pray that you will have an easier adjustment with your next "promotion."

Today's prayer to continue: Lord, help me make the adjustments necessary to continue following Your will, like the one I need to make soon . . .

September 4 Happy Labor Day

One day this month we will celebrate Labor Day. The subject of labor brings some interesting news:

• From New York – "Worker Dead at Desk for 5 Days"

• From Japan – "Japan to Pay Widow of Man Worked to Death."

• Sign in the store window: NO HELP WANTED.

The celebration of Labor Day is another matter – Originally set aside to honor labor's contributions to the U.S. – it has come to mean for most, just another day off from work and for some "work" is just another four-letter word. According to one poll, only 43 % of American office workers are satisfied with their jobs. Each day in the USA 50,000 people quit their jobs. For many, work has a less-than-profound meaning:

• Lawrence Peter, *The Peter Principle* – "In time, every post tends to be occupied by an employee who is incompetent to carry out its duties . . . Work is accomplished by those employees who have not yet reached their level of incompetence."

• Sign seen in a workaholic's office: "Thank God it's Monday."

• Observation of a Dairyman: "The hardest thing about milking cows is that they never stay milked."

Jesus said, "I must work the works of Him who sent Me while it is day; the night is coming when no one can work" (John 9:4). Enjoy your day off on Labor Day, then back to the work God has given you to do.

Today's prayer to continue: Not everyone has a job, so Lord I am happy to have a work that You have allowed in my life. May I function today in this God-given work as I . . .

September 5 Rewind and Replay

What is there in your past you would give everything to re-live again? The country song tells of a young rodeo cowboy who longs to be able to ride for eight seconds and make it all the way to the national finals rodeo in Las Vegas. The song ends with the man, now grown old, dreaming of his four world championships and affirming that, "he'd trade it all today for one ride in Vegas." When I was young, my Dad used lots of film on my brother and me. When we watched the film, there were certain scenes that we loved to rewind and replay, over and over again. I'm not sure what I'd be willing to give, but there are certain scenes from my past that I'd sure enjoy re-living again. Jesus was perfect, but I wonder if in his early morning quite times he ever thought about His past and longed to relive some special experience. We know that the Apostle Paul grieved over his wasted years (Galatians 1:13) but I wonder if he ever wanted to relive any experience in his post-conversion years? Surely Peter regretted some of his early actions, but did he ever think of reliving any of his high spiritual moments? John had a lot of free time on Patmos. I wonder if he spent any of it wishing he could re-live some pre-exile experience. How about you?

Today's prayer to continue: Thank You Lord for the gift of memory. May I learn much from re-lived memories of past days, so that today, I can serve You better as I . . .

September 6 God's Will . . . My Will

We divide and categorize people in many ways – politically, racially, economically, denominationally, geographically. The Bible divides people into two groups – those who follow God's will and those who don't. Many use their God-given freedom of choice to choose their own way. When my granddaughter graduated from college she shared with me her feelings of doing something different with her life than her college major prepared her to do. My response was that you do what you feel God is leading you to do and watch to see how everything you've thought was God's will (including a college major) is used by God in your future. Examples of this truth are legion. God has a plan, a purpose for your life. Accept and follow, or reject and refuse to follow. The Bible says it this way: "The Lord of hosts has purposed, and who will annul it? His hand is stretched out, and who will turn it back" (Isaiah 14:27)? Written by Bo and Dick Baker for a youth camp in the mid-1950s, "His Way . . . Mine" became a favorite for many a youth and young adult who discovered God's will for their life, myself included:

"Now in His will my soul finds life worth living Each day new blessings from above Tho' shadows come and valley's seem unending Still I know He makes a way for me."

Today's prayer to continue: I sincerely want to follow Your way for my life, Lord . . .

September 7 Understood

I once had a friend who responded to almost everything said to him with a one word reply – "Understood!" It was his way of assuring the talker that he had listened and processed what was said. I sometimes wondered if he really understood or if he was just in the habit of giving that response. Then I came across a quote from Stephen Covey, "Most people do not listen with the intent to understand; they listen with the intent to reply." Ouch! As one who has made a living by speaking (preaching/teaching/advising/consulting/etc.), I plead guilty. In fact I have lately caught myself replying with what I thought was a better story, a stronger point, a funnier joke. Many years ago, I memorized a verse that I need to refresh in my thought process. "Let every man be swift to hear, slow to speak" (James 1:19). It was Epictetus, an ancient Greek sage and Stoic philosopher who said, "We have two ears and one mouth so that we can listen twice as much as we speak." Understood!

Today's prayer to continue: Speak Lord, I am listening now rather than talking. I'm waiting to hear . . .

September 8 From Tablet to Tongue

The skeptic asked me, "Why do Christians talk so much about God?" Good question. Everyone talks about what is important to them, what is in their heart. Maybe it's about kids or grandkids, or the weather, or ball scores, or the latest movie or song, or a new found friend. So the path is from the heart to the tongue. While Christians do the same, something additional is in our heart. Moses wrote God's laws/commands on tablets of stone (Exodus 24:12). Twice, the writer of Proverbs used the phrase, "The tablet of your heart" (Proverbs 3:3; 7:3), indicating we are to write God's laws/commands on our hearts – the true inner self which determines who we really are – to be felt, remembered, and shared. Jesus added, "Out of the abundance of the heart the mouth speaks."

(Luke 6:45). So, here's the Christian path – God's law/commands given in a lasting, permanent, unchanging manner (tablets of stone), transferred to us (tablet of your heart), and then shared from our heart with others. What a wonderful opportunity we have today to share with others – from tablet to tongue.

Today's prayer to continue: Today, Lord, I want to share your law/commands, so lead me to . . .

September 9 You Jus' Like Us

At the conclusion of my Interim Pastorate in an East Texas town, he said to me, "Bro. Dan, I didn't think I was gonna like havin' a Seminary Professor for an Interim Pastor, but you know what? You jus' like us." To this day, several interim pastorates later, it is one of my most treasured compliments. There is a sense in which leadership needs distance between leader and led, but there is a far greater sense in which, if you can't be like 'em, you can't lead 'em. In reality there was a world of difference between him and me – educationally, socio-economically, politically, personally – but somehow we had enough in common for him to pay me a great compliment. I wonder how he liked heaven upon arrival there. First impressions often change, but I suspect one of these days, he will walk up to Jesus and say, "You know what Lord, you jus' like me." In that moment, he will be both correct and incorrect. It is that tension, between difference and likeness that makes for effective leadership and "followship." Perhaps the most unique man in the New Testament (other than Jesus) said it this way: "I have become all things to all men' (1 Corinthians 9:22).

Today's prayer to continue: I confess Lord, that I need to balance difference and likeness with . . .

September 10 Alone, but not Lonely

Sometimes it's best to be alone. Advice comes from everyone from popular authors to television talk-show hosts. Well-meaning friends propose insights. Educated professionals offer counsel. But the bottom line has to come from you and that can come much easier in the stillness of solitude than in the noise of company. In his famous sermon, "Payday Someday" Dr. R.G. Lee described the Old Testament prophet Elijah as, "God's preacher, often alone, but never lonely." The discipline of early morning aloneness in the life of Jesus is described as "in the morning, having risen a long while before daylight, He went out and departed to a solitary place; and there He prayed" (Mark 1:35). Paul Tillich, a German-American philosopher and theologian, widely regarded by some as one of the most influential theologians of the 20th century, wrote: "Language... has created the word 'loneliness' to express the pain of being alone. And it has created the word 'solitude' to express the glory of being alone." So find some glorious place, some quiet, out-of-the-way location, to be alone with God. It will be time well spent, decreasing your lonely days, and filling every day with more meaning.

Today's prayer to continue: Today Lord, I am going to find a place of solitude to be alone with You, and I will begin looking in . . .

September 11 9/11 Plus

Today we observe the anniversary of the events of 9/11/01. Like every adult American I remember exactly where I was and my reaction when the first news came. I also remember the questions of that day – Why, where was God, why didn't God prevent this, what happens now? And I remember the haunting question asked the next day in my Seminary class. "Dr. Crawford, would you comment on Romans 8:28 in light of yesterday's events?" In times of crisis, Romans 8:28 is an oft quoted and sometimes mis-quoted verse, even more often mis-applied. The verse, "And we know that all things work together for good to those who love God, to those who are called according to His purpose" does not say that all things work together for good for all people. Nor does it say that all things are good. And it certainly does not say that all things are God's will. In a world of God-given choice, in order to have God's will, there must be a not-God's-will. A violation of God's law can never be transferred into God's will. Murder is a violation of God's law; it is not God's will. To those who love God and who are called according to His purpose, the verse says, things work together for good. Not our definition of good, which usually has to do with finances, health, education, etc. But God's good – the good of all of God's family. The next verse says God meets us in the midst of our tragedies and uses "all things" both "good" and bad to conform us into the image of our older brother, Jesus Christ. So what have we learned from 9/11 or other crises of the years following? Simply this: Continue to allow God to conform us into the image of Jesus Christ and when crisis comes, small or great, trust God whose truth is relevant in all situations, whether we understand it or not.

Today's prayer to continue: Lord, I don't want to wait till crisis time to communicate with you, so today, I'd like to talk with You about . . .

September 12 Looking Beyond in Joyful Praise

Have you ever been stuck in your circumstances? In one set of circumstances we are distressed, while in another set, we are ecstatic. Sometimes the best way to get beyond current circumstances, be they positive or negative, is to look beyond in joyful praise. In her frustration Hannah prayed for a son and when God granted her request, she said: 'My heart rejoices in the Lord'" (1 Samuel 2:1). She looked beyond the gift, and praised the Giver.

After describing his enemies, David said: "My soul shall be joyful in the Lord. It shall rejoice . . ." (Psalm 35:9). The Psalmist looked beyond the skirmish, and praised the Savior. When told she would give birth to the Messiah, Mary sang: "My soul magnifies the Lord, and my spirit has rejoiced in God my Savior" (Luke 1:46). Mary looked beyond the miracle, and praised the Master. How do you get beyond today's circumstances, be they good or not so good? You look joyfully to Jesus.

Today's prayer to continue: I'm looking at You today Jesus, and I'm seeing . . .

September 13 God on Speed Dial

One of my new, favorite compliments came this week. I had communicated with a former student and good friend during a difficult time in his life and assured him of my prayer support. He replied with thanks for the prayer and concluded with, "I've always thought you and God had each other on speed dial." For you non-techies, Wikipedia defines speed dial as, "a function available on many telephone systems allowing the user to place a call by pressing a reduced number of keys. This function is particularly useful for phone users who dial certain numbers on a regular basis." While I appreciate the compliment and understand its meaning, the same should be said of every believer. God said, "Call to Me, and I will answer you" (Jeremiah 33:3). There is no reference or even implication of a delay – hold, busy signal, automated voice mail, or an answering machine (Wouldn't you hate to hear a deep voice say, "This is your Heavenly Father. I can't talk right now, but please leave a message at the sound of the harp?") I am reminded of an old gospel song, using an analogy from an earlier day, "Jesus on the main line, tell Him what you want. You can call Him up and tell Him what you want. His line ain't never busy, tell Him what you want." So, if He's not already there, how about adding God to your speed dial today and "tell Him what you want."

Today's prayer to continue: Lord, I know I need to communicate with You more often, so today I am beginning to . . .

September 14 Decisions During the Journey

Life has often been compared to a journey. While there is truth in this analogy, there is also truth in the fact that the journey is filled with forks in the road, where decisions have to be made on which road to take. Those of us who grew up in or around a church were challenged early to decide to follow Jesus vs. Satan; God's way vs. the world's way. The youth evangelists of those days told dramatic stories of lives filled with drugs and alcohol, until they decided to follow Jesus. Most of my friends decided to follow Jesus, a few chose the other road. The most popular seminar subject in college retreats and conferences was how to decide on God's will for one's life – as to a mate, a career, friendships, etc. Adult life is filled with decisions, from medical to material to management of time and resources. Retirement years bring a whole new set of choices – continue working, play more golf, spend more time with grandkids, or take a long trip to get away from it all? In Acts 20:16, Paul, "decided to sail past Ephesus" and in Titus 3:12 he "decided to spend the winter" in Nicopolis. Decisions are everywhere. It's possible you will face a decision today. Chose well. The big thing about decisions is that, while you can make adjustments, you seldom, if ever, get a redo.

Today's prayer to continue: Lord, the current decision I am facing is . . .

September 15 Laughter Lines

One of the good things about visiting the office of a medical doctor is seeing what is on the walls. Often times it is pictures or shadow boxes of medical instruments or practices of long-ago. That's what I saw this week – a picture of an old-time method of facial care. It was an instrument to be used on the face with the following instructions: "Pat across the corner of the mouth, across the laughter lines toward each ear." Laughter lines? As soon as I got home I starting to research what was a heretofore unknown term to me. I discovered I knew the condition better as "Crow's Feet" - the tiny wrinkles at the outer corners of the eyes resulting from age, sometimes called laughter lines. Further I learned that new research shows they don't just make you look old, but the wrinkles make you look angry as well. Then I discovered a song entitled "Laughter Lines" with the following lyrics: "I'll see you in the future when we're older and we are full of stories to be told. Cross my heart and hope to die, I'll see you with your laughter lines." As I age, I want my laughter lines to represent happiness, not anger. When God's people returned to Zion from captivity they sang: "Then our mouth was filled with laughter, and our tongue with singing. Then they said among the nations . . . the Lord has done great things for us, and we are glad" (Psalm 126:2-3). The Lord has done "great things" for me also, and I am glad. So let my laughter lines show joy.

Today's prayer to continue: Lord, today I pray that my "laughter lines" would show . . .

September 16 Joy Entered In

What a joy to share another's joy! When you enter into the joy of another, their joy overflows back on you, making you joyful as well. Perhaps it's enjoying a child or grandchild open a present with joyful expressions, or observing someone complete a perfect musical presentation. Maybe it's tearing-up with the Olympic athlete as they stand on the gold medal podium or sharing with someone you love as they receive good news. Better than all of this human joy is the experience of entering the joy of the Lord. In the parable of the talents, the Master rewards the two faithful servants for their investment and increase by encouraging them to "enter into the joy of your Lord" (Matthew 25:21 & 23). "The joy of your

Lord" may mean either the rejoicings at His return, or the present rewards which the Lord prepares for his faithful servants, or both. Whatever the meaning, it is an awesome thought that we could actually enter into His joy and have it overflow into our lives. Have a joyful day.

Today's prayer to continue: Your joy Lord, is something I really want to experience today as I . . .

September 17 A Tribute to my Professor

It was my first semester as a seminary student and I had a new professor. How could this happen to me? In a faculty full of distinguished, tenured scholars, I had a rookie, teaching evangelism, no less. He had no notes. He just told one story after another and threw in a few sermon outlines. When the first exam came, I was shocked. None of his stories/sermons were on the exam. That's when I realized we had books to read. I don't remember who else was in that class, but if it was a typical seminary class, there are alumni of that class who have served all over the world. Twenty years later, I found myself on the same faculty, and in the same department, as my rookie professor. For twenty-six years we served together. He was my professor, my mentor, my colleague, my friend, and last week we sent him home to heaven. If there was a receiving line in heaven, consisting of those who were influenced because of his ministry and witness, he may not have arrived at the throne yet. Even as he worships around the throne, he will be continually interrupted by those who remind him that they are there because of an interim pastorate, a revival meeting, a random seat assignment on an airline flight, a student preacher he sent to preach a revival meeting. And the line of his former students circles the globe today, touching every tribe, and nation, and tongue, and people. It was written of another, but could easily be said of Roy J. Fish, "he being dead still speaks" (Hebrews 11:4).

Today's prayer to continue: Thank You Lord for those who have influenced my life. I'm thinking today of . . .

September 18 Decision Making: Faith or Sight?

Two specialist surgeons in my county accept my type of medical insurance. I used Dr. X on my first surgery and despite the fact that he was very highly rated and recommended by my physician assistant, I was not pleased. It was not just him, but his entire staff that made me uneasy with their attitude and comments. So, on surgery #2, I went with a prayed-up, faith-based decision rather than the prevailing logic, and chose the lesser rated, not-recommended-by-my-physician-assistant, Dr. Y. On the day that I was awaiting surgery #2, I discovered that Dr. X had suspended his practice and all his patients were being referred to Dr. Y. Is there a lesson here? Absolutely! Sometimes the rightness of faith-based decisions are known before the fact; other times, after. But we have two choices when making decisions – we can walk by faith or by sight. In the case of surgery #2, I walked by faith and it turned out to be the right decision. Come to think of it, that's biblical. "For we walk by faith, not by sight" (2 Corinthians 5:7).

Today's prayer to continue: There are ways Lord that I can walk by sight today, but I'd rather walk by faith, especially as I make a decision related to . . .

September 19 Morality, or Spirituality, or Both?

Over the years, I've had friends who had strong spiritual convictions but low moral standards. The results of such lifestyles have been displayed widely in the media. I fear what has been revealed in the spotlight is only a fraction of what has been practiced in the shadows. More recently I have developed friendships with those who have strong moral beliefs, but not much spirituality. Must it be either/or? Can it not be both/and? Jesus found a way to incorporate both spirituality and morality into one lifestyle, so much so that his spirituality infuriated the religious leaders, who likely lacked moral convictions. His solid morality was described as, "in all points tempted as we are, yet without sin" (Hebrews 4:15). Expounding on this balance, Martin Luther King, Jr. said, "If we are to go forward, we must go back and rediscover those precious values - that all reality hinges on moral foundations and that all reality has spiritual control." However you say it, the ideal is a God-intended, Jesus modeled, lifestyle balance of healthy morality and solid spirituality.

Today's prayer to continue: Lord I need both the moral and the spiritual in my life today as I plan on . . .

September 20 Lo and Behold!

I've heard it all my life, but when I heard the expression again the other day, I paused to reflect on the exact meaning of, "Lo and behold!" It's actually an exclamation meant to draw attention to something. It is used especially to announce things that are considered important, thus it is often written with an exclamation mark. The word "lo" is a shortening of "look". So, "lo and behold" has the meaning of "look! – behold!" "Lo" is also akin to "O", and has been in use since the first millennium. In the early 1970s Bob Dylan sang: "Lo and behold! Lo and behold! Lookin' for my lo and behold," and said the words were based on an oft-repeated phrase of the Old Testament prophets. Something not very far removed from "lo and behold" appears in the Bible in Genesis 15:3 (King James Version): "And Abram said, Behold, to me thou hast given no seed: and, lo, one born in my house is mine heir." The person using the phrase (that originally sent me wondering) was giving their testimony, and said "Lo and behold, I discovered that God loved me more than I loved myself." "Lo and behold" indeed! Have you had any "Lo and behold" moments lately? This might be a good time to pause and thank God for the "Lo and behold" experiences in your life.

Today's prayer to continue: Lo and behold, Lord! Today I need to have my attention focused on You as I . . .

September 21 The Levity of Brevity

Having been retired from the seminary classroom for several years, it was a bit awkward recently to find myself in a substitute role for a former student, now teaching the same course he learned from me. One of the things I remembered during the class time was that, when teaching, I always prided myself in finishing on time or perhaps a few minutes early. In all my classroom years, I never had a student complain about getting out of class early. I often told my wannabe preachers, there were three rules of preaching: stand up, speak up, and shut up. Sadly some of my former students have abandoned my advice and now preach seemingly forever in each sermon. I always felt it was better to leave others wanting more than to exhaust the subject. I'll never forget the advice I received from my advisor as I was writing my doctorial report. "Eliminate every word you don't' need" he said. What if we applied these bits of communication advice to everyday conversation? Ever get in a conversation that seemed to go on forever and you couldn't find a way out of it? The Apostle Paul spoke of writing "briefly" of the mystery (Ephesians 3:3). Simon Peter wrote, "I have written to you briefly, exhorting and testifying that this is the true grace of God in which you stand" (1 Peter 5:12). If Paul and Peter could communicate "briefly" then perhaps we can also. Not that every communication needs to be brief, but some could certainly be shortened. So remember the five B's of good communication: Be Brief Beloved, Be Brief.

Today's prayer to continue: Briefly Lord, I just need You today as I . . .

September 22 Number One or Other

During my first year in high school I was relegated to the Junior Varsity baseball team. The next year I was determined to make the varsity. When the uniforms were passed out I was given #25, not one of my hoped-for numbers. When I asked the coach why I got #25, he replied, "Because we only have twenty-five jerseys to hand out." In other words, I was player #25 to make the team. My wife was engaged to another guy before we became engaged. I was the second choice to be the Director of Baptist Student Ministries at the University of Texas. When I was hired by the Southern Baptist North American Mission Board (then called Home Mission Board), I was told they had been interviewing people for one year. Two professor candidates were interviewed for the position I occupied for twenty-two years at Southwestern Baptist Seminary. So, what's the point? You don't have to be #1 to be chosen. Our first choice at manager of our own life is our self. That's why we have to reject self and, "accept" Christ, making Him Lord of our lives. But here is the really good news, Jesus said, "You did not choose Me, but I chose you" (John 15:16). With God, I am #1, and so are you!

Today's prayer to continue: Thank You Lord for choosing me. Guide me today as I share this good news with . . .

September 23 Declaring Kindness and Faithfulness with and without Music

Decisions of how to serve God occasionally turn on very small hinges. While my father wanted an athlete for a son, my mother desperately wanted a musician. I'm not sure of the content or length of their discussion on the subject, but in the early days of my athletic career, my mother asked me if I would like to play a musical instrument as a way of serving God. I volunteered to play the saxophone. Since my godly mother could not envision me playing a godly saxophone in church, she purchased a trombone for me and hired a teacher. During the first lesson, the teacher showed me the positions on the slide, and the sounds made by each position. During the second lesson, I surprised him by playing "Whispering Hope." Then he surprised my mother by resigning with the comment, "I can't teach someone who plays by ear." That ended my budding musical career and corresponding service to God via music. Several years later, having given up all hope, my mother sold the trombone in a garage sale and gave my younger brother voice lessons (which, by the way, served him well to this day, contrary to my short-lived athlete career). Small hinges; lifetime directions! The Psalmist said, "It is good to give thanks to the LORD, and to sing praises to Your name, O Most High; to declare Your lovingkindness in the morning, and Your faithfulness every night, on an instrument of ten strings, on the lute, and on the harp, with harmonious sound" (Psalm 92:1-3). If you're like me, and don't play an instrument, nor sing very well, I'd encourage you to join me today in finding ways to serve God by declaring loving kindness and faithfulness.

Today's prayer to continue: With the skill and talent You have given me Lord, I praise You today, especially through my . . .

September 24 Making Satan Mad

I never understood spiritual warfare until I got heavily involved in global evangelism and intercessory prayer. Two things that greatly irritate satan and cause him to attack are the sharing of the Christian faith with intent to convert and intercessory prayer for the non-believer and the backsliding believer. When Christians do things that lead non-Christians to change their affiliation from satan's kingdom to God's kingdom, satan gets upset and goes on the attack. When Christians do things that cause wandering believers to return to their first love of Jesus, satan gets upset and goes on the attack. Concerning satan and witnessing, Martin Luther said, "Where God built a church, there the devil would also build a chapel." Concerning satan and prayer, Corrie ten Boom said, "When a Christian shuns fellowship with other Christians, the devil smiles. When he stops studying the Bible, the devil laughs. When he stops praying, the devil shouts for joy," and William Cowper wrote, "satan trembles when he sees the weakest saint upon their knees." When Paul finished describing the armor of God, he wrote, "praying always with all prayer and supplication in the Spirit, being watchful to this end with all perseverance and supplication for all the saints— and for me, that utterance may be given to me, that I may open my mouth boldly to make known the mystery of the gospel" (Eph. 6:18-19). Let's make satan mad today.

Today's prayer to continue: Lord, if I could make satan mad today, it would be through . . .

September 25 A Helpful Refuge in Hard Times

The car in front of me had numerous bumper stickers and the light turned green before I could read all of them. The one I remember said, "Life is hard. Get over it." It reminded me of a quote from Sydney J. Harris, an American journalist, syndicated in many newspapers throughout the United States and Canada, who once wrote, "When I hear somebody sigh, 'Life is hard,' I am always tempted to ask, 'Compared to what?'" Good point. Yes, life is hard, but where were you ever promised it would be easy. You say, "But I'm a Christian. That's supposed to make life easy." Show me that verse! Life is hard whether you are a Christian or not. The advantage the Christian has is a refuge that the non-Christian does not have. J.B. Coats wrote a hymn that was recorded by everyone from Elvis Presley to Emmylou Harris to the Gaither Vocal Band. "Where could I go but to the Lord . . . Seeking the refuge for my soul. Needing a friend to save me in the end. Where could I go but to the Lord." The Psalmist wrote, "The LORD also will be a refuge for the oppressed, a refuge in times of trouble" (Psalm 9:9). Hard times? Sure! But give thanks, Christian! We have a helpful refuge in hard times.

Today's prayer to continue: Recently, Lord, I have needed a refuge and I am thankful that You provided it through . . .

September 26 Further Along

The book began with the words, "This book is by the one who thought he'd be further along by now, but he's not." It doesn't matter who wrote the book, for its author is legion. Nor does it matter the title of the book, for the opening line describes the book everyone hoped to write someday. How have we learned so much, yet applied so little? How have we grown so much, yet matured so little? Oh, I know a few whose ego allows them to believe they have arrived at perfection or at least they camp out in its vicinity. I remain their friend because I figure they need someone who sees through them and still likes them. I know many who are still on pilgrimage, struggling ever upward to their goal, however they understand it. I remain their friend also for we are sometimes on the same stretch of road and it's good to fellowship with the like-minded. I also know of an Apostle named Paul who wrote, "For the good that I will to do, I do not do; but the evil I will not to do, that I practice" (Romans 7:19). I thought Paul would have been further along on his journey by the time he wrote this. Press on fellow pilgrim!

Today's prayer to continue: Lord, this journey I'm own has me always wishing I were further along. It would assist me greatly if today, I could . . .

September 27 But, What About My Left Hand?

"All in favor raise your right hand." I was left-handed until the third grade when a teacher thought left-handedness was a sign of a slow learner and switched me. Did that mean I was discriminated against, because we always voted with our right hands? In church we were always implored to greet new members with the "right hand of Christian fellowship." Was there no such fellowship in my left hand? I learned later that the right hand was the favored hand in most cultures, a symbol of power and authority in many. The "right hand" was the hand of blessing in Genesis 48:17. It was described as a cherishing embrace in Song of Solomon 2:6. Paul describes Jesus as "sitting at the right hand of God" (Colossians 3:1). In Revelation 1:16, John talks about Jesus and His relationship to the Church ("the seven stars") and says He held them "in His right hand," then writes, "He laid His right hand on me, saying to me, 'Do not be afraid'" (Revelation 1:17) reminding the reader of Isaiah 41:10, "Fear not, for I am with you; be not dismayed, for I am your God. . . I will uphold you with My righteous right hand." So, what about the left hand? Injure your right hand and you will quickly learn the value of your left. The good news is that the left hand is as much a part of the body as the right and that's true of the physical body, as well as The Body of Christ, for we are "many members" but are a part of "one body" (Romans 12:4-5, 1 Corinthians 12:12, 20). Let's hear it today for the left-handed saints of God!

Today's prayer to continue: Lord, I know someone who is left-handed, so today, I pray for . . .

September 28 The Lost Art of Loyalty

A casual observance of society reveals loyalty is a lost art. In earlier days, sports fans could expect professional athletes to remain with one team for the life of their career. Now loyalty yields to a "show me the money" mentality. My grandparents believed, to guarantee a long marriage they should leave the word "divorce" out of their vocabulary. Now loyalty gives way to no fault, easy access divorce. A recent survey showed 57% of workers are dissatisfied with their jobs and would change employers immediately if a better position were offered to them. So much for vocational loyalty. At the first hint of disagreement or dissatisfaction, loyal church members transfer membership down the road or across town. An old favorite hymn, written for the first convention of the Baptist Young People's Union in 1894 would no longer be popular if we sang, "From over hill and plain there comes the signal strain, 'Tis loyalty, loyalty, loyalty to Christ; Its music rolls along, the hills take up the song, Of loyalty, loyalty, yes, loyalty to Christ. 'On to victory! On to victory!' Cries our great Commander, 'On!' We'll move at His command, We'll soon possess the land, Through loyalty, loyalty, Yes, loyalty to Christ." The Bible says, "Let your heart therefore be loyal to the Lord our God, to walk in His statutes and keep His commandments" (1 Kings 8:61). May this kind of loyalty never be a lost art.

Today's prayer to continue: Lord, I want to display my loyalty to You today as I . . .

September 29 Back of the Line

"Putting on the uniform never gets old." Those were the words of the new manager of the Fort Worth Cats minor league baseball team, but with an adjustment or two, they could have been my words. I feel that way about my academic regalia. Long ago I lost count of the graduations and convocations in which I marched in my cap and gown. On those occasions, my attention was often drawn to the back of the line where the retired professors walked, those who had given their lives to the training of the called-out ones, my academic heroes, men and women, "of whom the world was not worthy." (Hebrews 11:38). I remember thinking, "the last will be first."(Matthew 20:16). I also remember thinking how honored I would someday be to walk at the back of the line, retired, accomplished, proud. But times change and traditions die. Once retired, I was never once asked to walk in graduation or convocation again. It's OK! There is a great line in an old spiritual that says, "All of God's chillun got a robe." My reservation is secure in a place where time never overrules tradition; my eternal robe has been fitted; my place in line has been assigned. Someday, I'll put on the heavenly uniform (celestial cap and gown) and it will never, ever get old again, even if I'm at the back of the line.

Today's prayer to continue: It really doesn't matter to me Lord, where I am in the line as long as You know where I am, so today, I want to honor my place in the line by . . .

September 30 God's GPS

I finally bought a Global Positioning System (GPS) but the pronunciation was so poor, I could hardly find my way out of my own neighborhood. And when it told me to exit on Azle Ave., but pronounced it "Ah-zel-avie" I gave it to my granddaughter and went back to a map. I do understand the value of a GPS and think it would have saved Moses forty years of hearing his wife say. "Why don't you just stop and ask someone?" Abraham could certainly have used one when God told him to pack up and hit the road, and then, and only then, would he know where he was going (Genesis 12: 1-3). I also thought of Abraham finding his way from Beer-Sheba to Mount Moriah with Isaac, two servants, a donkey, wood, fire, and knife. But on Mount Moriah, when God spared the life of Isaac by providing a ram for the sacrifice, Abraham named the place, Jehovah Jireh, meaning, "God provides" (Genesis 22:14). Then it hit me. God has a GPS = God Provides System. With all due respect to the Global Positioning System (and I'll probably buy another one eventually), I like God's GPS better.

Today's prayer to continue: Lead me Lord, in the paths You would have me go today, and I will do my best to . . .

October 1 When Should a Pastor be Appreciated?

This is Pastor Appreciation Month. There was a time when pastors were appreciated because of their title. They were called Reverend because they were revered. They were called Brother because they were loved. No more. Because of the abusive actions of a few, and the investigative desires of many, today's pastors must prove themselves before they are appreciated. As one who has served as an interim pastor in more than twenty churches, I have seen the "calling" process take longer and longer, often including intensive background checks and painful question and answer sessions, often before the entire congregation. We no longer deeply respect the position. Now we thoroughly evaluate the person. Is this what Paul had in mind when he wrote to the believers in Thessalonica, "And we urge you, brethren, to recognize those who labor among you, and are over you in the Lord and admonish you, and to esteem them very highly in love for their work's sake" (1 Thessalonians 5:12-13). To "recognize" means to appreciate, to have a regard and respect for. Who they were is not mentioned. It is evident however, that the church was not left without appointed persons to minister to it. They were there "in the Lord"; called, gifted, and appointed. They did not take this position for themselves, nor were they appointed by men, but they were made able ministers by God. Christian ministers, who proclaim the whole truth, and labor in the service to others, are entitled to more than simply respect. They are to be "esteemed" abundantly "in love". But, if Pastors are to be appreciated these days, they have to earn it, "for their work's sake." It no longer goes with the title. Sad, but true.

Today's prayer to continue: In appreciation of the pastors who have blessed my life, today Lord, I want to . . .

October 2 A Gift for Pastor Appreciation Month

Some have labeled this Pastor Appreciation Month. Should you not give a gift during a time of appreciation? Then what gift should you not give your pastor? In my years of serving as a seminary professor, I also served more than twenty churches (two of them twice) as Interim Pastor; some for a few months, others for a few years. Interim pastors are sometimes appreciated, sometimes not so much. While they fill a crucial role in the life of a church, allowing for transition, sometimes for periods of healing, giving the church time to find the right pastor, they are occasionally seen as merely fill-ins, pulpit fillers, or as I was once introduced to a congregation, "our new temporary pastor." I can easily identify the churches where I was most successful in providing them the pastoral leadership needed. They are the ones who intentionally and consistently prayed for me – in public and in private. One church actually requested that I stop by their prayer room on the way to both morning worship services where a small group of people waited to pray for me. A recent internet article entitled, "Top Ten Gifts to Give Your Pastor" listed prayer as #1. J.C. Ryle, prolific writer and British pastor in the late 1800s, wrote, "If we would have good ministers, we must remember our Lord's example, and pray for them. Their work is heavy. Their responsibility is enormous. Their strength is small. Let us see that we support them, and hold up their hands by our prayers." The Apostle Paul wrote, "We urge you, brethren, to recognize those who labor among you, and are over you in the Lord and admonish you, and to esteem them very highly in love for their work's sake" (1 Thess. 5:12-13). Pray for your pastor this month, and then make it routine for every month thereafter.

Today's prayer to continue: Especially today, Lord, I want to pray the following for my pastor and other pastors . . .

October 3 Pastor Appreciation Night

In addition to "Pastor Appreciation Month," may I propose a "Pastor Appreciation Night"? A sleepless Saturday night was complicated by what one minister-friend calls, "Intestinal uncertainty." For me at least, it is a rather frequent Saturday night experience when I am preaching on Sunday morning. Even though I've spent Sunday mornings doing just that for more than fifty years, the butterflies keep coming and some nights they turn into buzzards. One can either resent this scenario or accept it as a way to keep from becoming self-sufficient on Sunday morning. This kind of night makes preachers extremely God dependent. Preaching on little sleep is a learned activity. During this Pastor Appreciation Month may I suggest that one of the ways you could show appreciation for your pastor is to pray for Saturday night rest? Maybe before you go to sleep on Saturday night you could pray for your pastor and if you awaken in the night, ask the Lord to "enlighten" the "darkness" (Psalm 18:28) of your pastor's possible sleeplessness. Most pastors could use more sentries of the night, especially on Saturdays.

Today's prayer to continue: Remind me Lord, to pray for pastors on Saturday nights and especially pray for . . .

October 4 Minister Appreciation

What some call "Pastor Appreciation Month" others broaden to "Minister Appreciation Month." The following applies to both pastor and church staff member, as well as to other ministers. When the team wins, the players get the credit. When they lose, the coach gets fired. That's the way it is in the sports world. Unfortunately, that attitude spills over into churches. I've known of far too many friends, former students, and acquaintances, who were terminated or sometimes, simply encouraged to leave, not because they misinterpreted their call from God, or were incompetent, or ineffective, but because things did not work out to the satisfaction of the followers (be that the church family, deacons, personnel committee, or some power group/person in the church). Granted there are situations where a minister, or a coach, needs to be assisted in moving on, but far too many are sent packing for wrong reasons. We ought not to need a special month to appreciate ministers, but October is "Minister Appreciation Month." Your act of appreciation will please both the minister and God, as well as fulfill the admonition of Paul to, "Recognize those who labor among you, and are over you in the Lord and admonish you, and . . . esteem them very highly in love for their work's sake" (I Thessalonians 5:12-13).

Today's prayer to continue: Lord, today I want to pray for ministerial staff persons who work alongside pastors and on behalf of the church. I pray especially for . . .

October 5 Called or Not?

I have communicated with a number of God-called ministers who are no longer in vocational ministry. While there are some understandable and legitimate reasons, there are also some not-so-good reasons. I've also met a few people who once felt called to be involved in church activities but now find themselves outside the fellowship of a local church and equally outside the service of the Lord. My response is to share two quotes; the first is from the Bible: "I have called you by your name; you are Mine" (Isaiah 43:1). The second quote is from television football: "It takes indisputable evidence to overrule a call on the field." If you have drifted from your call, I ask you, what is your indisputable evidence for overruling the call of God? Get back in the game and help others do the same. If you are, as best you can determine, in the middle of where God wants you to be, look around, identify and minister to those who are not.

Today's prayer to continue: I pray today for those who have felt called to ministry but are no longer serving in a ministerial position. May they . . .

October 6 Give the World a Smile

During my college days, there was a local radio program of Southern Gospel music that always began with the Stamps Quartet singing, "Give the world a smile each day, helping someone on life's way." During those same college years (actually 1963), Harvey Ball, a commercial artist from Worcester, Massachusetts created the smiley face. That image went on to become a recognizable symbol of good will and good cheer. The smiley face knows no politics, no geography and no religion. Harvey's idea was that for at least one day each year, neither should we. He declared that the first Friday in October each year would henceforth be World Smile Day. The "Day" actually began in 1999. You say you don't feel like smiling on the first Friday? Job, who had less reason to smile than anyone I know about, was in the midst of his sorrows – having lost all his material possessions, suffered various calamities, experienced the death of his sons and daughters, seen his house destroyed, suffered painful boils on his entire body, watched his wife lose her faith and challenge him to curse God and die – when he exclaimed, "I will forget my complaint, I will put off my sad face and wear a smile."(Job 9:27). Now, if Job can smile in those circumstances, perhaps, we can smile on World Smile Day. Come on, join me and let's give the world a smile.

Today's prayer to continue: I'm smiling Lord, partly because of all You have done in my life. As I share a smile, may I also share Your love today with . . .

October 7 Comments and Compliments

Those of us who preach receive a variety of post-sermon responses. One of my most remembered, was a good-intentioned, yet devastating comment from a dear lady who said, "Bro. Dan, every sermon you preach is better than the next one." Think about it. That's a comment, not a compliment. We who preach cringe when someone comments that they enjoyed our talk. Not complementary. Speeches are talked. Sermons are preached. There is a huge difference. Fellow-preachers also know that skill in sermon preparation is crucial, yet secondary. To paraphrase a verse, "Unless the Lord builds the sermon, they labor in vain who build it" (Psalm 127:1). Delivery is yet another challenge to a mixed-age audience where the young members do not understand the significance of a Pearl Harbor illustration and the older members do not understand the use of hi-tech terminology. And yet we preach on, fearing with Paul, that when, "I have preached to others, I myself should become disqualified. (1 Corinthians 9:27). A few Sundays ago, I received one of my best responses. Following a sermon, a man I did not know, came to me and said, "Dr. Dan, when you preach, God speaks." Now that's a compliment – a compliment that needs no comment. So preachers, preach on! And listeners, consider whether your post-sermon responses are compliments or comments.

Today's prayer to continue: Help me today, Lord to share compliments, not just comments, with those I meet, especially . . .

October 8 Fuel for the Journey

What fuels your day-to-day Christian life? Theological understanding? Trendy spirituality? Hyper-active servanthood? One of the most interesting Bible studies is to pose this question to what is written about the day-to-day Jesus. Especially during the early days of His public ministry, the record is punctuated with multiple references to Jesus leaving His disciples and finding a quiet place for the purpose of prayer (Mark 1:35). Furthermore, the Gospel record implies that Jesus needed this private time with the Father, not only for His own spiritual sustenance, but to strengthen and equip Him for the mission to which He had been assigned. Those who work with people quickly learn that to survive, it is necessary to get away from people occasionally. And not just get away for the purpose of relaxation, but also for the purpose of refueling, communicating with the Father. What does your calendar look like today? More important question: With what will you fuel yourself for today's journey?

Today's prayer to continue: For the tasks of today, Lord I need . . .

October 9 ACTS or MIGHTY ACTS?

There is a popular acronym that some use to assist them in the content of their prayers. The origin of ACTS (Adoration, Confession, Thanksgiving, Supplication) as a prayer outline is unknown, although some believe it is displayed in and derived from The Lord's Prayer (Matthew 6:9-13). Spiritual leaders, including such well-known personalities as Billy Graham, have promoted its use. While this is a good, helpful prayer-starter, there is much more to prayer than adoration, confession, thanksgiving, and supplication. Acknowledging that every acronym has its limitations; may I suggest a longer version? The Psalmist made reference to "the mighty acts of the LORD" (Psalm 106:2). So let's work with MIGHTY: Meditation, Intercession, Giving Up (as in fasting. Remember how often prayer and fasting are mentioned together?), Humbling ourselves, Travail (remember this lost word?), and Yielding (the "nevertheless, Your will be done" idea). It's not much of an acronym, but its mine. Feel free to substitute your own words, but let's acknowledge that while prayer is ACTS, it is more than ACTS.

Today's prayer to continue: Today, Lord I want to expand the content of my prayer to include . . .

October 10 Agreeing to Disagree Without Being Disagreeable

A Zulu proverb says when a thorn pierces the foot the whole body must bend over to pull it out. I was reminded again this week of the diversity within the Body of Christ and how, in our diversity, we must be one body with many members, working together to fulfill the plans of God. Paul said it this way, "For as we have many members in one body, but all the members do not have the same function, so we, being many, are one body in Christ, and individually members of one another" (Romans 12:4-5). A pastor arrived home only to hear his young daughter and her friends loudly disagreeing and criticizing each other. Walking into her room, the pastor asked if everything was all right, to which his daughter replied, "It's OK Daddy, we're just playing church." What have we taught the children and youth of the church, when adults, even in their diversities, fail to demonstrate the unity of the Body of Christ? As long as the church is made up of human beings, we will have disagreements. Let us agree to disagree, without being disagreeable, all the while, affirming the uniqueness of each. We really do need one another.

Today's prayer to continue: Lord, I have agreed and disagreed with my fellow believers, but today, I want to . . .

October 11 Known by Our Office

How is a person to be known? Various quotes indicate they are known by their silence, deeds, the company they keep, friends, books they read, tastes/distastes, and thanks to Jesus, "by their fruits" (Matthew 7:16). May I add another? A person is known by their office. Early in my ministry, a "decorator" looked at my office and almost had cardiac arrest. "Too stuffy, too uncomfortable" she said, plus a few other terms I dare not repeat. I guess it relates to who your office is for, you, or those who visit you. Since I seldom ever closed my door my office was always open to whomever wandered by. So what does my office look like? No plants, because I hate to water them. Erma Bombeck said, "Never go to a doctor whose office plants have died." Books? Yes, for reference. Mostly un-read, or read only until boredom set in. Every shelf of books is interrupted with an object that causes guests to comment. Pictures? Yes, of family, of significant scenes, and, of course, baseball. A corner with a prayer bench and multitudes of prayer prompters from places I've been and pictures of people I've taught or known. Framed money around the upper walls from every country I've visited, 57 and counting. Coffee mugs from every university campus where I've spoken or ministered, quotes, too many stacks of paper. And, of course, a space for my brain to work, remembering a quote by Robert Frost," The brain is a wonderful organ; it starts working the moment you get up in the morning and does not stop until you get into the office." I attended a funeral service recently where a video was shown of the man's office. I like that. Someone do that for my funeral. Among other things, I want to be remembered for my office.

Today's prayer to continue: Lord, memory is so important. Today, I pray that I might be remembered for . . .

October 12 That Could Have Been . . .

Our tour bus stopped for a photo opportunity at the beautiful little fishing village of Neils Harbour, located on the Cabot Trail of Cape Breton Island in Nova Scotia. The Cabot Trail is called the most photographed highway in Nova Scotia and further described as nature's longest roller coaster. Shortly after we resumed our tour, another tour bus lost control, ran off the winding road, and turned over, killing one passenger and injuring twenty others. One of my first thoughts was, "That could have been us." Then my mind raced back several years when I missed my flight after a speaking engagement because the driver couldn't find the right entrance to the airport terminal. While I was having my private pity party, and waiting on the next flight, I discovered that the flight I missed had crashed on arrival at my next destination. Again, the thought was, "That could have been me." In both circumstances, and other similar scenarios, why was it not me? The only answer I can give is that God planned it differently for me. Does that make me better than those who were not so fortunate? Not at all; just different. On another day, in another place, with another person, God said, "I, the Lord, have called you in righteousness, and will hold your hand; I will keep you" (Isaiah 42:6).

Today's prayer to continue: Thank You, Lord for "keeping" me. Today I need to live in appreciation of that as I . . .

October 13 Sleepless, but not Prayerless

Often, when I am preaching on Sunday morning, I have a sleepless Saturday night, or at least partly so. But this was Thursday night and there appeared to be nothing of great significance on my Friday agenda. Poet Maya Angelou wrote of sleepless nights, "There are some nights when sleep plays coy, aloof and disdainful. And all the wiles that I employ to win its service to my side are useless as wounded pride, and much more painful." So it was for me that Thursday night. I simply did what I learned from my prayer-warrior mother, I prayed for everything and everyone I remembered. I've seen the quote on bumper stickers, bookmarks, on wallpaper, and wall plaques, on coffee cups and clothing, on church bulletin boards and in church bulletins – "Don't count sheep, talk to the Shepherd." It is a popular subject and I knew I was not alone in my sleepless state. Even Paul, twice wrote about his own "sleeplessness" (2 Corinthians 6:5 and 2 Corinthians 11:27) and added in the second reference, "in sleeplessness often" implying it happened to him more than a few times. Next time you have a sleepless night, I highly recommend prayer. Even if it doesn't put you to sleep, it will be a night well spent.

Today's prayer to continue: Lord, next time I have a sleepless night, remind me to pray for . . .

October 14 Canadian Thanksgiving

On Thursday, January 31, 1957, the Parliament of Canada proclaimed: "A Day of General Thanksgiving to Almighty God for the bountiful harvest with which Canada has been blessed – to be observed on the 2nd Monday in October." So, today, or someday soon, Canadians will observe Thanksgiving. My sixth grade teacher assigned us a paragraph on what we wanted to be when we grew up. I wrote, "I want to be either a missionary to Canada or a professional baseball player." I never really became either (although I was reimbursed once with free meals for playing summer baseball for a restaurant sponsored team). However, seminary students who sat in my classes, and especially those who traveled with me to Vancouver, knew of my love for Canada. Sometimes one person's passion enlightens another's call. Often when one goes on site, they gain insight. Today I am thankful for those who went with me, those who were already there, and those who went on their own, all of whom allowed me, as their professor, to be a small part of God's Canadian plan for their lives. So on this Canadian Thanksgiving – for allowing me to fulfill my sixth grade calling to be a "missionary to Canada" – I express thanks to former students who have served or continue to serve in metro Vancouver or on Vancouver Island plus other former students who serve/have served across Canada. "I thank my God upon every remembrance of you" (Philippians 1:3). Give thanks today, for those whom God used to help influence you along the way.

Today's prayer to continue: Today, I am remembering those who influenced my life, Lord. I'm especially thankful for . . .

October 15 Following God's Call with Passion

Once, on Canadian Thanksgiving, I wrote of my gratitude for former students who serve in Canada, in part because of my involvement in their lives and I said, "Sometimes one person's passion enlightens another's call." Let me elaborate. In my pre-teens and early teen-age years I was a member of a very progressive church, one of the first, if not the first, Southern Baptist church to build an Activities Building and hire a full-time Minister of Activities. We laughed because if built by anyone other than a church, it would have been called a Gymnasium, but churches didn't build such in the 1950s, especially ones with ping-pong and card tables. So, even though it smelled like a gym, it was an Activities Building. Where would such a church go to find a full-time Activities Minister? Obviously, no seminary offered classes in the field. But Bob Boyd, a committed Christian, called by God to ministry, had been trained in secular institutions in the area of recreation. Our church added him to the ministerial staff, and he became a monumental influence in my life. One statement will never be forgotten by me. In his testimony, he said, "I prepared for a job that did not exist during my preparation." His passion, that led him under the call of God, to prepare for something that did not exist, enlightened my calling – to be unique and to follow God's calling where no one else was prepared to follow. Others will have to determine the degree of success I've had with that, but it was influenced by Bob Boyd, who like Caleb, had "a different spirit" and followed God "passionately" (Numbers 14:24, MSG).

Today's prayer to continue: Lord, make me willing to go anywhere, and do any task, in obedience to your call on my life. Today, I am particularly thinking of . . .

October 16 Anxious Reunions

I recently attended my college reunion. Psychologist Joyce Brothers says, "Ninety-nine and nine-tenths of people have some anxiety about going to a reunion. The rest are people who are so secure and have done so well they have no intention of going back." I guess I fit the majority.

There are several things you ought not to say at a reunion:

- What happened to you?
- I thought you were dead.
- Didn't you date my wife?
- Is that your husband or your son?
- Working yet?
- Can I borrow a couple of dollars?

"Reunion" is not in the Bible as a word, but it is as a concept. Paul told the believers in Rome, "I long to see you" (Romans 1:11) and told the believers in Philippi, "God is my witness, how greatly I long for you" (Philippians 1:8). It is good to re-unite with friends we have not seen in a while. Thankfully God occasionally allows for reunions in our lives. Of course there is coming a wonderful heavenly reunion. Until then, we'll have to settle for anxiety-filled earthly reunions. Why not make contact this week with an old friend with whom you've not communicated in a while?

Today's prayer to continue: Lord, I appreciate friends from earlier years. Today I give thanks for the friendship of . . .

October 17 Golden Friendships

Speaking of reunions, once at my college reunion, I dropped in on the Golden Luncheon, for those celebrating their 50 year class reunion. These were the sophomores, responsible for initiating us into college life, hated by those of us who were freshmen. They were our tormentors. I went to see if any of them had grown horns in the past 50 years. To my surprise, they had grown, more gentle, kind, and even friendly. I have made many friends over the years, but these college friends, even these who made my freshman year so miserable, have stood the test of time. Today they are dear friends, with whom I share the golden years. John, separated from his friends, wrote of seeing them "shortly" and called them "friends" (3 John 1:14). Joseph Parry wrote:

"Make new friends, but keep the old; Those are silver, these are gold. New-made friends, like new wine, Age will mellow and refine. Friendships that have stood the test-Time and change -- are surely best; Brow may wrinkle, hair grow gray; Friendship never knows decay. For 'mid old friends, tried and true, Once more we reach and youth renew." Join me today in thanking God for long-time friendships.

Today's prayer to continue: Thank You, Lord for long-time friends like . . .

October 18 Sabbath Rest

Some years ago I read in a psychology journal of a widespread, rather expensive survey that determined that man needed to rest one day in every seven. The Tokyo City Zoo discovered the animals were showing signs of stress until they let them have a day of rest from human interaction. It's amazing how humans discover what God knew all along. Early on, the Bible declares, "On the seventh day God ended His work which He had done, and He rested . . . Then God blessed the seventh day and sanctified it, because in it He rested from all His work . . ." (Genesis 2:2-3). The

Bible speaks often of a "Sabbath-rest" (Exodus 16:23; Leviticus 23:24) and even promises an eternal Sabbath rest (Hebrews 4:9). Everyone needs a Sunday, a Sabbath, even if, due to job and other responsibilities, it doesn't come on Sunday. Albert Schweitzer, a German—and later French—theologian, organist, philosopher, physician, and medical missionary in Africa, said, "Do not let Sunday be taken from you. If your soul has no Sunday, it becomes an orphan."

Today's prayer to continue: Thank You for rest, Lord. May I not ignore its importance in my life. I need Sabbath rest because . . .

October 19 The Long and Short of Separation

"The long and short of it" is an American idiom, said when one wants to get directly to the point of something without giving details. I'd like to do that with the idea of separation. When he was alive, my father and I attended a host of athletic events together. Occasionally, when an athletic event ends in a surprise victory for the home team, I still reach for the phone to call my Dad and share the celebration. Then I remember, he is gone, and I grieve once again. Why do Christians grieve at the loss of a friend or loved one to death? Most would answer, "separation." Granted, believers do not "sorrow as others who have no hope" (1 Thessalonians 4:13), but we nonetheless sorrow. We sorrow because we miss the departed. The younger the grieving one is the longer the separation seems before they are united again. But why does the departed one not grieve? Basically the new arrival in heaven is no longer subject to time or space. "There will be no night there" (Revelation 21:25; 22:5) and if there is no night in heaven, it is one continuous day. Even if the departed one does sense the loss of earthly friends and loved ones, they do not grieve for long because to them, we will simply arrive later in the day.

Today's prayer to continue: I'm looking forward to heaven Lord because it will end my separation from . . .

October 20 Fight or Focus?

The church seemed to always be fighting someone – city zoning office, neighborhood association, building contractors, other churches, etc. Once I asked the pastor about such fights and his reply was to the effect that if he could keep his church members busy fighting an outside entity, they wouldn't turn on him. One day they ran out of outside targets and turned on the pastor. His strategy proved to be effective but short-term. The culture of this particular church was one of survival fighting. It fed their purpose for existing. The late management consultant, Peter Drucker was famous for saying, "Culture eats strategy for breakfast." In this case, the church's DNA of always needing someone to fight, caused them to turn on their pastor and his strategy. May I propose another strategy? How about focus in the place of fight? How about, "Seek first the kingdom of God . . ." (Matthew 6:33)? How about, "Looking unto Jesus, the author and finisher of our faith . . ." (Hebrews 12:2). It seems to me that focusing on Jesus rather than fighting a common enemy, is a better way to grow the kingdom of God.

Today's prayer to continue: Lord, I guess I have occasionally been guilty of fighting rather than focusing. Today, help me to focus on . . .

October 21 God's Got This!

It took most of the week to process Monday's news. A summer biopsy showed a small skin cancer on my right temple. MOHS Surgery (that had twice before been 100% successful for me) was, this time, unsuccessful. Seems a part of the cancer had wrapped itself around a nerve. To expedite healing I was sent for plastic surgery, then to the Oncologist for radiation treatment. I was totally unprepared to hear that I would have treatments five days per week for the next six weeks, ending the day before Thanksgiving. Engagements had to be cancelled. Other than Sunday events, my calendar had to be cleared. Five days a week, for six weeks – with no guarantee that the radiation would kill all the cancer cells. I experienced heavy co-pays, since the seminary had recently cancelled its participation in retiree health insurance. It was almost too much to process, but as I sat in the Oncology waiting room, thinking about all the days and dollars till Thanksgiving, I realized how thankful I was. Names were called and people with much more involved cancer, went through doors to more extensive treatment than I was enduring. My cancer was, at least for now, skin cancer. Then this verse came rushing out of past experiences, "We know that all things work together for good to those who love God, to those who are the called according to His purpose" (Romans 8:28). I ended a long, confusing week knowing, God's got this!

Today's prayer to continue: Thank You, Lord that You have all of our experiences under control, including . . .

October 22 When Noise Needs a Silence Break

I've always enjoyed silence. Early on, God told Isaiah, "In quietness . . . shall be your strength" (Isaiah 30:15). Jesus had a pattern of rising early to enjoy the stillness of the morning and occasionally retired to the "mountain to pray, and continued all night in prayer to God" (Luke 6:12). Living in a world of noise, silence is more and more difficult to find. Indeed, my younger friends know little about a world that includes silence. Writing what he calls a, "faith-based theology of technology" Archibald Hart says, "Studies have shown that the average person today, surrounded by the cyber world, can only bear about fifteen seconds of silence" ("The Digital Invasion"). How sad! While I have made a living out of words, spoken and written, I treasure the quiet, wordless times. I guess some of those young friends would refer to me as a "throwback," but not everything in the past is bad. Without periods of silence, one tends to burn-out on noise. Mary Nelson Keithahn has written a moving verse, "Come away with me to a quiet place, apart from the world with its frantic pace, to pray, reflect, and seek God's grace. Come away with me. Come away." Since I often need a silence break, I treasure the times away.

Today's prayer to continue: Lord, a time of silence in my noisy world, would be helpful, since I . . .

October 23 A Personal Benediction

One of my early pastors closed every worship service with the same benediction. It was the one chosen by Paul as he closed his writings to the church at Corinth, "The grace of the Lord Jesus Christ, and the love of God, and the communion of the Holy Spirit be with you all" (2 Corinthians 13:14). What is a benediction anyway? One source defines it as "a memorable prayer, commending ourselves to God's care, and announcing His blessings upon the people." From the earliest church, Christians adopted ceremonial benedictions into their worship, particularly at the end of a service. Such benedictions have been regularly practiced ever since. Not all benedictions are corporate, nor are all so serious. Comedian George Carlin offered this benediction: "May the forces of evil become confused on the way to your house" and musician Bob Dylan offered, "May your heart always be joyful. May your song always be sung." You may not be called upon to offer a benediction in a worship service this week, but how about a personal benediction for friends or family? May you be blessed in so doing.

Today's prayer to continue: Lord, I want to commend the following friends to Your care today . . .

October 24 Loving in the Day; Singing in the Night

How do you spend your day . . . and your night? The Bible has a suggestion. Love in the daytime – both receiving and sharing God's love. In his *Ragamuffin Gospel*, Brennan Manning wrote: "We should be astonished at the goodness of God, stunned that He should bother to call us by name, our mouths wide open at His love, bewildered that at this very moment we are standing on holy ground." Then we pass that wonderful love on to others. Thaddeus of Vitovnica, a Serbian Orthodox elder and published author, wrote, "When we talk to our fellow men and they tell us about their troubles, we will listen to them carefully if we have love for them. We will have compassion for their suffering and pain, for we are God's creatures; we are a manifestation of the love of God." But what of the night? Songs! Songs from God, as stated in Job 35:10, "God my Maker, Who gives songs in the night." Songs that get you through a rough night. Songs that get you through a good night. Sing yourself to sleep. Awake singing. Then love. How do these two – loving and singing – go together? In the Psalms: "The LORD will command His lovingkindness in the daytime, and in the night His song shall be with me" (Psalm 42:8).

Today's prayer to continue: I will sing in the night time, Lord, and I will love in the day time. Today, that love will be expressed as I . . .

October 25 You Can't Judge a Book, or a Person, by the Cover

In 35 years of teaching at the university and seminary level, I learned this – you can't always tell when a student is learning, nor can you accurately predict their level of future achievement. Some of those I thought would surely fail now serve significant positions of leadership and ministry. Some I thought were "can't miss" types, have been disappointing. I wonder what the Lord thought about Peter. The meaning of disciple is "learner." Did it ever appear to our Lord, the ultimate teacher, that Peter was learning anything; anything that would help him become a success in his calling? And what about Judas? Eugene Petersen wrote, "Among the apostles, the one absolutely stunning success was Judas, and the one thoroughly groveling failure was Peter. Judas was a success in the ways that most impress us: he was successful both financially and politically . . . and Peter was a failure in ways that we most dread: he was impotent in a crisis and socially inept." It's true, you can't judge a book by its cover, nor can you judge a person by the outer appearance. Jesus saw people not as they were, but as they were becoming, and He gave them "the right to become . . . (John 1:12)." I want to be like that, don't you?

Today's prayer to continue: Forgive me Lord for judging just because of the outer appearance, and help me today to be affirming to . . .

October 26 Walking by Faith

He walks by my house every Saturday morning on his way to worship - black slacks, white shirt, black Yamakah on his head, black walking cane. His faith prevents him from driving on the Sabbath, so he walks, with a slight limp, for 22 blocks (3 miles round trip). Rain or shine, hot or cold, he walks. Lately, I've had bulging disks in my lower spine that create pain in the sciatic nerve of my right leg. I've thought of scaling back my activities, especially those that require excessive walking. But then I see him walking by my house again. If he can walk to worship the God of the Old Testament, surely, I can walk to serve the God of the entire Bible. We used to sing a children's song, "Walking in the sunlight, walking in the shadow, walking everyday walking all the way, walking with Jesus alone." Even while praying that the doctors can find something to ease my pain, I will continue to "walk by faith" (2 Corinthians 5:7). How about you?

Today's prayer to continue: Lord, may my walk with You today be . . .

October 27 Influence That Continues

Two men were instrumental in my joining the Southwestern Baptist Seminary faculty in 1985, and in my teaching there for more than twenty years. We've recently buried both Dr. Roy Fish and Dr. Justice Anderson. Both were my professors during seminary studies, then they were my colleagues on the faculty, and always, they were friends and mentors. Quite honestly, I was blessed less by class content than I was by their role modeling. I was reminded recently of that very fact when I encountered a former Seminary student of mine. He reminded me that he had taken a class from me a number of years ago and assured me that I had meant much to his ministry since that class. When I asked which class, he could not remember. This serves as a reminder to those of us who attempt to teach, whether it be in formal, academic settings, or informal, casual settings. We teach more by who we are than by what we say. Today I am grateful for the influence of two men who taught me so much – both inside and outside the classroom. Both were perfect models of Paul's mentoring instructions to Timothy: "The things that you have heard from me among many witnesses, commit these to faithful men who will be able to teach others also" (2 Timothy 2:2). May their influence continue.

Today's prayer to continue: I realize my influence is important to the lives of others, so today, Lord, may I be a positive influence to . . .

October 28 Patience When Needed

Time passes slowly when you're waiting on an airplane departure, especially when a mechanical issue has caused a four-hour delay. The airline kindly requested that we be seated and have patience. They offered a meal voucher since they were keeping us past the noon hour, a welcome offer since I had arisen at 4:30am and consumed a very early breakfast in order to be on time at the airport for the beginning of my flight delay. Mid-way through the delay a fire alarm sounded and an announcement was made to remain in our seats until further instructions. Where else was I to go with my plane under re-construction? Once the mechanical issue was fixed we were further delayed because the flight crew had not yet arrived. I wondered where they had been during the four hour delay. Finally, four hours and forty minutes late, we pushed away from the gate and were on our way. The tempers of the passengers leveled off at about the same time as did the aircraft. Somewhere out of the blue, in the midst of my frustration, came a reminder of the "fruit of the Spirit" in Galatians 5, especially fruit #4 – "longsuffering" or as some translations have it, "patience" (Galatians 5:22, NASB). What an interesting word for a patience-stretching flight delay. Remember that word during your next patience-needing time.

Today's prayer to continue: Lord, when my patience wears thin, remind me of longsuffering, and help me be able to . . .

October 29 Serenity or Courage?

The quote hung on my wall as a teen-ager. I would not know much about the author until Seminary days when his name was prominent on reading lists. "God grant me the serenity to accept the things I cannot change; the courage to change the things I can; and the wisdom to know the difference," so wrote Reinhold Niebuhr in his Serenity Prayer. American theologian, and professor at Union Theological Seminary for more than 30 years, Niebuhr offered me my first motto. Over the years I would learn that there were many more things that I could not change than there were that I could change. I found a fine line between serenity - the state of being calm, peaceful, untroubled and acquiescence - the reluctant acceptance of something without protest. Sometimes I didn't know which I had experienced until after the fact. Courage was different - the quality of mind or spirit that enables a person to face difficulty, danger, pain, etc., without fear. Moses said to Joshua, "Be strong and of good courage, do not fear nor be afraid of them; for the Lord your God, He is the One who goes with you. He will not leave you nor forsake you" (Deuteronomy 31:6). In my early, eager years, I mostly needed serenity. Today, I need courage. The Lord has been ever-present with me in both.

Today's prayer to continue: Thank You, Lord, for both serenity and courage. You know which one I need most today, so help me with . . .

October 30 A Little-Celebrated Special Day

Today is a very special day. October 30 is National Forgiveness Day. Begun in 1998, some attempts were made to change the name to Global Forgiveness Day and there are those who refer to it as that. The stated purpose of the day is: "To create an awareness and understanding of the power of love and the joy of forgiveness in producing good health, happiness, and stress-free living in the lives of individuals and our home, work, and worship environments." Various organizations will try to encourage people today to "take the pledge of forgiveness." In His Model Prayer, our Lord instructed us to both ask for forgiveness and grant forgiveness (Matthew 6:12; Luke 11:4). Of all people, who but Christians should celebrate a day of forgiveness? Not only should it be a Christian day, but everyday should be a day of forgiveness.

I challenge you to spend some time today making a list. Then take some time to both ask for forgiveness and grant forgiveness.

Today's prayer to continue: Lord I need forgiveness for myself today, but first I want to offer forgiveness to . . .

October 31 Facing Fear with Faith

I have always had fears. When I was a child, I feared being separated from my parents. When I was a teen-ager, I feared being unaccepted by my peers. When I was a college student, I feared not finding the perfect mate for life. When I was a seminary student, I feared not finding God's will for the perfect profession. When I was a young adult, I feared not raising my kids correctly. When I was a median adult, I feared being unsuccessful in ministry. When I was a senior adult, I feared retirement. As a retired adult, I fear uncertain health and financial issues. I have always had fears. So, it's a good thing that I discovered Psalm 56:3 early on: "Whenever I am afraid, I will trust in You." One reason I love the Psalms is that David never hesitated to share his fears. In fact, he may have shared them too often. Fear often makes us feel that we need God, and leads us to Him when we realize that we have no power to protect ourselves from impending dangers. I appreciate David teaching me that it is possible for fear and faith to occupy the mind at the same time. Like the Psalmist, I discovered trust in the Lord as the best antidote against fear. Join me today as we face our fears with faith.

Today's prayer to continue: Lord, I offer today's greatest fear to You in faith believing that You can . . .

November 1 Day of the Dead and the Living

Today is Día de Muertos. I first encountered Day of the Dead when we lived on the Mexican border, and later on a visit to Spain on this same November day. It is now practiced around the world in many cultures, often for a three-day holiday, October 31-November 2. On this holiday, traditions include building private altars, making face masks of the deceased with their names on them, consuming the favorite foods and beverages of the departed, and visiting graves, leaving possessions of the deceased. For many, it is a time of partying and celebration; for others, it is a time of introspection. While it is good to remember deceased loved ones, I prefer not to grieve, but rather celebrate their ongoing life. The Apostle Paul wrote, "I do not want you to be ignorant, brethren, concerning those who have fallen asleep, lest you sorrow as others who have no hope" (1 Thessalonians 4:13) or better paraphrased in "The Message," "Regarding the question, friends, that has come up about what happens to those already dead and buried, we don't want you in the dark any longer. First off, you must not carry on over them like people who have nothing to look forward to, as if the grave were the last word. Since Jesus died and broke loose from the grave, God will most certainly bring back to life those who died in Jesus" (1 Thessalonians 4:13-14, MSG). Because the hope of the believer goes beyond the grave we don't go about it in the same way as those who believe that death is the final end. Someday, it will be said that Dan Crawford is dead. Do not believe it. On that day, I will be more alive than I have ever been. Grieve earth's departure yes, but also celebrate new life in heaven.

Today's prayer to continue: As I remember those who have gone on to their heavenly reward, I give thanks, Lord, for the promise and hope of heaven, and the assurance of who is there . . .

November 2 Praying Through

As word spread of my radiation treatments, the responses began to flood in – via emails, Facebook entries, Twitter posts, cards, telephone calls, personal visits, text messages – everything from a simple, "Praying for you" to much more creative, imaginative expressions of support. One particular response caught my attention. "We're praying you through," a friend wrote. It caused me to remember what God said to His promised people, "Fear not, for I have redeemed you; I have called you by your name; you are Mine. When you pass through the waters, I will be with you; and through the rivers, they shall not overflow you. When you walk through the fire, you shall not be burned" (Isaiah 43:1-2). My collection of words comes up short when I try to explain what it feels like to pass through six weeks of five-day-a-week radiation treatments. Whether the cancer is severe or as simple as mine, words fail one in a time like this. What I find myself needing, perhaps as much as anything else, is accompaniment on the journey. I know God is with me. Beyond that, it really helps to know friends are with me also, praying me through. Have you prayed anyone through lately?

Today's prayer to continue: Lord, today I want to pray through for . . .

November 3 Praying for Pastors and Football Coaches

I am not interested in being an interim football coach, even though several universities have fired their coaches recently due to sexual misconduct. Having been interim pastor for churches with similar circumstances is enough. Fortunately, most of my more than twenty interims have been for good churches with good circumstances, but not all. Whether a pastor is guilty of sexual contact with children, extra-marital sexual relations, sexual harassment, mishandling of church funds for personal gain, or abuse of the position of pastor, sin is not limited to the secular. Nor is godly character limited to the church, I might add. I've known some very godly football coaches, at high school, university and professional levels. I know a young pastor whom God is using in amazing ways. He is personable, handsome, winsome, authoritative, and has a beautiful, sweet wife. Recently, I said to him, "I want you to know specifically how I am praying for you. I'm praying that God will lead you from temptation and deliver you from evil (Luke 11:4). Satan has a target on you as big as West Texas and there are females (and males) that are available for him to use to bring you down and destroy what God is doing through you." He looked at me like a deer caught in headlights and said, "Thanks." Every pastor needs someone praying a similar prayer for them. You don't necessarily need to tell your pastor (or a fellow pastor) that you are praying that prayer, but why not voice it this week. And, oh yes, pray for football coaches also.

Today's prayer to continue: When I think of temptation I want to ask your deliverance, Lord, for . . .

November 4 Explosivity

Listening to a so-called "football commentator" describe an explosive running back, I was surprised to hear a new word – "explosivity." Actually, it was not a real word, but an attempt to find a new way of describing a powerful running back. It reminded me of a Greek word – dunamis (from dunamai). It refers to intrinsic power or inherent ability, the power or ability to carry out some function, in some explosive way (might, strength, ability). From this Greek word, we get our English word, "dynamite." Acts 1:8 says "you shall receive power (dunamis; dynamite) when the Holy Spirit has come upon you; and you shall be witnesses to Me in Jerusalem, and in all Judea and Samaria, and to the end of the earth." This is the power which God used in our redemption, which God uses in our preservation, and which God will someday use in our glorification. Have you ever been in a power failure? Many spiritual power failures happen on Sunday mornings under steeples. When will we learn that programs, promotion, and pleasant personnel, are not enough? There must be power. J. Hudson Taylor affirmed this as follows: "Depend upon it. God's work, done in God's way will never lack God's supplies. All God's giants have been weak men who did great things for God because they reckoned on His being with them. God uses men who are weak and feeble enough to lean on Him." Paul assured Timothy and us "God has not given us a spirit of fear, but of power and love and discipline" (2 Timothy 1:7). You and I have dynamite-like power, given to us for the accomplishment of God's purpose in and through our lives. So, let's see some "explosivity" today!

Today's prayer to continue: There are things Lord, that I cannot do alone, so endue me with Your power today as I attempt to . . .

November 5 Is Praying "Thank You" Really Enough?

Lately, I've seen an interesting quote circulating. "If the only prayer you said in your whole life was, Thank you, that would suffice." Is that true? How does one reconcile this idea of only saying thank you, with Jesus' comment to Peter, "I have prayed for you" (Luke 22:32), Paul's frequent reminder to those to whom he wrote that he was praying for them, or James' instruction to "pray for one another" (James 5:16). A colleague, who took the time to count, says 78% of the prayers in the Bible are prayers for someone other than self. So, who made this questionable quote? The quote is attributed to Meister Eckhart, also known as Eckhart von Hochheim, a German theologian, philosopher and mystic, who lived in the late 1200s and early 1300s. In later life he was accused of heresy and brought up before the local Franciscan-led Inquisition, and tried as a heretic by Pope John XXII. I encourage you to pray lots of "thank you" prayers, but don't stop with the advice offered in a popular quote from a heretic theologian. Go ahead and practice biblical praying through intercession, petition, and supplication.

Today's prayer to continue: As thankful as I am, Lord, I also want to intercede today for . . .

November 6 Eating and Sinning

I've had a long-time food love affair with authentic Mexican beef tacos. More recently, I've started liking fish tacos. High on my non-love affair food list is cabbage. In fact, I only eat cooked cabbage with corn beef. Recently I was in a restaurant where I saw West Coast fish tacos on the menu. Being a long way from home and craving tacos, I ordered the West Coast variety. There were a few small bites of fish and a whole lot of raw cabbage. I should have reacted with a, "to each his own" opinion, but instead I reacted with a "why don't they list this in their menu as cabbage tacos with hidden fish bites." I know you may be wondering how I'm going to make a spiritual lesson out of this experience. I Corinthians 8:13 says, "If food makes my brother stumble, I will never again eat meat, lest I make my brother stumble." Application? I was so outraged at the cabbage tacos I continued to complain about it within my group, no doubt causing them to commit the sin/stumble of resentment, or perhaps the "I wish you would just shut-up" sin/stumble. So, lest I cause my brother to stumble, West Coast fish tacos will never again sit on my plate. Taco Bell today!

Today's prayer to continue: Lord, keep me from causing my brother to stumble, especially as I . . .

November 7 Making Melody in Your Heart

My mother used to worry about me since I exhibited zero musical skills. She actually bought me a trombone and hired a teacher. He showed me the positions on the slide and the sound each made, then quit during the second lesson, when I played "Whispering Hope" by ear. I sang in the church's youth choir because I was the pastor's son. I should have suspected something was wrong when the director suggested that I shouldn't feel forced to sing in the choir. Yet I love music. Most of my family and some of my best friends are musicians. My father was the only family member with less music talent than I, and he whistled everywhere he went. As a seminary professor some of my best friends were music professors. I enjoyed going to lunch with them because they didn't have to mix theology with their vegetables. For a segment of my life I awoke every morning with a song in my head. My mother said it was an answer to her prayer and claimed God had given me her song. I've actually put new words to existing hymn tunes, so I'm not totally music-less. Oliver Wendell Holmes, Jr. said, "Alas for those that never sing, but die with all their music in them!" I don't want to do that. Neither do you. So, bottle it up no longer. Somehow, someway, let your music out, "making melody in your heart to the Lord" (Ephesians 5:19).

Today's prayer to continue: I'm singing (or at least humming) for You today Lord, and the song I have in my heart is . . .

November 8 Pressing On in a Slow Burn

If I took time to list all the medical/dental issues I've had in the past two years, readers would get depressed and I'd go beyond my intent to share a one paragraph spiritual jump-start. Needless to say, it's good that I retired so I'd have time for all my medical/dental appointments. The problem is I keep getting invitations to speak/teach/consult/mentor and the medical/dental issues sometimes cause me to have to cancel my engagements, and I hate cancellations. I need to remember some advice from an early colleague who said when unwanted or impractical invitations come, open your calendar in front of you, cover both eyes, and say, "I don't see any way that I can accept your gracious invitation." But that is incredibly difficult for me to do, having been raised and mentored by workaholics with a degree of perfectionism mixed in. I confess I need help with this – when and how to say "no" especially when everything in my calling says, "say yes." Research is mixed on who first said, "I rather burn out than rust out" but I confess to be on a rather slow burn, struggling with Paul's advice, "Don't burn out; keep yourselves fueled and aflame" (Romans 12:11, MSG). So I will press on slowly– in between medical/dental appointments. In the words of Robert Frost, "I have promises to keep, and miles to go before I sleep."

Today's prayer to continue: Lord, please don't let me use my medical/dental condition as an excuse to keep me from ministry that You have ordained, such as . . .

November 9 The Sweet Aroma of Friendship

The medical procedures were not major, but were enough of a concern that I shared my anxiety with friends on social media. The three epidural injections were scheduled over a period of time and designed to relieve pain. I had opted to skip the pre-shot sedation. Sometimes, with no ill intent, "friends" increase the anxiety level. One friend replied, "I had the series of three; two out of the three weren't bad." Another commented, "A friend of mine was unsedated for the first shot, chose sedation the second time!" Still another testified, "Hope they work for you. I've had more than I can remember and none worked for me." One well-meaning friend wrote, "I hope this is your last injection." Wow! One could take that as sounding a bit terminal. But one long-time friend assured me all would be well and encouraged me to just breathe correctly, passing along a soon-to-be favorite Spanish phrase, "Huele la flor y sopla la vela." (Smell the flower, blow out the candle.). It reminded me of a proverb: "Perfume and incense bring joy to the heart, and the pleasantness of a friend springs from their heartfelt advice." (Proverbs 27:9). The procedures went quickly and well, and I once again thanked God for friends who were supportive, even if some shared more encouraging words than others.

Today's prayer to continue: Lord, today I am thankful for supportive friends, especially . . .

November 10 Productive Sleep

I confess that sometimes I fall asleep while praying on my bed at night. I have often felt guilty of this, especially when I wonder how excited God is about my prayer, when I can't even stay awake to complete it. On other occasions, I feel OK with it, since sometimes God responds to my prayer while I sleep, and I awake refreshed, with a new answer. After all, the Psalmist says that God, "Shall neither slumber nor sleep" (Psalm 121:4). Furthermore, since God is awake while we are sleeping, "He gives to His beloved even in his sleep" (Psalm 127:2). I'm not alone. For instance, as far back as the late 1800s Saint Thérèse of Lisieux, also known as "The Little Flower of Jesus" and one of the most popular Catholic saints of the early 20th century, wrote in her autobiographical manuscripts, "A Story of a Soul" that she often fell asleep while praying. She was of the opinion that like all parents, God probably loves His children best when they are asleep. She also popularized the theory that if you fall asleep while praying, your guardian angel finishes it for you. I'm not so sure about the angel part, but it is good to have company in falling asleep while praying. I've seen this idea on t-shirts, bumper stickers, coffee mugs, and posters, and it's been attributed to any number of authors/speakers. I'm not sure who originated it, but I like it: Some fall asleep while counting sheep, I prefer to fall asleep talking to the Shepherd. Give it a try hopefully you'll wake up with an answer.

Today's prayer to continue: Forgive me Lord, for falling asleep when praying, because I really wanted to talk with You about . . .

November 11 Responsibility and Reason

During my teaching years I often wondered why those who were saved as college students or older, were more aggressive with their evangelistic witness than those who were "born in church" and became believers as a child. Then later I suffered sciatic pain stemming from bulging disks in my lower back. For nine months I tried multiple cures – MRI, X-rays, meetings with specialists, epidural injections in the lower back, discussion with back surgeon, de-compression table, physical therapy, chiropractor visits, dry needling, cryotherapy, and various prescription pain meds. Nothing relieved my pain. One day I was introduced to deep tissue laser therapy and the pain was gone. I wanted to tell my story, and especially my healing, to everyone who would listen. Then I understood. Those of us who were raised in Christian homes, grew up in church, and became believers at an early age, never suffered the pain of sin as did those who were saved later in life, after sin had taken a toll on them. They had a more dramatic story to tell and told it with more intensity. Their pain was gone. They had found healing. Both groups were equally saved, but those who had suffered from the pain of sin, seemed more ready to talk of the cure and their relief. Both have a responsibility to share their story – "You shall be witnesses" (Acts 1:8); one group has a more deeply felt reason.

Today's prayer to continue: Lord, I understand the biblical instructions to be a witness, and today I want to find a way to witness to . . .

November 12 Coping with Conflict

Spiritual conflict! You have likely thought about this subject in terms of something that happens elsewhere–such as on the front lines of missionary service. After all, isn't the heat of the battle always on the front lines? It is until the front lines reach your front door. Conflict is no longer something for other people in other places. It is here and now, up close and personal, and at just the time when you were trying so hard to grow in your discipleship. How do you know when you are growing in discipleship? Measurement is not just in the number of hours spent in Bible study, the disciplines involved in your prayer life, the amount of money given to spiritual causes, the miles of missionary journeys you have traveled, or the number of persons to whom you have witnessed, but it is often in the way you respond to conflict. Just as true metal is tested in the fire (Proverbs 27:21, MSG), so the believer is tested in the conflicts encountered. Many a believer, successful in the eyes of the world, has failed in the face of conflict and thus negated much of the ministry entrusted to him or her. Conflict that could have propelled them toward God instead drove them away from God. Cope well with your conflicts this week.

Today's prayer to continue: Lord, use my conflicts as a means through which I might minister to . . .

November 13 What I Teach in my Class on Prayer

I was asked in a recent internet interview, "What key concepts (of prayer) do you present to your students; future leaders in the church?" I teach first that prayer is biblical, throughout the Bible from the first mention in Genesis to the final verses of Revelation, as well as modeled by Jesus to the extent that the disciples sought to be taught to pray (Luke 11:1). The most often used verb in the ministry of Jesus is not preach, teach, or heal, but pray. There is a popular bumper sticker that reads, "The Bible says it, I believe it, and that settles it!" Well the Bible teaches prayer and that settles it whether you believe it or not. I also teach the principles and methods of corporate prayer and personal prayer. I teach simple, often overlooked truths, like – We don't talk "to" God, we talk "with" God. And never talk to people about God until you've talked to God about the people. Then I always teach the global implications of prayer. If God's purpose is for the nations, then how can we pray for less? The bottom line, like with other disciplines, is that prayer is more caught than taught. So, in addition to my classroom teaching, I try to model a life of prayer for my students.

Today's prayer to continue: May I model a life of prayer for those around me, Lord, and while I am praying for the nations, I remember . . .

November 14 Jim Didn't Quit!

I first knew Jim as a seminary student in my urban evangelism practicum. We became good friends due to common interests. He was a walking baseball encyclopedia and a serious runner. I followed his career as a church planter in Ohio until he developed Parkinson's disease and took early retirement back to Fort Worth. But Jim didn't quit. He became Chaplain of the Fort Worth Cats minor league baseball team and invited me to assist him. When his voice faded he still didn't quit but began to write. Two books were produced plus a most interesting blog. Recently Jim's challenges (which he called opportunities) increased. Surgery on his neck was followed by a fall, resulting in emergency surgery followed by a stay in the intensive care unit. On Saturday, Jim's race ended. Cause of death - aspiration pneumonia – God's way of taking folks home who refuse to quit the race. Jim ran an outstanding race and he finished the course without quitting. Jim's life verse was, "I run in the path of your commands, for You have set my heart free" (Psalm 119:32). Heaven is now even more special because Jim is there.

Today's prayer to continue: Lord, I don't want to ever just quit, so help me today as I run the race with . . .

November 15 Loyalty, Where Have You Gone?

Events of recent days brought back to my memory a hymn from my youth. Anyone old enough to remember: "Loyalty, loyalty, loyalty for Christ?" Whether it's a university's athletic department switching conferences for the almighty TV dollar, a spouse switching partners for the lure of youth or status, or an institution cancelling the insurance premium coverage of its retirees for the sake of budget balancing, loyalty is a missing ingredient in today's society. The seeming disappearance of loyalty in society should be a warning to believers to revive both the word and the practice in their relationship to God. In the midst of His sermon on the mount, Jesus proclaimed, "No one can serve two masters; for either he will hate the one and love the other, or else he will be loyal to the one and despise the other. You cannot serve God and mammon" (Matthew 6:24). "'On to victory!' Cries our great Commander, on! We'll move at His command. We'll soon possess the land, through loyalty, yes loyalty to Christ." Revive it! Sing it! Live it!

Today's prayer to continue: More than anything else, Lord, I want to be loyal to You and I will demonstrate that today as I . . .

November 16 When Life Gives You a Parenthesis

A parenthesis is an explanatory word or clause inserted in a sentence for clarity, focus, direction, limitation. However, parentheses are not limited to grammar. Sometimes life gives you a parenthesis. Don't resist the parentheses of life. If Moses had rebelled at a forty-year dessert parenthesis, we might not have the Ten Commandments (Exodus 20:4-17). If Paul had resisted a prison parenthesis, we might not have the prison letters –

Ephesians, Colossians, Philippians, Philemon. If John had balked at a Patmos island parenthesis, we might not have The Revelation. When life gives you a parenthesis, God offers a lesson. It is a lesson that provides clarity, focus, direction, limitation. Accept it with gratitude. Pass it on with passion.

Today's prayer to continue: The most recent parenthesis in my life, Lord has been, and the lesson learned was . . .

November 17 Proper and Improper Celebration

I watched a celebration this week. It happened to be a victory parade for the champion Dallas Mavericks of the National Basketball Association. It could have been for any reason. Celebration is celebration, right? Maybe; maybe not. In the Old Testament, David announced, "I will celebrate before the Lord" (2 Samuel 6:21, NAS). Some translations read, "I will play music before the Lord." Being a non-musician, I like the idea of "celebrate" better. A few verses earlier it says, "David danced before the Lord" (2 Samuel 7:14). I don't think we were allowed to read that verse in my very conservative Southern Baptist upbringing. Worshipping in a Nigerian church in Benin, West Africa, I watched the people dance down the aisles to give their offering to God. To the other extreme, I was once a member of a church where the Pastor forbade clapping in the new worship center. Shouting "Amen" to his sermons was OK, just no clapping. I've been in so-called contemporary worship services where clapping was accompanied with whistling and shouting. The question is, how do we "properly celebrate before the Lord?" You say, as long as the celebration is sincere, it is proper. Is it then OK if one's sincere celebration, offends another?

Today's prayer to continue: Lord, may my worship honor only You and offend no one, since my worship is accompanied with . . .

November 18 Redeeming the Time

Yesterday was time-change Sunday. Maybe it's my advancing age, but I seem to like changes in time less, each time they happen. Today I will fly west and change time zones, only to fly back on Wednesday and change time zones again. Twice I have flown all the way around the world – once in three weeks, once in two weeks - and both times it took my body several weeks to catch up. Whatever the time zone or time frame in which we find ourselves, the Bible twice encourages us to be "redeeming the time" (Ephesians 5:15-16; Colossians 4:5). The word "redeem" means to make the most of every opportunity, to buy up those moments which others seem to throw away; steadily improving every present moment. Some of us remember "redeeming" savings stamps in years gone by. We traded in something of value (stamps that we carefully collected and attempted, usually without success, to lick into in a stamp book. The worst tasting glue in history was used on the back of those stamps as I remember, and they never stuck. That's why we used rubber bands around the books to hold the stamps in place). We took our stamp books to a Redemption Center and traded them in for something of greater value. The Bible encourages us to trade-in our time for a more valuable use of time, for spiritual time management. So, whatever the time zone, whatever the time change, while we've still got time on our minds, let's be in the time redeeming business.

Today's prayer to continue: Lord, when You desire to "redeem the time" for me, that means . . .

November 19 When the Spirit Departs

Something happened to Saul that I fear. 1 Samuel 16:14 says, "The Spirit of the Lord departed from Saul." We Baptists believe strongly that once a person is saved they are always saved - the eternal security of the believer. However once one is filled and controlled by the Holy Spirit, one does not always continue to be filled and controlled by the Spirit. One can lay their "all on the alter," then crawl off. In his wonderful devotional book, "This Day with the Master", Dennis Kinlaw writes, "A person who has known intimacy with the Holy Spirit can lose that intimacy. This is why it is never safe to find security in merely talking about the Holy Spirit without obeying him." Talk about the Holy Spirit? If you dare! Obey the Holy Spirit? Absolutely!

Today's prayer to continue: Lord, to "obey the Holy Spirit" today means for me to . . .

November 20 From This River

Last week I was near sea level in the Rio Grande Valley of Texas. Being in the Valley was "déjà vu all over again" for me. Having graduated from seminary and resigned the small church where I was pastor, my wife and I set up housekeeping in the this same Valley to work along this same river, primarily as the Baptist Campus Minister and Head of the Bible Department at Pan American University (now, the University of Texas at Pan American). In one of my first days in the Valley, I came across Psalm 72:8, "From the River to the ends of the earth." I know the Psalmist was likely referring to the Euphrates River and most definitely not referring to the Rio Grande River, but the verse lodged in my brain. Looking back, I have now been in 57 countries. God, who took me to the river, many years ago, has taken me to the "ends of the earth." I've seen the high places and the low places – geographically, emotionally, financially and spiritually – of this earth, all because I've tried to be a faithful follower. I recommend "following" to you today.

Today's prayer to continue: Lord, to "follow" You today means for me to . . .

November 21 Death, Where is Your Calendar?

Three days before her biggest moment on the ice, her mother died unexpectedly at the age of fifty-five. As a nation held its breath, the Canadian athlete skated twice in the Olympic Women's Figure Skating, winning a Bronze Medal in memory of her Mom. Death is never convenient. When my Grandfather died, I was in Mexico and could not be contacted for two days. When my Father-in-law died I was paged over the Public Address system at a professional baseball stadium. When my Mother died, we were in an ice storm of such size that her burial had to be delayed. My Father died thirty minutes before my birthday. While death never makes a previous appointment, it is always certain. When we die is less important than how we die. "It is appointed for men to die once and after this comes judgment" (Hebrews 9:27). When we die is up to God. How we die and face judgment is up to us. Live today as though it were your last. Celebrate, as though it were your first.

Today's prayer to continue: I'm not sure when I'm going to die, Lord, but You know, and that is enough to motivate me to . . .

November 22 Trust in God and Push Along

Be careful what you teach others. They may remember it. Sitting in a college Sunday School department at Coggin Avenue Baptist Church in Brownwood, Texas, I heard the department director, tell a warm, fuzzy story about a little Indian boy named

TIGAPA. His parents named him that because the letters in his name stood for "Trust in God and Push Along." Maybe because it matched my favorite Old Testament passage, Proverbs 3:5-6 or maybe because it was such a simple story, but last week I remembered it. My Howard Payne University cheerleading granddaughter sent me a text message as she was leaving Brownwood on a trip to the Christian Cheerleaders of America National Competition in North Carolina (during which they won the national championship in their division). I replied, "OK, TIGAPA," then explained the meaning. I am amazed that I remembered such a simple story. Makes me wonder (and fear) what my former students remember me saying. So be careful what you teach, lest someone remember it more than 50 years later.

Today's prayer to continue: I trust in You, Lord, and I want to "push along." For me today, that means . . .

November 23 Thanking a Teacher

She kept saying, "There's greatness in this class." Looking around my sixth grade classroom, I concluded she must be talking about me. I have no idea if anyone in that class accomplished greatness, but my sixth grade teacher motivated me to seek excellence in all my endeavors. So, when my first book was published I dedicated it to her. A few years later I received a phone call from her son-in-law. She had seen my book and assigned him to find me. Confirming me as the correct person, he put her on the phone. A feeble ninety year-old voice said, "I told my doctor I couldn't die till I found you, and thanked you for remembering me." After her long teaching career I was sure that many former students had returned to thank her, and I expressed that to her on the phone. Her reply broke my heart. "No" she said, "You're the first one." The Bible says, "In everything give thanks" (1 Thessalonians 5:18). Surely that includes the influence of sixth grade teachers. Is there someone in your life that you need to thank? You may be the only one who does.

Today's prayer to continue: Lord, this reminds me of someone who had an impact on my life and I want to thank You for . . .

November 24 Expressions of Gratitude

"Your sermons have meant so much to my husband since he lost his mind." Those words were shared with a former seminary student of mine from one of his church members. In my laughter, I remembered a statement shared with me in the early days of my ministry. Following the morning worship service, I was told, "Every sermon you preach is better than the next one." Think about it. Not good. What do you say to one who ministers to you? One critic said to their pastor, "Next time you have a weak sermon, yell louder." Thanksgiving is upon us. How will you express your feelings for your minister? Hopefully with none of the above. I assure you, the words you choose will mean less than the attitude with which you share them. God-called ministers deserve expressions of gratitude every day, but Thanksgiving affords you an opportunity to say something special to them. "Thanksgiving Day comes, by statute, once a year; to the honest man it comes as frequently as the heart of gratitude will allow." So wrote Edward Sandford Martin, founder of the "Harvard Lampoon." It is a time of remembrance with gratitude. Short memory makes thanksgiving difficult. Good memory makes thanksgiving inevitable. Think about it. Surely the encouragement to "be thankful" in Colossians 3:15 includes being thankful for those who minister to you. How will you express your gratitude this year?

Today's prayer to continue: In order to express my gratitude to those who minister to me, Lord, I need to . . .

November 25 Thanksgiving – A Shared Blessing

A few Thanksgivings ago I re-read Paul's comments in Philippians 1:3, "I thank my God upon every remembrance of you . . ." Then I decided to do an out-of-the-ordinary thing, which has become an annual ritual. I selected a few people for whom I had been especially thankful that year and let them know it as a part of my Thanksgiving observance. While I was thankful to God, I also wanted these special people to know of my gratitude for them. I assumed it would be a private thing and the blessing would be mostly mine. About the third year I did this, one of the recipients of my Thanksgiving messages was a former student of mine who was successfully serving as pastor in a town of some long-time friends. Although they were not members of his church these friends shared with me the high regard in which my former student was held by all in the town. I simply wrote him and thanked him. The Sunday before Thanksgiving, I challenged the members of the church where I was serving as Interim Pastor to join me in this practice of sharing gratitude. Two Sundays following Thanksgiving, the "small, small world" syndrome kicked in. My former student, the recipient of my thanksgiving letter, was the pastor of my church member's mother. On the Sunday after Thanksgiving, my former student had shared my letter in the pulpit as an example of how to add meaning to Thanksgiving. And word spread. My Thanksgiving blessing was no longer mine alone. Why not join me this year. Select a few special people and let them know your gratitude . . . and don't forget to also thank God for the role these special people have played in your life.

Today's prayer to continue: Lord, I need to express thanksgiving today to . . .

November 26 Making an "F" on Thanksgiving

I made an "F" on Thanksgiving again. I can't seem to do any better than family, food, and football. I overdosed on all of them, even to the point of digging out my old model train set to show my grandson, who was recently enamored with trains. My Dad attached my model train village to two large pieces of plywood, so it could be stored in the attic in the "off-season." On the day after Thanksgiving each year we would bring the train set down and set it up for Christmas. I could always count on Santa adding to my train collection. I still have most of that collection. Wonder what old 40s and 50s style Lionel trains are worth these days? Probably worth a fortune. There's another Thanksgiving "F" – fortune. Thanksgiving memories! I have collected a fortune in memories. Repeatedly the idea of being "called to remembrance" appears in the Bible, as in Ezekiel 23:21. So, before we get too far removed from Thanksgiving, let me call you to remembrance for a fortune of times, events, and people, for which you are thankful.

Today's prayer to continue: Events Lord. I need to express thanks to You for the following events in my life . . .

November 27 One Out of Ten

In most circumstances, one out of ten is not very good. A student who answers one question correctly out of ten will fail the test. A quarterback who completes one pass out of ten is most likely on the losing team. A salesperson who completes one sale out of ten good prospects may need a second income. A church member who attends only one Sunday out of ten is not considered a faithful member. Jesus experienced this unwanted ratio on at least one occasion. In Luke 17:11-19, ten lepers cried out to him for healing. They were outcasts, forced to live outside the city walls. The law required them to cry out, "Unclean" when someone came within a few feet of them. They often were forced to wear bells on the bottom of their robes to warn unsuspecting persons of the danger of being exposed to leprosy. Yet cries offered to Jesus were never unheeded, nor are they today. Jesus healed them and sent on their way. Only one returned to express thanks. The other nine went merrily and ungratefully on their way. It seems the thankful are often in the minority. We've observed Thanksgiving Day. Were you a part of the thankful minority or the ungrateful majority?

Today's prayer to continue: Lord, I want to always be counted in the grateful minority, so once again, I thank You for . . .

November 28 A Gratitude Attitude

I'm not real sure who originated the phrase, "An attitude of gratitude," but many a preacher has preached a sermon with that title, most delivering it around the Thanksgiving season. One source attributes the origin of the phrase to motivational speaker Zig Ziglar, who said, "The more you recognize and express gratitude for the things you have, the more things you will have to express gratitude for." An internet search reveals numerous books with this phrase in the title. Brian Tracy, a Canadian entrepreneur, public speaker, author and development trainer, well known through his seminar training and training audios said, "Develop an attitude of gratitude, and give thanks for everything that happens to you, knowing that every step forward is a step toward achieving something bigger and better than your current situation." I am a strong believer in giving credit where credit is due. So I prefer to site the origin of the phrase with the Apostle Paul who wrote, "Let the message about the Messiah dwell richly among you, teaching and admonishing one another in all wisdom, and singing psalms, hymns, and spiritual songs, with gratitude in your hearts to God" (Colossians 3:16, HCSB). But that's enough research. How about if we practice an increased gratitude attitude today?

Today's prayer to continue: Lord, for me to have a gratitude attitude today, I will need your help in . . .

November 29 Given and Required

American Thanksgiving has come and gone. We did what most Americans did – slept late, ate big, watched football on TV, took a nap, ate again, watched more football, thanked God for the blessings, and went to bed feeling full. All the while, more than 800 million people in the world did not have enough to eat, and one in nine people on our planet went to bed hungry on Thanksgiving. The majority of the world did not watch TV on Thanksgiving because a majority of people in the world do not own a TV. With two-thirds of the world not claiming to be Christian, the majority did not thank God for Thanksgiving blessings. Approximately 100 million of the world's population went to bed homeless on Thanksgiving night. While all these statistics might make us feel guilty, we most definitely ought to feel blessed. But a comment from Jesus haunts my Thanksgiving memories. In speaking of those who were blessed and faithful, Jesus said, "To whom much is given, from him much will be required" (Luke 12:48). Thanksgiving is once again gone. Much was given. The season of giving approaches. Much is required.

Today's prayer to continue: Lord, I have been given much, and I know I need to give accordingly. So today, I want to give . . .

November 30 Post-Thanksgiving Praying

For 364 days each year many people complain to God that roses have thorns. On Thanksgiving Day, they thank God that thorns have roses. Why do we do that? Why do we not thank God all year around for everything? I read the other day about a man who complained to God because his car was slow starting one morning, making him late for an appointment. The reply was that the car starting slow was delayed because God was preventing the man from being involved in a twelve car pile-up on the freeway. I remember missing a flight from Florida to New Orleans a few years ago because the person driving me to the airport was slow and uncertain of all the correct turns. While I was waiting on the next flight and telling God how upset I was, I learned that the flight I missed had run off the run-way during its landing in New Orleans, injuring several passengers. Now, listen to Paul talk about a 365 day thanksgiving prayer, "We give thanks to God always for you all, making mention of you in our prayers" (1 Thessalonians 1:2). Thanksgiving prayers have now been voiced. Keep it up!

Today's prayer to continue: Lord I am thankful for the times You have blessed and protected me, and I did not even know about it. What I do know about You is . . .

December 1 The Uncommon Use of Common Sense

In my many years of attending faculty meetings, I found them to be both informative and boring. Every so often something would happen that enlivened the meeting. In one such meeting during a curriculum discussion a favorite colleague of mine said, "What we really need is a course in common sense." Unaware of how such a course would fit into a theological curriculum, there was silence in the room. Then he added, "Unfortunately, we have no one on the faculty qualified to teach the course." A few of us laughed – partly because it was funny and partly because he was at least partially correct. A frequently observed anonymous quote seen on social media sites these days says, "Common sense is a flower that doesn't grow in everyone's garden." Well said. I often said to students in my classes, it doesn't matter how much theology you learn here, if you miss three things, you will fail in ministry – how to pray, how to use common sense, and how to laugh at yourself. Unfortunately, I've seen far too much failure due to a lack of common sense. While earlier versions use the word "wisdom" *The*

Message paraphrases Colossians 3:16, "Instruct and direct one another using good common sense." The use of common sense is far too uncommon, and the failure to use it, is unbiblical. Think about it!

Today's prayer to continue: Lord, common sense tells me that today I need to . . .

December 2 Background Checks and Second Chances

When I received the e-mail informing me I had been nominated to the Alumni Association Board of Directors of my alma mater, Howard Payne University in Brownwood, Texas, I only had one question - Do they do background checks for these positions? Like many, my college years were not the brightest lights on my tree. New found freedom resulted in too low grades. Too many creative ideas resulted in too many pranks. Cheap gasoline prices (I actually pumped it at $14.9 per gallon on one occasion) resulted in too many road trips. Late night card games resulted in a few missed early morning classes. But what great memories and what great friends I made. Now it appeared one of those "friends" had nominated me for the Alumni Association Board. I owe much to my school. I spent four very formative years there and somehow, in spite of myself; I learned much that served me well later in life. I majored in Bible and learned early that the Bible is a book of second chances. I remember an Old Testament professor who thrilled us with his version of Jonah and the line from Jonah 3:1 stuck with me, "Now the word of the Lord came to Jonah the second time." I'm glad I've been given a second chance to make a contribution to my alma mater. Aren't you glad God speaks a second time, and a third, and a fourth . . . in spite of the background checks?

Today's prayer to continue: Thank You, Lord for speaking to me several times on the same subject. Today I need to do something about it, perhaps . . .

December 3 Mountains and Canyons

I finally did it. I took a week's vacation that was not connected in any way to a ministry assignment. It took me more than forty years in the ministry before I accomplished this feat. I know, I know. Save the sermons! I've preached those same sermons to others. But I finally did it. My wife and I took the Copper Canyon Train tour into Mexico - a train ride through six canyons, five of which are larger than the Grand Canyon. As I sat on the hotel balcony, more than 8000 feet above sea level, overlooking the canyon at sunset, I remembered a passage of Scripture. I guess you can take me out of a ministry situation, but you can't take the ministry out of me. The Psalmist declared of God, "Your righteousness is like the great mountains; Your judgments are a great deep" (Psalm 36:6). While God's righteousness is as easily visible as the mountains in all their majesty and strength, God's judgments are often as unknown to us as the secrets of the deep canyons between the mountains. Charles Spurgeon wrote, "God's dealings with men are not to be fathomed by every boaster who demands to see a why for every wherefore." While we are privileged to walk by sight in the high mountains, we must walk by faith through the deep canyons. That's a good thought for today since it could be filled with both mountains and canyons. Walk on!

Today's prayer to continue: May lessons learned on the mountain tops, be applied in the canyons of my life, Lord. Especially today, as I . . .

December 4 Why I Like Senior Adults

I spoke recently at a Senior Adult Conference. As one who spent a few years serving on university campuses in collegiate ministry, then a few more years teaching at the graduate school level, I now find myself doing senior adult ministry things. Guess I can throw away my youth revival sermons. Now I can understand the conclusions drawn by another former student minister who is currently a senior adult minister. He listed reasons why he enjoyed working with senior adults more than working with students, and I've added a couple to his list: (1) you don't get phone calls after 10:00 p.m.; (2) you never have to deal with angry parents; (3) you never have to counsel with an unwanted pregnancy; (4) you can use the same materials over again and not fear they will remember, and (5) they're supposed to be on drugs. Whatever your age group, I hope you can laugh at yourself today. In the Bible you can only arrive at the seventeenth chapter of Genesis before reading, "Then Abraham fell on his face and laughed" (Genesis 17:17, NKJV). And the Psalmist proclaimed, "He who sits in the heavens shall laugh" (Psalm 2:4, NKJV).

Today's prayer to continue: Someone said, Lord, that laughter is a good medicine. I need to laugh today at . . .

December 5 Honored with Honors

It seems like only a few nights ago, I was honored to substitute and take my young granddaughter to the Father/Daughter Banquet at our church. I remember it well. She was wearing her Strawberry Shortcake dress with the ever-present bow in her hair. I must have taken a Rip Van Winkle type nap, because she recently graduated from college – with honors. Now she's planning a wedding that I'll be honored to officiate. Where did those years go – years filled with so much fun and meaning – yet so quickly gone? I really want to seize the day, carpe diem, as stated in 23BC by the poet, Horace. Yet I fear that I may doze off again and who knows what will be there when I awake? So I look back with fond memories while time moves forward with furious speed. Time is good. It is what God created on the first day of the creative process (Genesis 1:3-5). Managing time is what is so difficult. Author, speaker, and pastor, John Maxwell stated, "Time management is an oxymoron. Time is beyond our control, and the clock keeps ticking regardless of how we lead our lives. Priority management is the answer to maximizing the time we have." So my priority is to seize the day and be honored with honors.

Today's prayer to continue: Lord, this is a special day, simply because You made it and gave it to me. Using my time wisely today, I want to . . .

December 6 Determining Attendance at a Funeral

I attended a funeral at my home church last week – largest funeral I've seen there. All parking lots full thirty minutes before service, all seats on lower floor full fifteen minutes before service, standing room only in a 1000 seat auditorium. Who was this, some famous politician? No, in fact the funeral home directors commented that the only funeral they had seen that was as large was for the former mayor of our city. Was this a famous entertainer, sports figure, military hero? No. It was the funeral service for a career school teacher/educator who was a faithful church member. When various groups were asked to stand, the largest group was that of former students and colleagues who had known her through her education career. Amazing that one so young (she died of cancer at age 52), could accumulate so many friends. Earlier that same day I had attended the quarterly lunch meeting of seminary retirees, where my friend and fellow faculty member, Dr. Jack MacGorman, who is almost 94, said to the group, "God can do mighty things through little people who serve a big God." In terms of status, the world would have considered the deceased educator, to be one of the "little people," but the attendance at her funeral proved it to be different. She faithfully served people on behalf of her "big God" and they came to pay their respects, to celebrate her life; grieving, but, not "like the rest of mankind, who have no hope" (1 Thessalonians 4:14, NIV). I've always said that the number of people who attend your funeral will be largely determined by the weather. On a cloudy, overcast, day, I was proved wrong once again.

Today's prayer to continue: Lord, I would like to be remembered by those who attend my funeral as a . . .

December 7 Quietly Pointing to the Victor

More than eight million people did Internet searches for John 16:33 in a four hour period. Would you believe it was during a football game? Last Saturday, during the Southeastern Conference Football Championship game, Florida Quarterback Tim Tebow had the scripture reference painted on his face, under his eyes. Every time the cameras zoomed in on his face, the scripture reference was clearly visible. Better than a guy in the end zone wearing a multi-colored hair wig and holding a scripture reference sign, better than an airplane flying over pulling a scripture streamer, better than a prima donna, beating his chest and pointing heavenward after a touchdown, this was an All-American Quarterback, a former Heisman Trophy winner, a role model deluxe, quietly displaying his faith. Son of missionary parents and frequent missions volunteer, Tebow displayed to the watching world, a message on the source of inner peace. He lost the game, but pointed to the ultimate victor, who has "overcome the world."

Today's prayer to continue: Lord, may I be found faithful today in displaying my faith as I . . .

December 8 Bright, Shiny Faces

Surely some of you remember the children's song we used to sing first thing in the morning: "Good morning to you, Good morning to you. We're all in our places with bright, shiny faces. Good morning to you." I had no strong feelings either way about the song, but I remember wondering if my face was really shining?

Then I began to hear phrases like, "Her face was radiant (radiant: sending out light; shining or glowing brightly) and, "He was beaming (beaming: shining brightly). Seems a bright, shiny face was one that shed light into the darkness around it. A few years later I came across a Bible verse about a shining face. It was actually part of the first benediction in the Bible, a benediction being a declaration of blessing from God upon His people. In this benediction prayer, spoken first to Aaron, and repeated at the conclusion of worship services through the ages, Moses said, "The Lord make His face shine upon you" (Numbers 6:25). The shining face of God was desired as opposed to God hiding His face, as with Job (Job 13:24), and with Israel (Deuteronomy 31:17-18); and as opposed to God's face being against someone (Leviticus 17:10, Psalm 34:16). I don't know about you, but I pray that God's face will shine upon me today to brighten my path, to give me direction, and to reflect off of me on to others.

Today's prayer to continue: May Your presence shine on me today Lord so that I can reflect it on to ...

December 9 Not Everything is a God Thing

In a group meeting we were discussing the negative features of a recent experience. One member blurted out, "It was a God thing!" When reminded of still other negative features, the self-appointed super-saint insisted, "Everything is a God thing!" I am aware of God's sovereignty, omniscience, omnipresence, and even the fact that it can be a God thing in the midst of multiple negative features, but "everything" is not a God thing. My first question would be, why did Paul label satan, "the god of this age" (2 Corinthians 4:4) if some "things" are not satan's? My second question would be, why could Jesus "do no mighty work" in Nazareth (Mark 6:5) if His visit there was totally His "thing." My third question would be what about murder (Exodus 20:13), which is clearly not one of God's "things" (commandments). You can't take a violation of God's law and suddenly make it God's "thing," My point is, with God's gift of free will, in order for there to be "God things," there must also be "not God things." That does not leave God out of "things," but simply means, He will not violate His own gift of freedom of choice, but will allow negative features to control some experiences, making them not His thing. What we do know is that "all things work together for good to those who love God, to those who are the called according to His purpose" (Romans 8:28).

Today's prayer to continue: Today I want to celebrate God's things and try my best to resist those that are not God's things, such as . . .

December 10 Faltering Near the Finish Line

What causes people not to finish well? The question lodged in my mind following an illustration used by my pastor in a recent sermon. Noah, served God faithfully, followed God's instructions to the letter (or maybe to the cubit), saved his family, then ended in a drunken stupor (Genesis 9:20-21). Jacob dreamed of God's promise and vowed a powerful vow to God (Genesis 28:10-22) yet later worshiped false idols in his home (Genesis 35:1-4). God described David as "a man after My own heart, who will do all My will" (Acts 13:22), yet David had an adulterous affair with Bathsheba and arranged the murder of her husband, Uriah (2 Samuel 11:1-4). Sarah served God faithfully, but in her advanced years, when told by God that she would bear a child, laughed at God in faithless doubt (Genesis 18:12). Gideon lived up to his name which meant "mighty warrior" and was listed in the great hall of fame of the faithful in Hebrews 11:32 yet he made an object of worship out of the gold won in battle (Judges 8:27) and bore seventy sons from his multiple wives and concubine (Judges 8:30-

31). Even the Apostle Paul had a fear that "when I have preached to others, I myself should be disqualified" (1 Corinthians 9:27). Nor is this just a biblical issue. There are ample examples of this late-life descent in modern day spirituality. Is the cause physiological, psychological, emotional, mental, spiritual, or all of the above? I'm not sure, but it has become my daily prayer to finish more like Paul who wrote, "I have finished the race, I have kept the faith" (2 Timothy 4:7).

Today's prayer to continue: As much as I want to be found faithful today, Lord, I also want to finish well, especially in the area of . . .

December 11 Introductions

I've had more than my share of introductions in life. From the pastor who read the entire seminary produced biographical information – both pages, to the man who said, "This man needs no introduction to us. So, here he is." Some times I've had to live up to my introductions, other times I've had to further introduce myself in the midst of my presentation in order for an illustration to be understood. Occasionally I've needed no introduction, like I got (or failed to get) preaching recently in my home church. It is told that the well-known boxer, Joe Lewis, was having difficulty checking into a hotel once and exclaimed, "If you have to tell 'em who you is, you ain't." Perhaps the first introduction in history was that of Adam introducing Eve, (obviously to no one in particular) in Genesis 2:23, "Adam said: 'This is now bone of my bones and flesh of my flesh; She shall be called Woman, because she was taken out of Man.'" The more famous biblical introduction was that of John the Baptist to his followers, when he saw Jesus and announced, "Behold! The Lamb of God who takes away the sin of the world" (John 1:29)! How do you want to be introduced? Better question, how do you want to be introduced at the final judgment before Almighty God? How about in the words of the early hymn text by James M. Gray, President of Moody Bible Institute, "Only a sinner, saved by grace." Or the later musical words by Gloria Gaither, "I'm just a sinner, saved by grace."

Today's prayer to continue: Lord, not only do I want to be faithful introducing You to others, I want to be introduced as . . .

December 12 Remembering Home Again

Bellmead, Texas – the home of my early childhood. Thomas Wolfe was correct, you can't go home again, but you can go through what's left of home again. I did that recently. The house where we lived is no longer livable. Many of the houses my grandfather built are gone. The family grocery story is no longer a grocery store. The school I attended is old, dilapidated, and no longer a school. Life was simpler then. I learned to ride a bicycle – without a helmet. I drank from a garden hose without fear of disease. I rode in the grocery store delivery truck without a seat belt. That's right, we delivered groceries to the homes, went in the back door, and put the milk in the refrigerator. I watched in amazement when a cow gave birth to a calf, just outside my bedroom window. The place where my cousins and I played football after Christmas lunch was grown up in weeds. Social media meant face-to-face conversations at the Post Office, Barber Shop or Café. Every night, the Lone Ranger did good deeds and ended his radio program by riding off into the sunset with a hearty "Hi-Yo Silver! Away!" Those days live only in precious memories. Life has moved on. I wonder what Jesus expected to experience when he took His disciples back to his boyhood home of Nazareth. I doubt He was expecting His home town to be "offended at Him."(Matthew 13:57) At least no one in Bellmead, Texas appeared to be offended at me. I doubt if anyone even remembered me. But I did go through what was left of home again, and thanked God for the wonderful gift of memory.

Today's prayer to continue: Reading this today, Lord, causes me to remember with gratitude . . .

December 13 The Full Presence of God

I was new on the Seminary faculty. He had been around awhile. I was honored that he and his wife invited my wife and I to their home for dinner. The meal was delicious and the fellowship around the table was even better. Then he said he wanted to show me something. Down the hall we went into what was originally designed to be a middle bedroom. As we entered the room he said, "This is my prayer room." In the room there was only a kneeling bench – an old pulpit that some students had cut lower so that the reading area was at eye level for one kneeling on the attached bench. On the reading area sat an open Bible and a note pad. The room was illumined with only indirect light. Stepping from the hallway into the prayer room, was an experience I could only liken to how the biblical priests must have felt when they entered the Holy Place of the Tabernacle/Temple (1 Kings 8:10-11). Speechless, all I could think was, "This is different, like entering the very presence of God." Then I thought, why not? If the only activity ever experienced in this room, was communion with God, then the special Shekinah glory, the presence of God, never left the room. Thus, it was felt upon entering. But it was just a suburban bedroom! My later reflection was that there is no holy ground, just ground made holy because we repeatedly meet God there. I expressed appreciation for allowing me to see the room, and we went back to the table for dessert, but I was not the same. Thank you, T.W. Hunt for your special friendship. Thank you for helping me to see more clearly, and to know more fully! We will miss you but rejoice that as you bow before our Holy God in a place prepared for your eternal dwelling; you now see and know the full presence (1 Corinthians 12:12).

Today's prayer to continue: Lord, I sincerely want to feel Your presence in my life today, especially as I . . .

December 14 A Christmas Prayer

One of my prayers this Christmas revolves around a word, actually two words. These two words make all the difference in how Christmas is observed. For many people, Christmas is an event – by definition, an observable occurrence, a gathering. It is an event marked by parties, gifts, parades, decorations, family gatherings, etc. While these event-related activities are often involved, Christmas for others is an advent. Advent comes from the Latin word *adventus* meaning coming or arrival. Christians celebrate Christmas as the arrival of the Christ-child, the world's Savior and Lord. While the actual date for the physical arrival of Jesus is debatable, the observance of that birth is at Christmas time. *Adventus* is the translation of the Greek word *parousia* which appears 24 times in the New Testament, 17 of which are used in reference to the second coming of Christ, as when the disciples asked Jesus for a sign of His second coming in Matthew 24:3. For Christians, the season of Advent serves as a reminder both of the first coming of Jesus, His physical birth, as well as Christ's return from Heaven. How you celebrate Christ's second coming, depends largely on how you celebrate His first coming – event or advent. So, for the sake of your preparation for the second coming of the Lord, I pray that you celebrate His first coming as an advent, not simply as an event.

Today's prayer to continue: Thanks Lord for Your first advent, which we will celebrate soon. In order to be better prepared for Your second advent, I will . . .

December 15 Do You Sing What I Sing?

As much as I love singing Christmas carols, I confess to not paying much attention to the meaning of the words at times. I saw a cartoon the other day that brought that truth home to me. There was a picture of the manger, baby Jesus and the wise men. In the picture were the words of the 1962 hymn, "Do You Hear What I

Hear" – "A child, a child shivers in the cold. Let us bring Him silver and gold." The caption underneath the picture was one of reality – "Couldn't you just have brought him a blanket?" The wise men gave gold, frankincense, and myrrh (Matthew 2:11). What will you give to the Lord this Christmas? We annually give monetary Christmas offerings for missions, for the homeless, for goodwill, and for numerous other worthy causes. The better question is, will what you give to the Lord this year be something of practical value or just more monetary value? Perhaps this Christmas, in addition to "silver and gold" we could give Him time and talent, work and worship. Only when our service matches our silver and our going matches our gold, can we hear what we should hear and sing what we should sing.

Today's prayer to continue: This Christmas season, Lord, I want to give You . . .

December 16 My Christmas List

The web site was entitled, "Top Five Christmas Gifts." Being a sucker for top ten and top five type lists, I quickly opened the site only to discover that it listed sixteen items and then asked me to vote on which five I wanted. I quickly ruled out the wedding dress, women's jewelry, the hair straightener, and lingerie. The other twelve really contained nothing I needed or wanted. So I decided to make my own list of gifts I'd like to give to my faithful readers this Christmas. Obviously I wish for you the greatest gift of all and join Paul in thanking God for the "indescribable gift" of Jesus (2 Corinthians 9:15). Beyond that, I wish for you a hot breakfast that you don't have to prepare, an unexpected email, Facebook post, text message, or phone call from a long-ago friend, being able to get in a drive-thru lane without the person in front of you needing to transact business or place an order for a small army, surviving all 35 TV football bowl games and then remembering who played in the first five, finding a guest in your favorite seat at church and having the grace to greet them rather than glare at them, and finally, showing gratitude for all your Christmas gifts even if you don't know why you received it or what exactly it is.

Today's prayer to continue: As I make my Christmas gift list this year, Lord, may I remember to give You . . .

December 17 What's in a Baby's Name?

I was named for two Baptist Pastors and the Chief of Police. My great, great Grandmother had five names. My daughter was named for a favorite aunt and me. My son was named for his two grandfathers. An international friend changed his name to Fred because when his foreign name was translated into English, his name was "Shovel." A popular book is entitled, *40,001 Best Baby Names*. Jesus had hundreds of names and titles, four of which were given to Him several hundred years before His birth. Isaiah said, "His name will be called Wonderful Counselor, Mighty God, Everlasting Father, Prince of Peace" (Isaiah 9:6). How are you feeling during this Christmas season? Are you confused or perplexed? Jesus is a Counselor who is wonderful. Do you feel weak or powerless? Jesus is a God who is mighty. Are you feeling bound by time or space? Jesus is a Father who is everlasting. Are you stressed or anxious? Jesus is a Prince who is peaceful. What's in a baby's name? All that we need.

Today's prayer to continue: Thank You Lord for being all Your names suggests You to be. I am especially drawn today to your name of . . .

December 18 What to do With Glory

One word I hear frequently spoken and sung at Christmas is the word "glory." Among other places, it comes from John 1:14. After describing the origin of Jesus the scripture states, "We beheld His glory, the glory as of the only begotten of the Father . . ." Later Jesus prayed that those whom the Father had given to Him might "behold My glory (John 17:24). Like with many subjects, we sometimes speak and sing that which sounds good but has little meaning to us. Why do we behold the glory of Jesus? I don't think it is because He needs it. If you owned the cattle on a thousand hills, the earth and the fullness thereof, would you need glory? Maybe we speak and sing glory to Jesus because He is the only one who knows what to do with glory when it comes His way. I certainly don't know how to handle glory when it comes my way, do you? Mostly, I just get the "big head" when someone tries to glorify me with earthly praises. While He doesn't need it, Jesus receives glory and encourages us to glorify Him even more. If Jesus doesn't need glory and yet encourages us to glorify Him, the benefit must be for us. Now there's a glorious Christmas thought.

Today's prayer to continue: I need to glorify You today Lord, so please accept . . .

December 19 The Cost of Christmas

Christmas is a costly celebration. It seems as though everyone from the lending institutions, to the counseling offices to the travel agencies makes money off Christmas. And the cost escalates each year. I read recently that if the gifts given in "The Twelve Days of Christmas" were purchased just once – from a partridge in a pear tree to a dozen drummers drumming - in today's markets, the cost would be in excess of $25,000 plus tax. Even the eight maids would earn minimum wage for milking. I was in a church once that spent an enormous amount of money on "The Greening of Christmas." I couldn't help but think about the real green in their greening. Come to think of it, Christmas has never been inexpensive. Think of the cost of that first Christmas (or at least the birth of our Lord, from which we derived the Christmas celebration). There were government costs due to the required census registration, travel costs for Mary and Joseph, likewise for the shepherds and the wise men, innkeepers' costs, the cost of pigeons and doves for consecration in Jerusalem, gifts from the wise men, the cost of an unexpected trip to Egypt. And when the earthly costs are tabulated, add in the cost to the Father in the giving of His only Son to mostly ungrateful humanity. And you thought your expenses were high at Christmas! "Thanks be unto God for His indescribable gift" (2 Corinthians 9:15).

Today's prayer to continue: Lord, since You paid the cost of my salvation, I want to share the cost of celebrating Your birth this Christmas by . . .

December 20 Another Way

Did you ever plan a trip and have someone or something rearrange your well-made plans? It happened to the wise men. I'm not sure how well-made their plans were but their instructions were clear. Herod told them to, "Go and search diligently for the young child" (Matthew 2:8). Somewhere along their star-directed way, they picked up a few gifts. They should have let their wives do the shopping for them. Gold is not a bad gift for any occasion. Frankincense was OK assuming no one was allergic to it. But myrrh was a commonly used funeral ointment. Hardly a gift fit for a new-born child. You know the rest of the story, or do you? Have you ever noticed the interesting words at the end of the account? "They departed for their own country another way" (Matthew 2:12). No one, wise or unwise, ever has a genuine gift-giving encounter with Jesus and goes back the same way. When we meet Him and give Him our lives, we can never walk the same path again. Those things we once loved we now despise. Those things we once distrusted, we now love. These two words may be the most descriptive of all the language used to explain the conversion experience and the subsequent following of Jesus. "Another way." The wise men experienced a divine interruption, followed by a divine revelation and then followed by divine directions. "Another way." In this season we celebrate the birth of our Lord. Are your gifts to Him appropriate for a Child/King? And having encountered Him again this Christmas, which way will you go?

Today's prayer to continue: The only way I desire to go is Your way, Lord. Guide me today to walk in . . .

December 21 A Pin Dropped

We stood at the very back of the magnificent Mormon Tabernacle in Salt Lake City while a tour host dropped a pin on the platform. In the silence and the semi-darkness, we clearly heard the sound of the pin hitting the floor. Such are the amazing acoustics of the Tabernacle. For four hundred years there had been silence. It's called the inter-biblical period, the time between the Old Testament and The New Testament. It was a time when no prophet spoke, no preacher preached, no writer wrote. It was a time of dark quietness. Then God dropped a pin. It was the birth of a baby in a quiet place, in a semi-dark manger, on a silent night. Such were God's acoustics, that all mankind eventually heard the angelic announcement of the birth of the long-awaited Messiah, the world's Savior. It was as Isaiah had prophesied, "The people who walked in darkness have seen a great light" (Isaiah 9:2). As the years have gone by that Light, that Good News, has been allowed to grow dim and quiet. Many people ignore it for eleven months out of the year then in December, they respond once again to the good news of a baby's birth. Now, once again, we enter the Christmas season, when we celebrate the birth of our Lord Jesus and once again much of the human race pauses in an attempt to be human again. Celebrate the season and the Savior it serves.

Today's prayer to continue: I know people who walk in darkness this Christmas season. Lord, help me be a reflection of the Light as I . . .

December 22 God with Us

"God's in His heaven, all's right with the world" is beautiful poetry written by Robert Browning. However, if God had remained in heaven, "all" could have never been right with the world. The story of Christmas is that God did not remain in heaven, but descended to earth in the person of a boy-child, arriving in a manger, on a silent night. The message is that He who dwelt in heaven without a heavenly mother, arrived on earth without an earthly father. He became "Emmanuel" (Isaiah 7:14) – God with us. The theological term is "incarnation" – which literally means embodied in flesh. It was the greatest and most stunning miracle that had ever been. It is the answer to the question: "Who is Jesus Christ?" The answer revealed by the incarnation is: Jesus Christ is fully God and fully man in one person. In other words, He is God with us. The better news is that Jesus not only existed prior to Bethlehem's manger, but that He continues to exist after the Garden's tomb. He is with us! That makes all the difference in the world at Christmas time – for those who worship Him. He is with us as we hang Christmas decorations, shop for gifts, send and receive Christmas cards, look at Christmas lights, wrap packages, open presents, eat delicious meals, sing carols, and enjoy the presence of family and friends. He is with us!

Today's prayer to continue: Thank You Lord for being with us this Christmas and all year around. I desire to experience Your presence especially as I . . .

December 23 Who's Watching O'er the Sheep?

A group of shepherds left their flock to follow an angelic announcement of "a Savior, who is Christ the Lord" (Luke 2:11). Among the well-known details, my question is: who kept the sheep? The shepherds left "with haste" for "the city of David". Sheep lost ground on the shepherd's priority list, when Jesus was born. Great events put routine into perspective. Nevertheless, the sheep could not care for themselves. Someone had to remain in the fields. Who decided which shepherds got to go to Bethlehem and which had to stay with the sheep? What a time to be a left-behind shepherd! Putting God first does not mean that second and third place items on the list suffer. No doubt God blessed the shepherds who went to the manger, however many of them there were (the Bible doesn't give a number, but Hallmark says three). But consider the blessing of those who remained with the sheep. Were they left out of God's blessing? I doubt it. It reminds me of a line from John Milton: "They also serve who only stand and wait." What is your service for the Messiah this Christmas?

Today's prayer to continue: Lord, I may not be at the front of the stage, but I want to be a part of the drama, just like the shepherds who remained with the sheep. So today, let me . . .

December 24 An Embarrassing Christmas Moment

It was surely one of my most embarrassing Christmas moments. It followed a gift of a Jingle Bell tie. Christmas Eve came on Saturday that year, so we had our family gift time that evening. My kids gave me a beautiful, if a bit gaudy, Christmas tie. It was black with green and red bells on it and when one mashed the middle portion, it played "Jingle Bells." Observing my somewhat reserved excitement, my kids asked me to wear it on Sunday morning in the church where I was serving as interim pastor. I reluctantly agreed to do so. So on Christmas Sunday morning, I semi-proudly wore the tie, but unfortunately leaned into the pulpit during my sermon, pushing the magic Jingle Bell button. What followed was a rousing rendition of Jingle Bells, picked up by my lapel microphone, and played over the church's sound system. If I remember correctly, the next words of my Christmas sermon were, "The Wise Men brought gifts to Jesus of 'gold, frankincense, and myrrh' (Matthew 2:11) and fortunately, they brought no Christmas tie for Joseph." It was one of my most embarrassing Christmas moments.

Today's prayer to continue: Thank You Lord that Christians have more fun than others do, and thank you for the laughter provided by the gift of a Christmas tie. May our Christmas laughter be contagious, and our joy spread to . . .

December 25 The Changing and the Unchanging

The observance of Christmas has changed, but the meaning remains the same. It all started with the wise men who followed a star to worship the new-born King, then "departed for their own country another way" (Matthew 2:12). Christmas celebration has been changing to "another way" ever since. I have childhood memories of real trees decorated with strings of cranberries and popcorn; hanging egg-shells with the insides blown out and the outsides painted bright colors; incoming Christmas cards displayed all over the living room. My Mother used to wrap and ribbon empty boxes and set them under the Christmas tree so it would look like we were having a bigger Christmas than we actually were. Christmas has changed. No more empty boxes under real trees. Credit card love provides many more gifts under nice, easy-to-store, artificial trees. In contrast, this year we'll go see yards decorated with hundreds of lights, blinking in sync with music heard only from a specific frequency on the car radio. We'll receive hundreds of Christmas greetings, but most will arrive via the Internet, only a few will arrive with a stamp on them. We'll go to a Christmas Eve candlelight service, but will be told by some that real candles now present a fire hazard, thus no Silent Night by candle light. We'll be reminded that the cost of the gifts mentioned in "The Twelve Days of Christmas" has increased another 6% over last year's cost. In the midst of changes, God remains the same, as does human nature. We will still give, because God gave. We will still worship the Christ-child, because He is worthy. Christmas observances change. Christmas meaning stays unchanged - Emmanuel – God with us! Merry Christmas to all.

Today's prayer to continue: Thank You, Lord for being the unchanging element in Christmas. May I share Your unchanging love with a changing world today, and I'm thinking specifically of sharing with . . .

December 26 Christmas Forever Changed

It was in a tiny church in a tiny German town. Thirty-five tourists happened upon a small group of German Christians rehearsing their Christmas music. Seated on hard wood pews, in a chapel that seated maybe fifty worshippers, we listened, few of us understanding the words, but all of us recognizing the tunes. Christmas tunes came from a long-used guitar. Christmas words flowed from untrained, but sincere voices. Then came the very familiar. The original lyrics of Stille Nacht, were written in German by an unknown Austrian priest, Joseph Mohr, the music by Austrian musician Franz Gruber, not known outside of his Austrian village. It would be two years later when the song was first performed on Christmas Eve, 1818, accompanied only by a guitar, No known celebrity performed it that night, nor was it performed in some great concert hall, but at a Midnight Mass in St. Nicholas Church. It would be more than forty years before Silent Night would be translated into English. Now recorded by over 300 artists and sung globally by multiplied thousands at Christmas time, its powerful message of heavenly peace has crossed all borders and language barriers. But it never sounded better than that night near Titisee, Germany. When we finally exited the small church, our tear-stained eyes were met with softly falling snow. Christmas has not been the same since.

Today's prayer to continue: Memories of Christ past flood my mind, Lord. Thank You again for Your birth and the fact that we can celebrate it during this season. As the calendar moves away from Christmas, don't let me forget . . .

December 27 A Second Meaning of the Manger

As good as the "Good News" (or "glad tidings") of the manger was, it was never meant to stay in Bethlehem or with the immediate recipients. In addition to the good news of Jesus' birth, the second key phrase of the manger addressed the good news "to all people" (Luke 2:10). Repeatedly this idea appears through the gospels, Acts, the letters of Paul, the general letters, and even in the book of Revelation. It was used by Jesus in the resurrection's great commission to, "all the nations" (Matthew 28:19), and around the heavenly throne, "to every nation, tribe, tongue, and people" (Revelation 14:6). So after you've gathered with family and friends this Christmas, remember the good news of the season stretches to the ends of the earth, leaving no person, nor group out of its reach. Let us not forget that some have not yet heard the news while others are still rejecting it, and the sharing of it often brings criticism, even persecution. Yet share we must. The fact that it is sharable with all is what makes the good news so good.

Today's prayer to continue: Motivate me Lord to share the good news of Your birth with . . .

December 28 Remember the Reason

"Remember the Reason" proclaimed the banner on my Christmas morning Facebook post. So, how did we do? In the midst of the now-normal Christmas activities, did we remember the real reason for the season, or did the birth of the Christ-child get lost in the tinsel and tunes of the holidays. I confess that I heard many more wishes for having a "Happy Holiday" than I used to hear. I guess wishing a "Merry Christmas" is becoming politically incorrect. I'm certainly not against having happy holidays, and I'm only in favor of the "Merry Christmas" greeting because it proclaims "Christ" as the reason for both the greeting and the season. I'm also aware that the origin of the December 25 celebration is not exactly Christian, and that Jesus was more likely born in the spring time when shepherds would have been "abiding in the field, keeping watch over their flock by night" (Luke 2:8). However, December 25 is when we celebrate the incarnational birth of our Lord. When the accompaniments are all stripped away, it is finally, all about Jesus, the only valid reason for the season. I hope you had a meaningful Christmas – for all the right reasons.

Today's prayer to continue: As the memories of Christmas fade toward the new year, Lord, help me to focus on the right reason for the season, especially today, as I . . .

December 29 Caught on Christmas

I got caught by the police! Red handed! On Christmas Day! Every year I purchase Starbucks's gift cards, drive around on Christmas Eve and Christmas Day giving them to police officers with a quick, "Thanks for working on Christmas." This is done anonymously in the tradition of one of the early versions of Santa Claus, St. Nicholas, a saint who was known for giving anonymous gifts, especially to children during the night as they slept. This idea, of course, was popularized by Clement Moore, who wrote a simple poem for his children in 1822 entitled, "A Visit from St. Nicholas," that begins with the now famous words, "Twas the night before Christmas . . ." And of course in the spirit of Jesus who told His disciples, "when you do a charitable deed, do not let your left hand know what your right hand is doing" (Matthew 6:3). For the first time, I got caught. One of the recipients apparently recorded my car license tag. My wife was surprised when a police vehicle pulled up to our front curb and gave her a hand-made note for me. It read, "Of all the gifts bestowed this year . . . the greatest is the appreciation of those like you" and it was signed by nineteen police officers, complete with their badge numbers. I wept. One of my greatest Christmas joys, passed onto to me by my Father, is the anonymous giving of gifts. This year, I was blessed to be caught on Christmas.

Today's prayer to continue: Lord, I would like to do something nice for someone today, without them knowing it was me, so help me focus on what to do and who should be the recipient . . .

December 30 The Spirit of Christmas Past

In "A Christmas Carol" by Charles Dickens, Ebenezer Scrooge, surviving partner of Scrooge & Marley, grudgingly gave Bob Cratchit his Christmas check and went home on Christmas Eve. He dreamed of Cratchit and three spirits – first, the spirit of the past, reminding him of his youth before he became miserly. Then he dreamed of the spirit of the present and finally the spirit of the future. Before leaving Christmas, consider "The Spirit of Christmas Past." In Luke 2:17-20 there are numerous past tense verbs. It speaks of proclaiming ("made widely known") the message of Christmas past. The passage speaks of Mary pondering the meaning of Christmas past. Finally the verses speak of praising God for the miracle of Christmas past – "they returned glorifying and praising God." So before we get too far removed from Christmas, let's make the truth of our Lord's birth widely known as we ponder on its meaning and praise God for its miracle. Merry Christmas past and Happy New Year to come.

Today's prayer to continue: Once more Lord, show me today, a Christmas meaning that perhaps I missed or overlooked this Christmas, and then allow me to share it with . . .

December 31 Last Year . . . Next Year

The last hours of a year are always a mixture of looking back and looking forward. What Ralph Waldo Emerson said about a past and future day, could well be applied to a completed and coming year: "Finish each day and be done with it. You have done what you could; some blunders and absurdities have crept in;

forget them as soon as you can. Tomorrow is a new day; you shall begin it serenely and with too high a spirit to be encumbered with your old nonsense." The Apostle Paul said it this way: "Forgetting those things which are behind and reaching forward to those things which are ahead, I press toward the goal for the prize of the upward call of God in Christ Jesus" (Philippians 3:13-14). So mix your New Year's Resolutions with some of last year's memories and let's begin again. Published in 1908, the following poem by Minnie Louise Haskins, is appropriate: "I said to the man who stood at the gate of the year: 'Give me a light that I may tread safely into the unknown.' And he replied: 'Go out into the darkness and put your hand into the Hand of God. That shall be to you better than light and safer than a known way.'"

Today's prayer to continue: In the New Year Lord, I resolve to . . .

Morning Manna – Scripture Appendix

Genesis 1:1 – March 9

Genesis 1:1-3 – April 22

Genesis 1:2 – April 16

Genesis 1:3-5 – December 5

Genesis 1: 5, 8, 13, 19, 23, 31 – February 22

Genesis 2:2-3 – October 18

Genesis 2:7 – July 15

Genesis 2:20 – July 8

Genesis 2:23 – December 11

Genesis 5:1 – February 17

Genesis 6:22 – July 23

Genesis 7:2 – March 29

Genesis 9:6 – August 3

Genesis 9:20-21 – December 10

Genesis 11:1-9 – May 20

Genesis 12:1-3 – September 30

Genesis 15:3 – September 20

Genesis 17:17 – December 4

Genesis 18:12 – December 10

Genesis 22:14 – September 30

Genesis 28:10-22 – December 10

Genesis 35:1-4 – December 10

Genesis 48:17 – September 27

Exodus 3:14 – June 15

Exodus 16:23 – October 18

Exodus 20:4-17 – November 16

Exodus 20:13 – December 9

Exodus 24:12 – September 8

Leviticus 10:3 – February 21; June 23

Leviticus 17:10 – December 8

Leviticus 19:18 – August 21

Leviticus 23:24 – October 18

Leviticus 23:32 – February 22

Leviticus 23:40 – March 15

Numbers 6:25 – December 8

Numbers 14:4 – February 12

Numbers 14:24 – October 15

Numbers 18:29 – August 6

Deuteronomy 8:2 – June 14

Deuteronomy 31:6 – April 29; October 29

Deuteronomy 31:17-18 – December 8

Deuteronomy 33:25 – April 18

Joshua 1:1 – July 17

Joshua 1:6, 7, 9 – August 8

Joshua 3:4-5 – June 4

Joshua 3:5 – January 1

Joshua 14:10-12 – August

Judges 8:27, 30-31 – December 10

Judges 17:6; 21:25 – March 21

1 Samuel 1:10 – May 5

1 Samuel 2:1 – September 12

1 Samuel 14:37, 45 – May 25

1 Samuel 16:12 – April 14

1 Samuel 16:14 – November 19

1 Samuel 19:1-6 – July 18

1 Samuel 30:6 – May 9

2 Samuel 6:21 – November 17

2 Samuel 7:14 – November 17

2 Samuel 11:1-4 – December 10

1 Kings 8:10-11 – December 13

1 Kings 8:61 – September 28

1 Kings 19:4, 10 – January 17

1 Kings 19:12 – July 6

1 Kings 22:48 – August 12

2 Kings 9:13 – March 15

2 Chronicles 20:12, 15 – February 3

2 Chronicles 32:20 – May 5

Nehemiah 9:28 – May 5

Job 1:21 – August 22

Job 2:13 – April 13

Job 9:25, 27 – August 16

Job 9:27 – October 6

Job 12:12 – July 28

Job 13:24 – December 8

Job 21:15 – March 7

Job 35:10 – October 24

Job 42:10 – January 3; February 19

Psalm 2:4 – December 4

Psalm 2:8 – May 11

Psalm 9:9 – September 25

Psalm 16:9 – April 8

Psalm 18:28 – October 3

Psalm 20:4 – January 5

Psalm 22:2 – June 25

Psalm 22:3 – January 11

Psalm 23:3 – January 9

Psalm 24:1 – April 22

Psalm 27:5 – January 10

Psalm 30:5 – February 5

Psalm 34:16 – December 8

Psalm 35:9 – September 12

Psalm 36:6 – December 3

Psalm 37:23-24 – August 1

Psalm 39:3 – April 15

Psalm 42:8 – August 2; October 24

Psalm 46:10 – February 26

Psalm 48:14 – February 2

Psalm 56:3 – October 31

Psalm 71:17-18 – September 1

Psalm 72:8 – November 20

Psalm 78:20-33 – February 1

Psalm 84:2 – January 24

Psalm 85:6 – June 26

Psalm 90:10 – July 16

Psalm 92:1-3 – September 23

Psalm 92:14 – June 6

Psalm 96:1 – June 2

Psalm 106:2 – October 9

Psalm 116:15 – July 12; August 11

Psalm 116:17 – August 27

Psalm 118:24 – January 4; February 10

Psalm 119:11 – July 14

Psalm 119:32 – November 14

Psalm 119:105 – February 26

Psalm 121 – July 14

Psalm 121:1 – April 9

Psalm 121:1-2 – January 25

Psalm 121:4 – March 25; November 10

Psalm 126:2-3 – September 15

Psalm 126: 5-6 – March 10

Psalm 127:1 – October 7

Psalm 127:2 – November 10

Psalm 139:1, 3 – March 4

Psalm 144:9 – April 10

Psalm 144:15 – June 13

Proverbs 3:3 – September 8

Proverbs 3:5-6 – January 22; March 9; September 1; November 22

Proverbs 4:7-8 – September 3

Proverbs 7:3 – September 8

Proverbs 10:7 – April 19

Proverbs 23:22 – June 18

Proverbs 25:11 – January 14; February 27

Proverbs 27:9 – November 9

Proverbs 27:16 – April 7

Proverbs 27:21 – November 12

Proverbs 29:18 – August 7

Proverbs 31:28 – May 12

Ecclesiastes 9:10 – April 3

Ecclesiastes 12:2 – January 23

Song of Solomon 2:6 – September 27

Isaiah 7:14 – December 22

Isaiah 9:2 – December 21

Isaiah 9:6 – December 17

Isaiah 14:27 – September 6

Isaiah 30:15 – March 19; September 28; October 22

Isaiah 30:21 – March 13; July 6

Isaiah 35:3 – July 10

Isaiah 41:9 – August 20

Isaiah 41:10 – September 27

Isaiah 42:6 – October 12

Isaiah 43:1 – October 5

Isaiah 43:1-2 – November 2

Isaiah 59:2 – February 8

Jeremiah 1:8 – February 24

Jeremiah 20:9 – April 15

Jeremiah 22:29 – April 22

Jeremiah 31:3 – May 17

Jeremiah 33:3 – February 28; March 28; September 13

Jeremiah 42:6 – July 27

Lamentations 3:22-23 – April 30

Ezekiel 14:3 – February 14

Ezekiel 23:21 – November 26

Ezekiel 37:9 – June 5

Daniel 4:22 – March 8

Hosea 6:6 – May 15

Joel 2:13 – March 21

Joel 2:28 – May 18

Amos 7:8 – May 27

Obadiah 1:15 – May 24

Jonah 3:1 – December 2

Micah 6:8 – May 16

Nahum 1:3 – May 26

Habakkuk 2:4 – June 8

Zephaniah 1:7 – February 9

Haggai 1:5, 7 – April 4

Zechariah 8:16 – June 17

Zachariah 9:9 – March 17

Malachi 3:10 – May 30

Matthew 2:8, 12 – December 20

Matthew 2:11 – December 15; December 24

Matthew 2:12 – December 25

Matthew 4:19 – June 11

Matthew 5:24-26 – April 22

Matthew 5:41 – August 14

Matthew 5:44 – August 21

Matthew 5:48 – June 19

Matthew 6:3 – December 29

Matthew 6:6 – August 25

Matthew 6:9-13 – October 9

Matthew 6:12 – October 30

Matthew 6:24 – November 15

Matthew 6:33 – October 20

Matthew 6:34 – March 5

Matthew 7:7 – February 25; April 23; May 25

Matthew 7:12 – May 24

Matthew 7:16 – October 11

Matthew 8:1 – February 23

Matthew 9:35 – June 21

Matthew 9:38 – March 14

Matthew 11:28 – June 11

Matthew 13:38 – February 13

Matthew 13:57 – December 12

Matthew 14:22-33 – January 16

Matthew 17:8 – January 18

Matthew 17:15 – February 23

Matthew 18:19-20 – June 16

Matthew 19:14 – May 1

Matthew 20:16 – January 27; May 19; September 29

Matthew 24:3 – December 14

Matthew 24:36, 44 – May 21

Matthew 25:21, 23 – May 29; September 16

Matthew 25:43-45 – June 7

Matthew 26:26 – May 4

Matthew 26:40 – April 28

Matthew 26:53 – March 12

Matthew 26:69-75 – April 21

Matthew 27:64-66 – March 24

Matthew 28:4 – March 24

Matthew 28:17 – April 5

Matthew 28:19 – March 23

Matthew 28:19-20 – February 23; December 27

Mark 1:17 – June 11

Mark 1:33, 37-38 – July 7

Mark 1:35 – February 22; September 10; October 8

Mark 5 – January 15

Mark 5:9 – August 28

Mark 5:15 – July 25

Mark 5:25-35 – March 31

Mark 6:5 – December 9

Mark 9:3, 7, 14, 17 – July 31

Mark 10:14 – May 1

Luke 1:46 – September 12

Luke 2:7 – January 7

Luke 2:8 – December 28

Luke 2:10 – December 27

Luke 2:11 – December 23

Luke 2:17-20 – December 30

Luke 2:41-52 – July 3

Luke 6:12 – August 2; October 22

Luke 6:45 – September 8

Luke 8:15 – January 12

Luke 8:35 – July 25

Luke 9:27-36 – January 13

Luke 10:2 – August 18

Luke 11:1 – August 15; August 18; November 13

Luke 11:2- July 4

Luke 11:4 – October 30; November 3

Luke 11:5-8 – July 9

Luke 11:9 – February 25

Luke 12:48 – November 29

Luke 17:11-19 – November 27

Luke 18:1-8 – July 9

Luke 18:16 – May 1

Luke 19:41 – March 22; May 14

Luke 22:19 – May 31

Luke 22:32 – November 5

Luke 22:44 – May 5

Luke 24:16, 31-35 – April 15

John 1:1 – March 9

John 1:12 – October 25

John 1:14 – December 18

John 1:29 – December 11

John 1:38 – June 11

John 2:1-11 – April 2

John 3:2 – June 11

John 3:8 – June 5

John 3:16 – March 9: March 16

John 4:10 – February 16

John 4:23 – April 27

John 6:35 – February 16

John 9:4 – September

John 9:31 – February 8

John 11:1 – July 29

John 11:35 – May 14

John 11:54 – August 26

John 12:12 – March 15

John 13: 4-5 – March 27

John 13:23 – March 26

John 14:2 – April 17; May 8

John 14:6 – June 1

John 14:8-9 – January 19

John 15:4 – July 2

John 15:11 – August 31

John 15:13 – May 28

John 15:16 – September 22

John 16:33 – December 7

John 17:24 – December 18

John 21:12 – March 30

Acts 1:8 – November 4; November 11

Acts 2:2 – June 5

Acts 4:13 – July 22

Acts 4:29 – August 30

Acts 4:36 – August 23

Acts 9:27 – August 23

Acts 13:22 – December 10

Acts 17:28 – September 2

Acts 20:6 – September 14

Romans 1:11 – October 16

Romans 3:23 – July 30

Romans 5:3 – May 6

Romans 7:19 – September 26

Romans 8:22 – May 5

Romans 8:24 – April 24

Romans 8:28 – March 9; April 7; September 1; September 11; October 21; December 9

Romans 10:15 – January 16

Romans 12:4 – January 21

Romans 12:4-5 – September 27; October 10

Romans 12:5 – February 6; May 7; June 3

Romans 12:11 – November 8

Romans 15:30 – May 5

1 Corinthians 3:16 – March 16

1 Corinthians 3:22-23 – July 24

1 Corinthians 6:19-20 – August 22

1 Corinthians 8:13 – November 6

1 Corinthians 9:22 – September 9

1 Corinthians 9:27 – October 7; December 10

1 Corinthians 12:12 – December 13

1 Corinthians 12:20 – September 27

2 Corinthians 2:14 – June 25

2 Corinthians 4:4 – December 9

2 Corinthians 5:6 – March 2

2 Corinthians 5:7 – September 18; October 26

2 Corinthians 5:17 – February18

2 Corinthians 6:5 – October 13

2 Corinthians 9:15 – December 16; December 19

2 Corinthians 10:7 – April 25

2 Corinthians 11:25 – April 26

2 Corinthians 11:27 – October 13

2 Corinthians 12:7-9 – July 11

2 Corinthians 12:8 – August 25

2 Corinthians 12:9 – May 9; August 10

2 Corinthians 13:5 – March 1

2 Corinthians 13:14 – October 23

Galatians 1:1 – March 3

Galatians 1:13 – September 5

Galatians 2:20 – April 6

Galatians 4:12 – February 15

Galatians 4:19 – May 5

Galatians 5:1 – July 5

Galatians 5:22 – October 28

Galatians 6:9 – March 10

Ephesians 1:4 – January 30

Ephesians 1:6 – February 4

Ephesians 3:3 – September 21

Ephesians 4:6 – August 9

Ephesians 4:29 – June 12

Ephesians 4:31 – January 26

Ephesians 4:32 – January 20

Ephesians 5:15 – April 1

Ephesians 5:17 – June 20

Ephesians 5:15-16 – November 18

Ephesians 5:19 – February 7; November 7

Ephesians 6:18-19 – June 9; September 24

Ephesians 6:19 – June 30

Philippines 1:3 – October 14; November 25

Philippians 1:6 – February 11; May 3

Philippines 1:8 – October 16

Philippines 1:21 – July 21

Philippines 2:9-11 – April 22

Philippines 3:12-14 – June 29

Philippines 3:13-14 – December 31

Philippines 4:4 – April 11

Philippines 4:6 – May 22

Philippians 4:8 – January 29

Philippians 4:11 – March 6; April 20; August 19

Philippines 4:13 – August 13

Philippians 4:19 – March 5

Philippians 4:13 – January 6

Colossians 1:16-22 – January 8

Colossians 1:28 – July 19

Colossians 3:1 – September 27

Colossians 3:15 – November 24

Colossians 3:16 – November 28; December 1

Colossians 4:5 – November 18

Colossians 4:6 – March 18

Colossians 4:12 – May 5

1 Thessalonians 1:2 – November 30

1 Thessalonians 4:13 – January 28; July 12; October 19;

1 Thessalonians 4:13-14 – November 1

1 Thessalonians 4:14 – December 6

1 Thessalonians 5:12-13 – October 1; October 2; October 4

1 Thessalonians 5:17 – April 8; June 22; July 9

1 Thessalonians 5:18 – November 23

2 Thessalonians 3:3 – March 10

1 Timothy 1:19 – April 26

1 Timothy 2:1-2 – July 1

1 Timothy 4:7 – April 7

1 Timothy 4:12 – June 27; July 26

1 Timothy 4:7-8 – May 23

2 Timothy 1:7 – November 4

2 Timothy 2:2 – July 18; October 27

2 Timothy 2:3 – March 11

2 Timothy 2:15 – February 20

2 Timothy 3:7 – January 31

2 Timothy 4:7 – January 2; December 10

Titus 1:5 – July 20

Titus 2:13 – April 24

Titus 3:12 – September 14

Hebrews 4:9 – October 18

Hebrews 4:15 – September 19

Hebrews 5:7 – May 5

Hebrews 6:1 – May 2

Hebrews 9:27 – November 21

Hebrews 11:1 – April 24; August 5; August 17

Hebrews 11:4 – May 13; September 17

Hebrews 11:13 – June 28

Hebrews 11:32 – December 10

Hebrews 11:38 – May 19; September 29

Hebrews 12:2 – October 20

Hebrews 12:12 – July 10

James 1:9 – February 9

James 1:19 – September 7

James 2:20 – June 10

James 4:3 – May 25; July 11

James 4:14 – April 12

James 5:16 – August 25; November 5

1 Peter 1:5-7 – July 13

1 Peter 2:11 – June 28

1 Peter 2:21 – July 26

1 Peter 5:12 – September 21

2 Peter 1:14 – August 4

1 John 1:5 – February 22

1 John 1:7 – May 7

1 John 4 – August 24

3 John 1:14 – October 17

3 John 5-6 – March 20

Revelation 1:5 – January 11

Revelation 1:11 – January 27

Revelation 1:16-17 – September 27

Revelation 5:9 – June 2

Revelation 7:9 – March 15

Revelation 14:6 – December 27

Revelation 19:9 – May 4

Revelation 21:1-3 – April 22

Revelation 21:25; 22:5 – October 19

www.ingramcontent.com/pod-product-compliance
Lightning Source LLC
Chambersburg PA
CBHW070532010526
44118CB00012B/1106